The Real Politics of the Horn of Africa

In Memoriam: Meles Zenawi 1955–2012

and for Hiroe, Hannah and Adan

The Real Politics of the Horn of Africa

Money, War and the Business of Power

Alex de Waal

polity

First published in 2015 by Polity Press
Reprinted 2016 (twice)

Polity Press
65 Bridge Street
Cambridge CB2 1UR, UK

Polity Press
350 Main Street
Malden, MA 02148, USA

ISBN-13: 978-0-7456-9557-0
ISBN-13: 978-0-7456-9558-7(pb)

A catalogue record for this book is available from the British Library.

Library of Congress Cataloging-in-Publication Data

De Waal, Alex.
  The real politics of the Horn of Africa : money, war and the business of power / Alex de Waal.
    pages cm
  ISBN 978-0-7456-9557-0 (hardback) – ISBN 978-0-7456-9558-7 (pbk.) 1. Political culture–Horn of Africa. 2. Political violence–Horn of Africa. 3. Political corruption–Horn of Africa. 4. Horn of Africa–Politics and government. I. Title.
  DT367.8.D4 2015
  306.20963–dc23

                                                              2015004483

Typeset in 10.5/12 12 Sabon
by Toppanleefung Best-set, Hong Kong
Printed and bound in Great Britain by Clays, Ltd, St Ives PLC

The publisher has used its best endeavours to ensure that the URLs for external websites referred to in this book are correct and active at the time of going to press. However, the publisher has no responsibility for the websites and can make no guarantee that a site will remain live or that the content is or will remain appropriate.

Every effort has been made to trace all copyright holders, but if any have been inadvertently overlooked the publisher will be pleased to include any necessary credits in any subsequent reprint or edition.

For further information on Polity, visit our website: politybooks.com

Contents

Contents

Figures and Maps

Figures

Maps

Acronyms

AU	African Union
AUHIP	African Union High-Level Implementation Panel for Sudan
AMISOM	African Union Mission in Somalia
CAR	Central African Republic
CEO	Chief executive officer
CPA	Comprehensive Peace Agreement
CSO	Civil society organization
DPKO	UN Department of Peace-Keeping Operations
DRC	Democratic Republic of Congo
ECOWAS	Economic Community of West African States
ELF	Eritrean Liberation Front
EPLF	Eritrean People's Liberation Front
EPRDF	Ethiopian People's Revolutionary Democratic Front
FIBS	Faisal Islamic Bank of Sudan
GoSS	Government of Southern Sudan
ICC	International Criminal Court
IGAD	Inter-Governmental Authority on Development
IMF	International Monetary Fund
JEM	Justice and Equality Movement
LJM	Liberation and Justice Movement
LRA	Lord's Resistance Army
NCP	National Congress Party
NGO	Non-governmental organization
NISS	National Intelligence and Security Service
OAU	Organisation of African Unity

PDF	Popular Defence Force (Government of Sudan)
PDF	Protection and Deterrent Force (IGAD/UNMISS)
PFDJ	Popular Front for Democracy and Justice
PSC	Peace and Security Council
RPF	Rwandese Patriotic Front
SFG	Somali Federal Government
SLA	Sudan Liberation Army
SNM	Somali National Movement
SPLA	Sudan People's Liberation Army
SPLM	Sudan People's Liberation Movement
SRF	Sudan Revolutionary Forces
TFG	Transitional Federal Government
TNG	Transitional National Government
TPLF	Tigrayan People's Liberation Front
UN	United Nations
UNAMID	United Nations-African Union hybrid operation in Darfur
UNMIS	United Nations Mission in Sudan
UNMISS	United Nations Mission in South Sudan
UIC	Union of Islamic Courts
USAID	US Agency for International Development
USC	United Somali Congress

Preface and Acknowledgements

This book is an outcome of thirty years' research and political engagement with the countries of the Horn of Africa. At its heart is an ethnography of contemporary politics, drawing on both the actions and analyses of its subjects – members of the political and security elite – and my own observations and analyses. My hope is that, in understanding this politics better, there is a chance to change it.

I had originally planned to write a more conventional political science analysis, both of the Horn and of the core concepts of the 'political marketplace'. Early drafts of this book spent much space and effort clarifying where I agreed with, and where I diverged from, leading scholarly accounts of the countries of the Horn, and the literature on conflict and state formation. At the risk of offending the many writers who have toiled away at this particular coalface, and who might justifiably expect to be credited here, I decided instead to invoke the ethnographer's privilege of theorizing from observation. The book opens up more pathways than it can travel, and raises more questions than it can answer. It is a reflection and an exploration intended to provoke debates and open new avenues for research, including my own.

To enumerate the personal and intellectual debts of the last three decades would require a long chapter in itself. However, let me single out some of those without whom this book would not have been possible.

Meles Zenawi, the ablest political intellectual of his generation, played a major role in provoking my thinking and writing: this book is in part a response to a challenge he laid before me. Among his comrades in arms, I have particular debts to Mulugeta Gebrehiwot and Tsadkan Gebretensae. For more than twenty-five years, Abdul Mohammed has been an unstinting force of creativity and optimism for the entire region. Among Sudanese and South Sudanese, my greatest debts are to Yoanes Ajawin and Abdel Salam H. Abdelsalam, who showed how it is possible to retain integrity amid the fierce turbulence that is Sudan. Other Sudanese and South Sudanese who have shaped my thinking include Yousif Kuwa Mekki, Suleiman Rahhal, Abdalla Hamdok, Suleiman Baldo, Francis Deng, Abdel Wahab al Effendi, Gamal al Tom, el Taj el Banan Tajelassfia, Hafiz Mohamed and Godfrey Bulla. My main guides for Eritrea have been Paulos Tesfagiorgis and Dawit Mesfin. For Somalia they have included Rakiya Omaar, Hussein Mursal and Abdi Baafo. Tajudeen Abdul-Raheem was an irreplaceable fount of political commitment, energy and frankness. I have also learned a huge amount from the African leaders with whom I have had the privilege of working: Thabo Mbeki, Pierre Buyoya, Abdelsalam Abubakar and Salim Ahmed Salim. Others involved in peacemaking, less prominent but no less wise or capable, include Elghassim Wane, Boitshoko Mokgatlhe, Pauline Olunga, Barney Afako, Dawit Toga, Itonde Kakoma and Vladimir Zhagora. Jennifer Klot has been a model of intellectual activism. Julie Flint has been invaluable to my engagement with the Nuba Mountains and Darfur. Neha Erasmus has been a voice of humanity for South Sudan.

Others without whom this work would not have been possible include my colleagues Kahssay Gebreyesus, Wendy Foulds and especially Lisa Avery. Nimco Mahamud Hassan has a special place.

Among my many academic mentors and collaborators, I must begin with Wendy James and Ahmed Karadawi, who were instrumental in setting me off on this intellectual journey. Among scholars of the Horn, I have learned much from Rogaia Abu Sharaf, Mark Bradbury, Richard Brown, Mark Duffield, Lidwien Kapteijns, David Keen, Andrew Mawson, Michael Medley, Alula Pankhurst, John Ryle and Eddie Thomas. A number of recent colleagues were particularly important in helping me shape the concept and arguments, including Jacek Kugler, Peter Uvin, Noel Twagiramungu, Isaac Williams, Laura James, Sarah Nouwen, Dave Mozersky, Bridget Conley-Zilkic, Tim Allen, Mary Kaldor, Tatiana Carayannis, Koen Vlassenroot, Marielle Debos, Sarah Chayes and Claire Smith. Rachel Ibreck has contributed especially thoughtful comments and ideas.

1

Introduction
Observing the Business of Power

The View from the Edge

The small town of Kurmuk lies under a rocky hill, a stray outcrop from the Ethiopian escarpment that is just across a small riverbed, inside Sudan; 25 miles to the west is the boundary with South Sudan. Development has bypassed this town: it has no two-storey buildings, no metalled roads. Kurmuk is on the edge – or on several edges. But it is also the cockpit of the Horn of Africa, where armies from those three countries – and also Eritrea – have been sent to fight battles that have determined the fate of the entire region. The Grand Ethiopian Renaissance Dam, just 50 miles to the north on the Blue Nile, is also a pivot for the future of the Horn and the Nile Valley, including Egypt. Just as the escarpment dramatically separates Sudanese plains from the Ethiopian mountains, so too the ethnic, religious and political lines are drawn sharply through this land. Here we find Muslims, Christians and followers of diverse traditional religions; people who identify as 'Arab', and others who assume a range of other labels including 'African'. Sudan's Blue Nile State was, in the 1990s, the place where Islamist cadres pioneered a total Islamic society and, after the 2005 Comprehensive Peace Agreement (CPA), where proponents of a democratic 'New Sudan' tried to build a model of equitable development.

Near Kurmuk is the customary land of a small community known as Uduk. They were caught on the shifting front lines of several wars and compelled to adapt as best they could. The Uduk are invisible in the high politics of the Horn of Africa, but their long-time ethnographer, Wendy James, has given them a voice. She reflects on a 'kind of tolerance towards persons' that applies not only to Uduk individuals who made their choice to join one army or another, or seek protection by marrying across religious lines, but also to the soldiers and administrators posted to their area:

> I have rarely heard, at the local level, of individuals in the front-line zones being blamed for supporting one side or the other...individuals on whatever side were praised for personal decency or blamed for personal cruelty, but not for being caught up in one or another armed organization.[1]

From the most powerless people we have a simple, human insight into the nature of politics. Similar observation and judgements are made by local commanders, administrators and chiefs, or by their superiors in Khartoum or the headquarters of the Sudan People's Liberation Army (SPLA). The view from the wrong end of the telescope is unexpectedly clear: people see *real politics* – pithily defined by Lenin as 'who, whom'.[2]

Throughout this book the focus of this telescope is turned to the men who conduct real politics in the Horn of Africa. It is a contemporary historical ethnography of these men: their power, their relationships with one another, and their norms and ethics. The dominant, and growing, system that orders their behaviour is what I call the 'political marketplace'. For the region's political entrepreneurs and business managers, this is not a metaphor. They actually exchange services and rewards, loyalty and money, for prices that are set by the elementary principles of supply and demand, and also influenced by whoever is able to regulate the market. Men who belong in different political camps, or who organize lethal violence against each other's followers, do not hate each other, any more than business rivals may dislike or feud with one another. People with no power simply do not feature in their calculus. These men may have political motives and goals – protecting communities, pursuing beliefs about a better society, or building states – but their political fortunes depend on how well they operate in the political marketplace.[3]

These politicians share one norm with the Uduk villagers, which is the value they attach to personal character. Ordinary, powerless people value personal integrity and human decency: when they imagine a better society, they think of 'better people' in positions of authority.[4] But for political bosses and security chiefs, decency or cruelty are less important than skill and reliability in political business. Members of this elite work on the assumption that human allegiance is tradable: individuals will serve others for reward. They are not always right, but they are correct for enough people enough of the time, that a system based on exchanging loyalty for money works. As we move from lower to higher levels of political business, the ethical codes change: political-business managers are more remote from ordinary people, and less amenable to sentiments such as community and humanity. In fact, the more that a political entrepreneur can discard humane norms and instead adopt a market-based calculus, the more likely he is to rise to the top and stay there. We will also see that, over the last decades, this auction of loyalties has been liberalized, dollarized and internationalized. This is the change I try to describe and explain in this book.

Political entrepreneurs operate in the political marketplace using money and violence. A politician needs money that he can use at his discretion without having to report or account for it – a 'political budget'. Every politician, in any system of government, needs such a political budget: in marketplace systems, getting this money and spending it is the very essence of political business. It is a complicated business, as this book will show. Most of this fund will be spent on buying (or renting) other politicians, especially those with armed followers. The public budget is the sideshow. Political-business violence is also complicated: the politician needs to own or hire its machinery and utilize it in a politically effective manner. Guns are themselves a currency.[5] Their political calibre is the power they can dispose through extortion, killing or destruction, which are demonstrations of their owner's power and determination. For the politician, the ideal is to have an armed unit whose members are personally loyal (for example, family members), but to operate at scale he will need to hire practitioners of violence. A recurrent trait among political-military business practitioners is that they overestimate their skill in using violence and make costly mistakes.

The marketplace has buyers and sellers, trading loyalty for resources. Each buyer is also a seller: a political entrepreneur or business manager will aggregate the loyalties he has bought or rented, and sell the package to a higher-level trader. In doing so, he tries not just to bundle them together but to add value. The market operates in essentially the same way from local to international levels. The political-territorial domain of each political merchant expands or contracts depending on market conditions and his business model and skill. Violence is intrinsic to the market: it is a means of bargaining and signalling value within the marketplace.

The Horn of Africa is an excellent place to investigate political markets. Political bargaining and political entrepreneurship can be seen naked, stripped of the flattering wardrobe of democracy, rule of law and state-building. Political budgets and the price of loyalty can be measured. The Horn is sufficiently diverse that it serves as a laboratory for different political-business strategies, some carried out under extreme austerity and others with relative opulence, some with intense and unregulated competition, others with attempts at tight control. It also is the location of serious efforts to challenge or reverse the marketplace, notably in Ethiopia. The Horn of Africa is important in its own right, but also, I suggest, its advanced political markets reveal emerging patterns of monetized politics elsewhere in the world.

I find this political system fascinating and repugnant. It is intellectually fascinating because it challenges important orthodoxies of political science, development and related disciplines. It is repugnant because it is fundamentally inhumane, reducing human beings to mere instruments and commodities, mutating public goods into private ones, and co-opting good intentions to achieve malign outcomes. We see politicians manipulating commendable policy goals such as state-building and peacekeeping as mechanisms to accumulate power and money, while perpetuating those same miseries that gave rise to those policies in the first place. But in accordance with the Gramscian precept of pessimism of the intellect, optimism of the will, it is essential first to understand and diagnose the pathology before starting treatment. Similarly, my challenge to theories of state-building is empirical, not normative. States, especially democratic ones, are a better way of meeting human needs. But in the contest between the most determined state-builders and the logic of the political marketplace, the state-builders are not winning.

A Vignette: The Darfur Negotiations

Shortly before dawn on the final day of the Darfur peace negotiations in Abuja, Nigeria, on 6 May 2006, I travelled from the venue of the talks within the grounds of State House to the Chida Hotel where the delegations were staying, sitting in the back of a car with the leader of the Sudan Liberation Movement (SLM), Abdel Wahid al Nur. Also dispersing after an all-night session were the assembled mediators: Salim Ahmed Salim, former Secretary General of the Organisation of African Unity who was leading the mediation team, the Nigerian President Olusegun Obasanjo, who was hosting, and the US Deputy Secretary of State Robert Zoellick, who had arrived to help seal the deal. Squeezed into the back seat of the car, speaking in English, Abdel Wahid told me all the reasons of principle why he would not sign the deal on the table. The deal was, he said, deeply unfair. Shortly after arriving in his hotel room, he took a call on his mobile. 'They offered me $30 million!' he said to his interlocutor (whom he didn't identify) in Arabic. 'I demanded $100 million. But I will negotiate.' He was referring to the first instalment for the fund for compensating the victims of the war, which, it was understood, he personally would allocate.

Later in the day, back at the hall, one of the more memorable moments of the negotiations occurred. Abdel Wahid had been consulting with his delegation at the hotel. The majority was in favour of signing the document – the Darfur Peace Agreement – on the table, but Abdel Wahid was holding out for a better deal, and especially one that gave him more than his rival, Minni Arkoy Minawi. He imagined that the Americans were bidding in the auction for his loyalty: his chief advisor, a Canadian citizen of Sudanese origin named Ahmed Mohamadein, had flown to Canada the week before, promising to go to Washington, DC, and get a better deal than that offered by Zoellick. After talking to his friends in the Darfur advocacy movement, Mohamadein phoned Abdel Wahid and advised him not to sign anything before he returned to Abuja. His call was intercepted by a CIA officer attached to the US delegation, who shared this information with the mediators, and later that week Mohamadein also bragged to me about his role. But at that moment – just after midday – all I could see was Abdel Wahid's defiant body language as he stepped out of his car and walked towards the hall, with his team following.

Not wanting Abdel Wahid to speak to the cluster of journalists on the steps of the hall, I went to intercept him halfway along the side of the building. Taking him by the hand, I said, 'I need to speak to you,' and pulled him through a side door. By sheer chance, Obasanjo was behind the door. The Nigerian President turned and confronted Abdel Wahid, jumping into the pose of a boxer with his fist in the Darfurian rebel's face. 'You let me down, boy!' he shouted, taking him by the collar and dragging him into a nearby room. Obasanjo had paid at least $1 million personally to Abdel Wahid a couple of days earlier. I discovered afterwards that Abdel Wahid had asked the Americans for hard cash as well, and had been rebuffed.

An hour later, with Abdel Wahid intransigent in the face of promises and threats from both the chief mediators, Zoellick asked me whether there was something psychologically wrong with the man. Abdel Wahid was vain and was vacillating, but he understood one of the fundamentals of Sudanese politics: if he joined the political establishment without enough money in his own pocket, whatever document he had signed would be worthless. If he could not reward his followers, his value would go down. However much the Americans promised development aid for the people of Darfur, this did not solve his political need. In fact, large-scale aid might even make Abdel Wahid's predicament more difficult, as others would become brokers for these funds and could threaten his position. As the day progressed, Abdel Wahid looked like an alcoholic desperate for a drink, offered everything but the one thing he craved, but could not admit he needed.

Over the previous five months, the peace talks themselves had been arranged according to a standard format. Tables in the main conference room downstairs in the Chida Hotel were arranged round a rectangle. The mediators sat across one, shorter side, with the government delegation on their right and the rebels on their left, facing one another. Representatives from the international community sat on the fourth side. The proceedings were formal, consisting of moderated exchanges of views on documents drafted by each side and by the mediators. Often the Sudanese negotiators made lengthy statements, usually for the benefit of an imagined public gallery, and sometimes they exchanged insults. There was a lot of posturing but little real negotiation – which was why the mediators were compelled, under the pressure of deadlines imposed by the UN Security Council, to prepare and present the proposals themselves.

Meanwhile, upstairs in the claustrophobic rooms of the Chida Hotel, political business was conducted differently. The discussions were of course all in Arabic, and while much effort was expended trying to generate an atmosphere of secrecy, almost all of what went on among the rebels was known to the government delegation.

The government's chief negotiator, Dr Majzoub al Khalifa, was a hard bargainer. He had been a trade unionist, the chief negotiator for the doctors' union, and it showed. He had a file on every individual in the hotel, and not only the rebels. He was as distrustful of his colleagues as he was of his adversaries, and was also keenly interested in the members of the mediation team and observers.

The Darfur rebels joked that Majzoub was a *'jellaba* politician', with reference to the class of traders known as *jellaba*, originating from the Ja'aliyiin and Shaygiyya tribes of the Nile north of Khartoum, who had spread out throughout the Sudanese provinces (and beyond) with small shops and lorries. Selling soap, matches and other basic consumer goods at slender profit margins, far from home, the *jellaba* nevertheless managed to accumulate capital that they invariably remitted back to the riverine regions.[6] In English, the best term for Majzoub might be 'retail politician', with reference to the way in which he bargained over the price of each individual on a case-by-case basis. He employed junior officials as thrift-store bargain hunters, who scoured the ranks of the junior rebel commanders looking for the abandoned and underpriced. Two terms they used were *al sanduq al siasi* ('political budget') and *al suq al siasi* ('political market').

Abdel Wahid did not sign that day. But he continued to negotiate for a week after the formal ending of the talks. Majzoub returned to Khartoum while Abdel Wahid stayed in Abuja, though he moved with his delegation to an even more dingy hotel where cockroaches scuttled across cigarette-burned carpets. They communicated by phone and by documents passed through the last remaining member of the mediation team in Abuja (me). Both men hoped that they would be able to agree an addendum to the agreement, one that raised the price payable marginally but sufficient for Abdel Wahid to join. The SLM leader did not see a future fighting in the mountains of Darfur. But neither of them foresaw the echo chamber of Darfurian public opinion, facilitated by mobile phones and the internet (perhaps a harbinger of the potential of social media in just a few years' time). The government's announcement of the peace deal, spun to appeal to its core constituency, was heard by leaders of the internally displaced persons (IDPs) in Darfur, who were bewildered and angered. That version was echoed and amplified by the agitation of diaspora rebels, prompting the AU mediation team to issue a public letter explaining the content of the peace deal – too late.[7] This resulted in demonstrations in the IDP camps against the African Union, and vociferous critiques of the agreement by western activists. Abdel Wahid seized the opportunity, repositioning himself as the principled opponent of making any deal with Khartoum. He became, over the following years, the exemplary 'hotel guerilla', moving from Nairobi to Asmara to Paris to Kampala, campaigning everywhere except in Darfur. Majzoub dismissed him as a hapless clown with an over-inflated sense of his value.

Vernacular Politics in Sudan

A few weeks after Majzoub and Minni signed the DPA, I went to see Majzoub, at his office in Khartoum next door to the presidential palace. In his home terrain, his operating procedure was plain to see. The office resembled a doctor's surgery (in professional practice, he had been a dermatologist), with the patients sitting outside waiting to be summoned in, one by one, to be given their prescriptions. Each supplicant was given detailed personal instructions, and a note to be redeemed for payment.

Majzoub had repeatedly complained during the talks that the rebels were overpriced: they were demanding too much and, if he complied, other constituents in Sudan would demand more. He was alternately baffled and angry at the way in which Chad, Libya and the Americans inflated the rebels' price. 'The price must come down,' he assured me, as a matter of political-economic fact.

One of Majzoub's motivations was not to repeat the mistake of his rival, Vice President Ali Osman Taha, who in dealing with southern Sudan had abandoned retail politics in favour of a wholesale deal: the CPA. For twenty years, Khartoum's security officers had run the war in the south by hiring the services of discontented members of the southern provincial elite one by one. This worked well enough to ensure that the SPLA's rebellion, headed by Colonel John Garang, was entangled in a series of bloody and destructive internecine wars. But they were not able to buy off Garang, who was astonishingly stubborn, and had built himself a series of regional and international alliances to compensate for the weakness of his internal mobilization. Garang would not be content with a provincial deal: he wanted power in Khartoum, where the real money was. In 2003, Ali Osman decided to deal directly with Garang and make an offer that was both political (power sharing) and financial (nearly half of the enormous funds becoming available through Sudan's oil boom). But, according to Majzoub, Ali Osman had overpaid and the government would regret it in due course. He made the case to President Omar al Bashir that the Darfurians could be bought off much more cheaply, and promised to prove this. Majzoub's political-business plan is standard for the Sudanese political and security elite, and it is unsurprising that he prevailed over Ali Osman.

An essential skill for a political leader in such a system is extremely wide and detailed knowledge of people. Bashir, who emerged as an unusually deft manager of his country's system, is well known for having an open door at his residence in the evening (at least for army officers), an extraordinary memory for people and events, and great sociability, including a famous sense of humour. Another skill is anticipating multiple possible configurations of people and circumstances, and taking them into account. When I discussed with Majzoub, I could almost see his brain calculating how each scenario would play out with the multiple actors whose machinations he had to consider. I had few encounters with Bashir, but I noticed the same characteristic. However, while Majzoub was usually bluffing when he spoke about his 'red lines' beyond which no compromise was possible, Bashir was both sparing and deadly serious when he marked out these boundaries.

Another accomplished practitioner of retail politics was the long-time director of the National Intelligence and Security Service (NISS), Salah Abdalla 'Gosh'. He was so capable that his political budget and the loyalties he rented thereby were a challenge to Bashir, who dismissed him in 2009. But one of the hallmarks of an astute operator is that his political funds, networks and intelligence persist whatever his formal position, and Gosh remained powerful even though his office was now a private consultancy. Opening a conversation in November 2010, I asked him, 'So, what is the price of a Darfur militia today?' Without blinking, he told me the going price of the day and how it had changed from the previous week. Gosh then went on to echo Majzoub's misgivings about the southern Sudanese: he said they were demanding too high a price for their cooperation. Their sense of ethnic nationalism (he used the term) and money from oil made them unreasonably expensive, he said. But, for Gosh, it was not a matter of different rules of the game, but simply that the tactical market conditions were not right. He was confident that playing divide-and-rent would work again in due course.

The vernacular of everyday politics in Sudan uses the vocabulary of the market. This is really how Sudanese politicians transact their business. And it is on this basis that it is necessary to construct a framework for how Sudanese politics actually functions.

From Political Vernacular to Political Theory

Since I first travelled to Sudan in 1984, the global organization of resources, violence and communication has changed substantially, such that political leaders in countries such as Sudan face immense difficulties preserving those public goods that exist, let alone creating new ones. The public goods in question include institutional political order, peace and security, and economic development. Over thirty years, the level of provision of public goods, and the source of those goods, has fluctuated wildly. But, on the whole, there has been a decline in the quality of public institutions and their command over the political sphere. This is true beyond Sudan: most members of the political elites of north-east Africa have failed to create basic public goods, and many have abandoned the effort and come to resemble gangsters rather than civic political leaders. Even those who are principled and selfless must contend for survival in a system that rewards those with ruthless political-business skills. In the strict sense of the word, as first applied to Nigeria in the 1960s by Stanislav Andreski, these are kleptocracies in which 'the functioning of the organs of authority is determined by the mechanisms of supply and demand rather than the laws and regulations'.[8]

Like many students of my generation interested in refugee issues, I went to Sudan because the University of Khartoum was the global intellectual centre for the study of humanitarian issues. Intellectual capital was produced in two modest buildings either side of Sharia Jamaa, the Institute for African and Asian Studies and the Commissioner of Refugees of the Sudanese Ministry of the Interior. From here, the academic product flowed to the academies of Oxford and elsewhere. Sudan was the source of scholarly and policy innovation in the field. Since then, a combination of academic penury and repression has meant that African universities have fallen far behind their European and American peers. Meanwhile, the Horn of Africa as a whole has become a fascinating crucible for political experimentation, and the best analysts of those realities have been the men and women who have to grapple with their political systems on a week-to-week basis. Unfortunately, too many of the creative thinkers of north-east Africa have been forced to live and work elsewhere, or survive through taking on consultancies for international organizations. Much of the creative vigour that used to characterize another modest place on Sharia Jamaa, the University of Khartoum Faculty Club, has been lost. This book is also an effort to encourage students in the region to regain the intellectual courage to study their countries' problems starting from their lived realities.

One of the region's most important political thinkers was Meles Zenawi, whom I had the privilege of knowing for nearly twenty-five years. The earliest drafts of the chapters of this book were written for, and discussed with, Meles. As a student activist, a liberation fighter and then head of government, Meles represented a different kind of political intellectual from the Sudanese politicians I have described above. For example, when I discussed with him a model of political bargaining developed by Jacek Kugler, Meles's response was to appreciate the predictive power of the model, but to ask about the theoretical precepts on which it was based.

My encounters with Meles began at dusk in November 1988, when I crossed Sudan's eastern border into part of northern Ethiopia held by the Tigrayan People's Liberation Front (TPLF), and climbed on to a Soviet-built Zil truck captured from the Ethiopian army, at that time led by Colonel Mengistu Haile Mariam, a military dictator allied to the Soviet Union. On the truck were several members of the TPLF leadership, including Comrade Seyoum, head of foreign relations, and Comrade Meles, in his pyjamas, returning from medical treatment in Khartoum. All travel was at night because of daily overflights by Ethiopian MiG fighter-bombers and the occasional helicopter gunship. During the day we rested under trees or in caves; during the night we travelled on roads hacked out of the mountainside by the guerrillas. Some of the hairpin bends were so tight that the truck had to make three-point or even five-point turns on the corners, the wheels just inches from the precipices. Near government garrisons, the drivers switched off their headlamps and drove by moonlight and keen eyesight. The journey was equally memorable as a travelling seminar, in which Meles, Seyoum and others discussed the history of European revolutions, theories of warfare, and peasant survival during famine and theories of economic development. At one point we stopped for almost an hour while Meles argued with some hunters we met by the roadside, on the importance of conserving endangered species.

Meles later gained fame and controversy for his prowess in grounding political practice in political theory. But others in the leadership, including Sebhat Nega, Mulugeta Gebrehiwot, Abadi Zemo and Tsadkan Gebretensae, were also fine intellectuals. They followed the principle that each problem they faced – political, military or economic – needed to be thoroughly analysed and understood, and a consensus established on this analysis. Having achieved this, accomplishing the task that followed was a straightforward matter. Tsadkan, the TPLF's leading logistician who went on to command the forces that captured Addis Ababa in 1991 and then became chief of staff of the national army, remarked to me that 'war is primarily an intellectual exercise'.

Among the decisions taken by the TPLF leadership, in 1984 as famine gripped Tigray and the survival of the rural populace was in doubt, was to give priority to famine relief.[9] Hundreds of thousands of villagers were evacuated to refugee camps in Sudan, and later brought back, and military operations were scaled back, with important exceptions such as a raid on a food depot near Lalibella in which they opened the storehouses and distributed the food, which the military government had been rationing to supply its militia and those farmers assigned for resettlement, to the general population. This organic connection between the welfare of ordinary people and security policy was later manifest in Ethiopia's white paper on national security, written by Meles.[10]

Meles possessed a detailed knowledge of his country, and of individuals who were politically active or who had positions in the administration. He was also a master of tactical manoeuvre, a skill that had allowed him to survive – by the narrowest of margins – an internal challenge to his position in 2001, when the TPLF was split

down the middle. However, Meles's thinking was never solely tactical, but rather derived from a theoretical framework, which joined
politics, economics and security in an integrated whole.

Twenty years after my first meeting with Meles, I was a member
of a group that regularly convened small seminars in his office in
Addis Ababa, to debate his theory of the 'democratic developmental
state' and issues of peace and security in the Horn.[11] In this seminar
I presented an early draft of the framework of the 'rentier political
marketplace', and Meles commented:

> [This] is a powerful tool for the archetypical African state, which
> demystifies politics on the continent. It needs to be elaborated further.
> It mostly deals with the political elite, it should bring in the mass in
> the rural and urban areas, how are they affected? We need to know
> which social forces generate deeper rent seeking, and which can assist
> us in finding a way out.[12]

His concern with the 'archetypical African state' was principally how
it could be superseded: how best to stamp out rent-seeking and
replace it with an ethos and practice of value creation – the 'democratic developmental state'.

Meles's analytical starting point was that Ethiopia (and indeed
Africa as a whole) lacked comparative advantage in *any* productive
sector. Ethiopian farmers could not produce and bring to market
cereals to compete with Kansas, and Chinese workers manufactured
textiles at a ninth of the cost of the work done by Africans. Only in
boutique products such as cut flowers and upmarket coffee, or in
natural resources such as hydropower, was Ethiopia competitive, and
those sectors had no prospect of supporting a population approach-
ing a hundred million people. In Ethiopia's small, open economy,
exposed to the global market forces, local businesspeople faced vast
hostile odds against success. Among those adverse odds was the likelihood that some minor tremor in the world economy would collapse
their businesses completely.

I was pessimistic that any African government could tame the
world's economic and political turbulence sufficiently to create the
conditions for building an institutionalized state. Instead, I argued
that marketized politics was an effective adaptation to the global
political economy, and it might well overwhelm institutionalized
political orders. Meles countered that he did not have the luxury
of pessimism when national survival was at stake, and prescribed
an 'activist state' dedicated to 'democratic developmentalism'. He
was a deliberate, deliberative and ruthless state-builder. But one of
the paradoxes of Meles's state-building effort was the extent to which

it relied on him as an individual. It is an ironic testament to the pervasiveness of the political marketplace that Ethiopian state-building was driven less by world-historic forces, and more by the energies and capabilities of an individual who briefly succeeded, through intellectual power and political skill, in centralizing control over rent in his office.

In our discussions, Meles liked to steer the topic away from current affairs into history and theory. One time when I complained that my duties with the African Union High-Level Implementation Panel for Sudan (AUHIP) had prevented me from redrafting my paper on political markets, Meles responded that the intellectual work of theorization was no less important than the practical work of mediation, and proposed that when he retired from active politics we would have the opportunity to develop our respective frameworks in tandem and as a debate. I argued that the globalization of political finance meant that the political marketplace was set to triumph, and Meles promised to prove me wrong. We never had the chance to complete our debate, and this book is a contribution to that unrealized aspiration.

Outline of the Book

Chapter 2 lays out the framework of the political marketplace, exploring it both as a real phenomenon found in certain countries, and also as a general principle of political life. It introduces the key problem of the book: how politicians operate as political entrepreneurs and business managers to seek and maintain power in an intrinsically turbulent and unpredictable system. I do not argue that *all* politicians operate in accordance with political market principles all the time, and still less do I claim that they all explain their actions in this way. Rather, I claim that the most skilled and successful politicians operate in this way, and understand perfectly well what they are doing. Quite often, politicians make mistakes, and some of those mistakes mean their political agendas fail, and other errors ignite violence that is excessive or counterproductive. Sometimes politicians try to resist the logic of the market, appealing to different principles, but the market will usually judge them harshly and they will either accommodate their political projects to the market, or they will fail. Very often, external actors fail to see how real politics functions in these countries, and doom their own projects to failure.

Chapter 3 provides an overview of the modern history of the Horn of Africa, as a laboratory of conflicts, unfolding over three acts, during which time each of the three large countries – Ethiopia, Somalia and Sudan – has been partitioned. During the Cold War, the entire region was embroiled in interlocking civil wars, while economies and governmental systems reached the point of collapse. In the 1990s, a contest between political Islam and an alliance of new revolutionary governments reconfigured the subcontinental struggle for supremacy. The third act, from the millennium to today, is a contest for position in a regional political marketplace, in the context of a rentierist global political economy.

The framework of the political marketplace initially derived from experience in Darfur. Chapter 4 analyses Darfur as a near-perfect political market, characterized by multiple purchasers of loyalty and fierce competition among provincial political-military entrepreneurs. It recounts the process of the marketization of Darfurian political life, the political-business management errors by the Sudanese government that led to war in 2003, and the way in which that war subsequently mutated into a multi-sided auction of loyalties.

Chapter 5 addresses the national Sudanese political marketplace, showing how politics has been structured around the generation and allocation of a political budget based on rents. This explains the long-term process of the decay of political institutions, the growth of the Islamist movement, the internal political management within the ruling elite, the dynamics of war and peace and the post-secession crises as the country's ruler faced a dramatically reduced political budget.

Chapter 6 takes South Sudan as a case study of an extreme and revealing exemplar of a polity in which institutions are fully subordinated to militarized patronage. It recounts how South Sudan's leaders developed a political system that translated oil revenue into political loyalty, by funding a vast military payroll, and licensing corruption. Such a kleptocratic system was possible only for as long as budgets were increasing, and when oil revenues stalled, crisis was inevitable.

Chapter 7 explains how Somalia has functioned as a political market for the last thirty years. In the 1980s, the Somali government was run as a militarized patrimonial system based upon superpower rents. Unable to regulate the private flows of political funds, President Mohamed Siyad Barre found himself priced out of his own political market, and government collapsed. Every subsequent attempt to put together a government has been based on rentier financing and has faced the same problem, and failed to resolve it. The Islamists' brief experiment in setting up a government based on Somali business financiers was destroyed by Ethiopian and American opposition.

The case of Somaliland shows how a viable political system can be established in these circumstances. Focusing on the circumstances and processes whereby domestic financiers struck bargains with political and military entrepreneurs, chapter 8 recounts how this came about.

Chapter 9 deals with Eritrea, explaining how President Isaias Afewerki has stayed in power despite military defeat, international isolation and an insolvent formal economy. It is a case study of skilled but brutal political-business management, and how Eritrea has transitioned to a criminalized rentier system. It is a sad illustration of how political projects succumb to the material logic of the marketplace.

Throughout the Horn of Africa, the political market is making it impossible to build states in the conventional manner. Chapter 10 turns to the country that has made the most sustained efforts to establish a developmental state and a working set of governance institutions, namely, Ethiopia. The demographic majority in the Horn consists of 90 million Ethiopians and their country has a strong claim to enduring statehood. Ethiopia's experiment in 'democratic developmentalism' – at once a reversion to central planning as practised in an earlier era and an assault on pervasive rent-seeking – poses the principal challenge to the logic of the political marketplace. In this chapter I briefly examine this experience and its prospects for success.

In the final two chapters, I explore the drivers of change across the whole of the Horn and beyond. Chapter 11 links the Horn to a global political marketplace, showing how the region is integrated as part of a global patronage system, in which political loyalties are instrumentalized and dollarized. I suggest that oil exports, security cooperation and aid have contributed to a 'shadow globalization', and that new models of peace support operation are becoming instruments of security patronage.

The final chapter deals with the public sphere – the politics of ideas and democratic debate – and political circuitry – political market information, convening and communication. The latter is a component of real politics no less important than finance or firepower. As political markets become more efficient, junior members of the political elite find it more advantageous to participate in them. This makes the market more competitive and inclusive, but also more firmly entrenched, thereby making ideas and public policy less relevant than money to political outcomes. This chapter also identifies resistance to the political marketplace, emerging from other social logics and practices.

2

The Political Marketplace
Politics is Business and Business is Politics

'No Condition is Permanent'

The 'political marketplace' is a contemporary system of governance in which politics is conducted as the exchange of political services or loyalty for payment or licence. The Horn of Africa is an advanced and militarized political marketplace, characterized by pervasive rent-seeking and monetized patronage, with violence routinely used as a tool for extracting rent. It is integrated into regional and global circuits of political finance.

To elaborate this, let me begin by drawing upon Jane Guyer's analysis of the West African economy, integrated into the Atlantic economic order over several centuries and exposed to recurrent shocks to the extent that instability is the norm. Guyer challenges the 'intellectual "homing instinct" towards equilibrium, systematicity, and slow directional growth' and observes, '[t]he logic of theories that index to Western experience would predict eventual total social incoherence for any society that was subjected for any length of time to the conditions expected in small open economies.'[1] She contrasts today's dominant paradigms in social science with William James's philosophy of 'pragmatism' that had its roots in the disturbed experience of post-Civil War America:

> The stable, cumulative, and systemic concept of institutions is a reflection of a later Western world, more sure of its direction. It becomes, however, blunt and illogical when applied to a reality that seems, to those who live it, altogether less settled. Like pragmatists, they have to apply reason and judgment to horizons of contingency rather than applying a narrow calculative rationality to given variables.[2]

The premise of an unsettled world is summed up in a favourite slogan painted on West African trucks and taxis: 'no condition is permanent'. This can also be described as 'turbulence', a term taken from fluid dynamics that refers to the way in which a system is unpredictable and chaotic from one moment to the next, lacking discernible pattern, but still maintains a recognizable structure over a longer period of time. Turbulence can be visualized as the currents, swirls and eddies of a fast-flowing stream, which produces moments of calm and tranquillity, before plunging into another vortex. Let me augment this with three other aquatic metaphors. The businessperson or national economic planner in a small open economy is like R. H. Tawney's peasant, up to his chin in water, who can be drowned by a mere ripple[3] – which could be caused by the wake of a distant ship plying its normal trade. Also, the national leader is like Robert Jackson and Carl Rosberg's early post-colonial ruler, for whom 'governance is more a matter of seamanship and less one of navigation – that is, staying afloat rather than going somewhere'.[4] Third, just as physicists and chemists find it much easier to investigate the properties of solids rather than liquids, so too social and political scientists prefer to study institutions and regularities, rather than individuals, transactions and contingencies. The scarcity of scholarship does not mean that the subject matter is less important.

Politics is fractal in the sense that the same patterns of authority and bargaining are reproduced at all levels: local, provincial, national and interstate. The turbulent and fractal characteristics intersect insofar as a disturbance at a lower level may generate an unpredictable change at a higher level. This is the political version of the climatologist's 'butterfly effect' whereby a miniscule phenomenon such as the breath of air caused by a butterfly flapping its wings can be the trigger for ever-larger weather phenomena ultimately creating a hurricane. Politics is also an open system: it is amenable to innovation. In the same way that a business entrepreneur can find profit within a weak and unstable economy, a creative and able political entrepreneur can find new sources of political income, change the political geography of patronage or exploit a new means of mobilizing a constituency.

Turbulence means that politics is often confusing and apparently patternless. It means that the newly posted diplomat or rookie journalist is easily excited by what appears to be imminent change. Turbulence gives rise to the standing joke about Sudanese political life: it changes from week to week but if you come back after ten years it is exactly the same. Short-term fluctuations obscure longer-term trends. Nonetheless those trends are there, some of them indeed shaped by the persistent patterns of political life, in the way that a turbulent stream can carve a channel through a hillside.

Political markets are well adapted to systemic turbulence. This gives us insight into one of the enigmas of modernity in Africa and the Greater Middle East: the parallel proliferation of governance institutions and a lack of popular confidence in those institutions. In most countries, there are far more governmental institutions than forty years ago, and they have a more intrusive impact on people's lives. The World Bank's 2011 *World Development Report* found that progress on key state-building indicators has not only been sustained, but has been even more rapid in recent history than previously.[5] It is harder to measure people's confidence in institutions and in the prospect that they will generate a modern state, but there is a widespread perception of the opposite. This was articulated by James Ferguson, writing about contemporary Zambia – once the most industrialized and urbanized country in sub-Saharan Africa – in words that resonate across the Horn:

> [S]ome contemporary Africans seem to feel a sort of nostalgia for the modern. In my own work in Zambia, for instance, mineworkers did not say, 'We are modern, but in our own, alternative way!' or even, 'We have never been modern'...They said, in effect, 'We used to be modern – or, at least, well on our way, but now we've been denied that opportunity.' Modernity, for them, was not an anticipated future but a dream to be remembered from the past. The real future was almost universally understood as bleak, even apocalyptic.[6]

I suggest that the enigma is explained because the political market has emerged as an alternative form of governance. A generation ago, Africans saw a contest between modernization and customary, patrimonial forms of governance. Even though perversions of the latter were common, people were confident that these were deviations on the path of progress. Today, they implicitly understand that political markets are becoming dominant while state-building fades.

The Political Marketplace and Real Politics

The concept of a political market operates at two levels: as one general feature of political life (everywhere) and as the central component of politics (in advanced political markets). Every political system involves interpersonal bargaining in which reward is exchanged for cooperation. The laws, social codes and institutional rules and regulations that provide the apparatus of political life in developed societies should not obscure the fact that everyday politics also consists of transactions that involve services/allegiance, resources/licence, and coercion/threat. Some of these transactions are labelled 'corruption' and others are permissible horse-trading. Political markets can thrive behind the facade of an institutionalized state. When a strong state (such as a well-regulated authoritarian government) is thrown into crisis, it may mutate into an advanced political marketplace, rather than transitioning towards democracy.

In advanced political marketplace governance systems, the conduct of political business as exchange is the central feature, and the prices of the commodities of cooperation and allegiance are determined by supply and demand. Resources are allocated accordingly. Real politics is the bargaining and coercion that constitutes these transactions.[7] These systems are found in locations (countries and parts of countries) in which the following conditions apply: (a) political finance is in the hands of individuals with political, military or business interests; (b) control over the instruments of violence is dispersed or contested; and (c) political disputes are not resolved by institutional rules and procedures (law is subordinate to political contingency). Additionally, (d) these countries are integrated into the global political and economic order in a subordinate position. Almost all of these locations are commonly characterized as weak, fragile or failing states, but, for reasons that will become clear, I do not find this terminology helpful – neither the adjectives nor the noun 'state'. Most are countries in conflict or where wartime political-business models and networks continue to prosper in the post-war regime. Elements or isolated exemplars of this kind of politics may be found elsewhere. For example, a big country with a well-governed core may have remote peripheries or urban enclaves in which governance is conducted as a political marketplace.

This form of advanced political marketplace is a contemporary form of governance and not an obsolete relic or a transitional system that is destined to be replaced by a Weberian state. It is flexible and dynamic. It is also a product of recent history, specifically economic and political globalization and the deregulation and monetization of the provision of public goods and services, notably security. Charles Tilly famously made the comparison between early states in Europe and organized crime:

> If protection rackets represent organised crime at its smoothest, then war risking and state making – quintessential protection rackets with the advantage of legitimacy – qualify as our largest examples of

organised crime. Without branding all generals and statesmen as mur-
derers or thieves, I want to urge the value of that analogy. At least for
the European experience of the past few centuries, a portrait of war
makers and state makers as coercive and self-seeking entrepreneurs
bears a far greater resemblance to the facts than do its chief alternatives: the idea of a social contract, the idea of an open market in which
operators of armies and states offer services to willing consumers, the
idea of a society whose shared norms and expectations call forth a
certain kind of government.[8]

In earlier eras, those ambitious political leaders who founded the
forerunners of modern states acted in ways *akin* to the heads of
criminal cartels. Today, their counterparts in poorly institutionalized
countries are accurately described as *political entrepreneurs* and
political-business managers, who *are* the chief executives and sometimes the owners of businesses, including criminal ones. They manage
a modern, dynamic system, which is neither a historic relic nor a
precursor to an institutionalized state.

Political Entrepreneurs and Business Managers

Understanding the political marketplace requires appreciation of the
skills and strategies of those who succeed within it. Political skill is
not an extraneous factor: it is central to understanding governance.
Some politicians are simply more talented and capable than others.
If we are to develop a framework for analysing political skill, the best
place to start is with the concepts and judgements of the politicians
themselves, and especially those who have a proven record of success.
They use a business lens, and so shall we. They mark a political
entrepreneur up if he knows a lot of people and can judge their
capacities well. They mark him down if he lacks those qualities, or
is timid or capricious. They predict a crisis when a political-business
manager is short on political funds or his claimants have upped the
price. In this book I outline these vernacular models. In a later exercise I plan to model them more precisely and test their predictions
against real people and real events: I hypothesize that they will come
out as more reliable guides to political trajectories than the metrics
of academic political science.

 If this approach has value, it follows that successful politicians will
operate according to business principles, and in turn that business
management models will be a useful guide to understanding these
governance systems and how they are changing. Isaac Williams[9] has
explored this and developed a model, drawing upon the 'five forces'

of Michael Porter,[10] used to describe the forces shaping industry competition.

The key concepts from business management transfer remarkably well to politicians in the political marketplace. Political businesspeople seek to increase revenue and limit costs. They can finance their operations through debt, equity, revenue from operations, or rent. The best income streams are rents – payments in excess of what would be determined by supply and demand. Political rents derive from owning land or natural resources, from the privilege of being able to assert sovereignty, from external patronage, and from using or threatening violence. The downside of rent is that dependence on external funds incurs potential risks of hostile takeovers from financiers. Consequently, politicians try to control as much information flow as they can, and prefer their foreign sponsors to be diverse and not in contact with one another. Politicians are invariably rent-seeking, but not all are rent-dependent: some obtain their funds through deals determined by market forces alone.

Political businesspeople also face choices between incurring direct costs or outsourcing/licensing to subcontractors, incurring risk of forward integration by new entrants taking over their market share. They seek to limit the entry of competitors into the market and discourage rival or replacement products. They try to develop customer loyalty through branding, typically by using identity labels, or by demonstrating their own long-term commitment by closing exit options, for example, by committing conspicuous atrocities. Extremist groups such as al Shabaab use these stratagems to keep their costs down.

Political-business managers may be executives who answer to a board, or they may be the owners of the business themselves. The structure of their political businesses determines not only how they manage and prosper, or fail, but also exit barriers. A political CEO who has built up a wholly owned firm, or who has become indispensable to a cartel, may face particular difficulties with exit. Bashir failed to overcome this problem in 2014. Sudan is fortunate that its long-time military rulers do not have biological children, but in other countries in Africa and the Greater Middle East, sons are political heirs apparent, as if their countries were family businesses.

Political businesses can expand. A political entrepreneur can increase his market share at the expense of his rivals. He can become so effective at renting the services of those lower down the chain and adding value to their activities, that he can challenge and displace his erstwhile patrons. As a larger-scale operator, especially if he takes a controlling stake in a recognized government, he can expand his reach across borders, even making formally sovereign rulers into his clients. He can expand into new sectors: taking on counter-terror contracts is a current favourite. In doing so he can repackage his business and try to rebrand his reputation. As the complexity of sources of revenue rises, so too does the time horizon of the businessperson, and the level of institutionalization of the firm and its contractual relations with its buyers and suppliers.

The concept of 'profit' is more complex. Political businesspeople are still *political* actors: their goals are rarely confined to personal material reward but commonly extend to enjoying power and fulfilling ambitions, including realizing aspirations for their communities and countries. Profit can be 'real' in the normal business sense but, in a *political* marketplace, those funds are typically reinvested into political and security budgets, and sometimes into vanity projects and public goods. 'Profit' is therefore convertible between power and money, and partly a metaphor. In reflecting on business motives, we should also not forget that many commercial businesspeople invest their profits in political careers or philanthropic ventures, for all kinds of reasons.

The business model is the entrepreneur's set of strategic choices which define the nature of his venture, including choices related to financing types, revenue sources, cost structure, market-entry, staffing, and responses to market competition. This is represented by Michael Porter with the graphic and Figure 2.1.[11] The way in which Williams adapts the chart in Figure 2.1 for the political entrepreneur or business manager is shown in Figure 2.2.

Specifying the Variables of 'Real Politics'

Politicians conduct their affairs within systems that can be specified according to the four variables mentioned in the previous section: political finance; control over the means of violence; the means for regulating political disputes; and the terms of integration into the global political economy.

The first variable is *political finance*. This has two elements, income and expenditure. Following Rudolf Goldscheid's enjoinder to develop a fiscal sociology, and his dictum, 'the budget is the skeleton of the state, stripped of all misleading ideologies',[12] we can identify the skeleton of the political marketplace, as the *political budget*. This is the money available for a politician to spend on whatever purposes he may choose – especially for renting the loyalty or cooperation of other politicians. The political budget is not the same as government

The five forces that shape industry competition

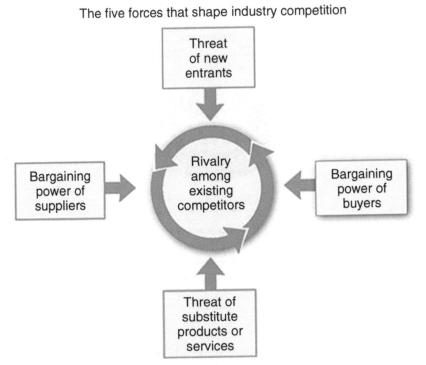

Figure 2.1 Michael Porter's 'five forces' of business

revenue: it is money for which no accounting is required. Governmental funds that are controlled by state institutions, which the ruler cannot control directly, are not part of the political budget. Therefore, it is not equivalent to the defence budget but consists instead in the bribes paid by arms contractors and the funds paid to commanders, accounted for as payments to 'ghost soldiers'.

In many countries – perhaps most – political payouts on the scale required to outbid competitors, and to turn executive decisions into real action, are far greater than the money that can legitimately be extracted from institutionalized public politics. So politicians are required to operate in a shadow world of illicit finance, or else legalize influence-peddling. The simplest form of getting political money is primary accumulation: theft and extortion, or selling licences for robbery. This was seen in the 1980s and 1990s in Somalia and Sudan. More complex forms are exacting payments from trade or local production, monopsony rentierism (for example, oil revenues or resources

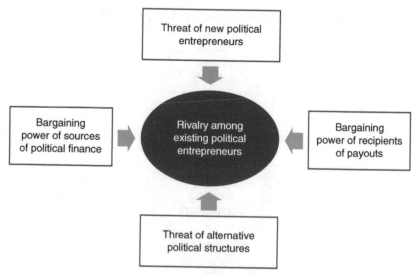

Figure 2.2   The 'five forces' of political business

provided from security cooperation), which are today dominant in South Sudan and Sudan. Various forms of organizing political power and business generate different levels and kinds of political financing.[13] Certain industries – oil, banking and arms, in particular – are ideal sources for political funds. Petroleum and financial services have vast amounts of money, and their profits are heavily influenced by government legislation. Weapons systems manufacturers sell chiefly to governments, and, unlike other government contractors, they conduct their deals in secret behind the soundproofed doors of national security. This takes place in every country in the Horn. If a politician is funded by national businesspeople, getting that money may involve competitive bargaining among his peers. Kenya and Somaliland offer examples of this. The most complex forms of political finance are derived from citizens' direct contributions (e.g., organized labour) and taxation: this was the case in Sudan forty years ago. These different kinds of political finance differ in their complexity, sustainability, reliability and size, which in turn determine politicians' options and strategies.

A useful trick for the political-business manager is to use the instruments perfected by transnational corporations for profit shifting and tax avoidance. He may offer a transnational corporation the opportunity to pay very low taxes (e.g., on crude oil exports or land acquisition), in return for depositing a bribe in the politician's account in a tax haven. The politician can then 'round trip' those funds into a political budget back home.

A politician's spending can be divided into three baskets: a personal security budget, a political budget and spending on public goods. The general rule is that a political CEO will first take care of his own security and political needs, and whatever remains may be allocated to public spending.

To vary Goldscheid's anatomical metaphor, political cashflow is the heartbeat of political-business management. The health of the political budget is the indicator of whether a political entrepreneur will thrive or fail, or whether a political CEO will sustain his empire, or be plunged into crisis. The life-sustaining element is loyalty payment. The *price of loyalty* is the prevailing market rate for ensuring the allegiance or cooperation of other politicians for a period of time or a particular activity. The price is determined by market forces, including the relative leverage of the buyer and the sellers, quality of information and expectations among the traders, the availability of coercion, and the barriers to entry for new political entrepreneurs. In week-to-week political management, the politician's challenge is sustaining political cashflow and ensuring that claimants are paid, at minimum cost, or persuaded not to demand payment. Tactical means of reducing or postponing payment include making promises (running up political debts), issuing licences (for plunder or corrupt deals), or making cheap appeals to common identity or common threat – each of which comes at a political price.

Political markets share the perverse feature of security markets,[14] namely, that competition increases the price. The more tightly regulated the market, the lower the price of loyalty and the higher the barriers to entry for new political entrepreneurs. The political CEO's strategic challenge is to control the market and thereby lower his loyalty spending. Success in this frees up funds for other things he may want to do, which can range from personal enrichment to political aggrandizement through buying weapons or building monuments, or spending on public goods such as education, welfare and development. Among the ways of reducing loyalty spending are intimidation, divide-and-rule, and invoking popular solidarities by appeals to ethnicity, nationalism or religion. Institution-building also serves as a way to reduce political payments, but it is a riskier and more difficult strategy.

The second variable is the degree to which *control over violence is centralized or decentralized*. Control over the organization of violence can vary between: fully centralized; distributed among governmental institutions (e.g., regular army, national security, police, presidential guard); and decentralized across society (to include militia, rebels, vigilantes and criminal gangs). Typically, the distribution of control over the instruments of violence is a product of history, specifically war, peace agreements and the strategies pursued by national political CEOs to create divided and rivalrous security institutions in an attempt to 'coup-proof' their regimes. Peace agreements do not usually dismantle wartime political-security networks, but consolidate them.

In a militarized rentier-political marketplace, the main instrument whereby a national political CEO can keep military entrepreneurs in line is financial patronage. Rulers have their own instruments of coercion, but very few of them can rule by force alone. In almost all cases, members of the provincial political elite, such as rebel commanders and tribal chiefs, can organize violence on their own account. So can those formally positioned within the state apparatus, such as army officers or heads of paramilitary and security forces, who nonetheless have sufficient autonomy to pursue their own political-business careers. Some have one foot in the governmental system and one outside.

By threatening or staging a *rent-seeking rebellion*, a commander, chief or local administrator attracts attention, advertises his intent and determination, and strikes up a round of bargaining. This is conducted through fighting and talking. Killing, and being prepared to send one's own followers to their deaths, is an index of seriousness in bargaining. The rebellion is settled through a *payroll peace*: its leader is given a promotion and his fighters are put on the army payroll: arrears are paid, pay rises awarded, and more soldiers – real ones and ghosts – are salaried.

Violence organized in this way intersects with identity politics. In north-east Africa, the most characteristic form of this is militarized tribalism. Armed groups are constituted on the basis of patronage and kinship: their leader simultaneously *rewards and defrauds* his soldiers. Because salaries are scarce, the leader employs his kin. Because each official involved in disbursing the cash for wages and allowances takes a cut, the wages received by a soldier are never as much as advertised. Each commander is short-changing his followers. Co-ethnicity is part of the bargain to minimize the risks of the payroll mutiny. And when leader or fighters stage a rebellion, those they kill first are members of other tribes – traders or officials from other ethnic groups, neighbouring communities – and the conflict takes on an ethnic character. Fighting itself reinforces ethnic bonds. Meanwhile, when a political entrepreneur invokes ethnicity he makes a pact with the custodians of that identity – such as tribal chiefs – who will try to assert their dwindling authority when the protagonists begin their political bargaining to settle the conflict. This haggling is dressed up as a peace process, involving community representatives, reconciliation and settlement of grievances.

The rent-seeking rebellion cycle is inherently inflationary, and the national political CEO faces the challenge of how to manage it without going bankrupt. Typically, his means include increasing the costs and risks of rebellion (by fighting it), enlisting the rebel's competitors to steal or destroy his asset base, and shutting off other sources of political funds by cutting deals with external financiers.

The third variable consists of the *rules, norms and mechanisms that regulate bargaining and dispute resolution.* A market is itself an institution. The formal and informal institutions for resolving political disputes vary according to the *degree* to which they are regulated. Some societies are more rigorously regulated than others, whether by law and regulation, or by custom and social norms. They also vary in the *kind* of regulation, whether it is by formal and impersonal rules and institutions or according to societal norms. Generally speaking, the greater the formalization of rules and procedures, the greater the potential for impartial voting, tax assessment and collection and access to justice that empower individual citizens. The less the formalization, the more that the application of law and procedure is governed by political expediency and judgement on the merits of the case.

Markets require information, and those with more timely, comprehensive and accurate information get better deals. Political CEOs invest in intelligence and in control over *mechanisms of convening and communication.* They seek to monopolize – or at least dominate – the capacity to call people together for political meetings, to have control over communication (including both speaking and listening, which includes the mass media, surveillance capacities and social media) and to be in a position to set an agenda for political talks and determine the speed and frequency of (re)negotiation. The *political circuitry* – where political bargaining occurs – may overlap to a greater or lesser degree with the *public sphere.* Communication and convening may be centralized or decentralized, regulated or deregulated. Thus, Ethiopia is tightly regulated by institutional procedures and opportunities for bargaining are few, while Somalia is regulated by custom and the political debate is open to all with renegotiation being frequent. In no country in the Horn is the real political circuitry accessible to the public.

The fourth variable concerns the conditions of *integration into the global marketplace*, including barriers to entry into the marketplace for new political actors. The generic political marketplace country is economically poor and vulnerable. Domestic businesspeople and its foreign investors are intimate with its politicians.

In a system financed by political funds from domestic sources (which here include foreign wage earners who provide remittances), politicians get their funds through deals with business leaders. This is not a rentier system in the sense that government revenues and political budgets are external rents. Nonetheless, political and business leaders remain rent-seekers. In such a case, the political manager needs to negotiate *both* revenue *and* spending, making a double bargain with financiers and clients. Hence, the political marketplace functions in a different and more complex manner. One of the features of this double bargain is that the key players in the business sector are able to regulate the supply of political finance to the entire political marketplace. These financiers therefore have the option of either sponsoring competitors in a patronage marketplace or taking the different approach of regulating political finance across the board. If commercial political financiers can agree on the latter approach, they have the possibility of establishing a stable system with a low price of loyalty.

A system financed from external rents demands a different skill set. A national political CEO will want to regulate incoming political finance, both to secure as much as possible for himself and to minimize the risk of it funding rivals or new entrants. His ability to do this will depend in part on the country's economic structure. Thus, oil companies will need to deal directly with the ruler, whereas traders and bankers may spread their favours more widely.

Increasingly, the political marketplace is *globally* integrated, not only through the institutions of formal globalization, but even more so through flows of rent. The nexus between foreign investment (especially in the minerals sector) and business practices that involve profit-shifting and the circulation of public funds into political budgets is one of the main mechanisms for this. Another mechanism is western security cooperation. Insofar as political instability, corruption and chronic violence are a product of a rentier political marketplace, these countries generate threats to the US and Europe, including terrorism, organized crime and migration. In turn, US and European security policies involve paying governments to combat these threats, or intervening directly themselves. In political markets, however, such assistance and intervention fund rentier political budgets while also increasing the price of loyalty, thus intensifying the very conditions whereby threats are sustained.

Regional political ambitions also fuel transnational patronage. The national political CEO's position in the regional hierarchy is key to his political prospects. A ruler who is more powerful and better funded than his immediate neighbours will discourage new entrants, whereas one who is less so will be challenged by political entrepreneurs with foreign sponsors. Examples will recur throughout this book.

Different values for the four variables of 'real politics' give rise to variant political systems. Throughout this book there is no attempt to theorize or catalogue them thoroughly. Each of the countries of the Horn will illustrate different elements of the political marketplace, or attempts to resist it. Another reason for avoiding a detailed categorization is that political markets are dynamic. This is an open system, in which skilled political entrepreneurs innovate to good effect, and in which each crisis creates new opportunities. Over time, however, most contingencies and most successful political-business ventures intensify the dollarization, integration and deregulation of the marketplace, and weaken the chances of non-market political projects.

State-Building versus Political-Business Management

Political science has been concerned with the transition from a patronage-based political system to an institutionalized one or a developmental state,[15] and the emergence of social movements, democracy and nationalism.[16] This literature contains rich insights regarding political systems that have not made this transition, including those at the cusp of it. The World Bank's *World Development Report 2011: Conflict Security and Development*[17] is an ambitious effort at bringing this powerful current of political science to bear on contemporary challenges of fragile states. However, the *WDR 2011* bears the hallmarks of institutional pressures to emphasize the potential for conventional state-building, not alternative trajectories of governance. My analysis differs in two main respects: the historical specification of the factors for state-formation and the main focus of attention.

The transitions identified by Olson, Tilly and North are derived from the history of state-formation in Europe and North America. At its simplest, this model contains a ruler who dominates the use of organized violence, and intermediate landowning and commercial elites that control most resources. This leads to a 'protection-racket' governing system in which the ruler abandons primary accumulation in return for regular tribute and taxation. The space for communication and convening is organized around national communication and convening infrastructures such as languages, newspapers and parliaments; it is contested on roughly equal terms between ruler and intermediate elites; and the opportunities for bargaining are scarce, so that once a deal has been struck, it is likely to remain in place for decades. These three factors generate a fourth: nationally distinctive political settlements can emerge, creating both nation and state through interwoven processes. Altogether, this allows stable rules of the political game to develop.

Figure 2.3 is a simplified version of Mancur Olson's 'stationary bandit', in which the ruler has the guns and the intermediate elite has the resources. Contemporary advanced political marketplace systems differ on all key variables. The ruler possesses (most of) the national revenue because of state rents. Control over organized violence is widely distributed among the intermediate elites, both those ostensibly within the governing system and those outside it. Third, these countries have historically governed their peripheries using a central-

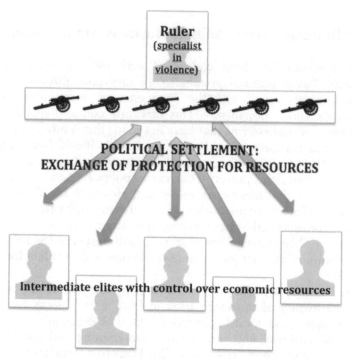

Figure 2.3 The 'stationary bandit'

ized monopoly over communication and convening, which has recently and rapidly been transformed by new transport and communications infrastructure and technology. And, lastly, all these factors operate across boundaries and are integrated into a global economic, security and political order, with aggressive transnational political patronage at its centre. State-builders contend with a new and more difficult environment.

Figure 2.4 is a simplified version of a 'militarized rentier political marketplace', in which the ruler has the money and the intermediate elite has the guns. Consequently, the main concern of the political marketplace framework is with the actual functioning of political systems that have not transitioned to institutionalized states, and which are not likely to make any such transition in the foreseeable future. Additionally, I am concerned with how the power and logic of political markets can influence relatively institutionalized or developmental states, to the point of corroding or overwhelming them.

The student of African politics has a rich literature to call upon. Perhaps because it has been a scholarly backwater, Africanist political

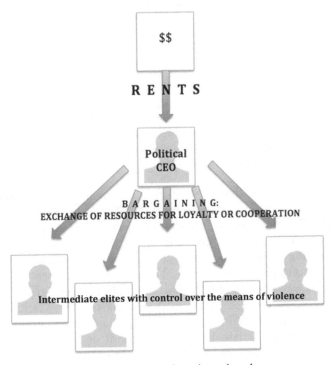

Figure 2.4 The militarized rentier political marketplace

science has had the opportunity to innovate to good effect, and the more 'Africanist' and the less mainstream, the more interesting and useful the results. There is a fine tradition of political ethnography,[18] or the thick analysis of contemporary politics with an anthropological sensibility, exemplified by writers such as Jean-François Bayart, Donald Donham, Stephen Ellis and Marielle Debos. But because most ethnographers are dedicated to studying the local, and because there are few opportunities for sustained participant observation of political elites, there are few such studies that focus on ruling elites, and none at all (of which I am aware) of how interstate politics is conducted. I hope that this book may spur more political ethnographies.

The vocabulary of clientelism, (neo-)patrimonialism, rentierism and big-man rule was already prevalent well before Africa's systemic crises of the 1980s. Neo-patrimonialism is a useful paradigm, sadly under-utilized outside the continent. It is usefully defined by Michael Bratton and Nicolas Van de Walle:

> In neo-patrimonial regimes, the chief executive maintains authority through personal patronage, rather than through ideology or law. As with classic patrimonialism, the right to rule is ascribed to a person rather than to an office. In contemporary neo-patrimonialism, relationships of loyalty and dependence pervade a formal political and administrative system and leaders occupy bureaucratic offices less to perform public service than to acquire personal wealth and status. The distinction between private and public interests is purposely blurred. The essence of neo-patrimonialism is the award by public officials of personal favors, both within the state (notably public sector jobs) and in society (for instance, licenses, contracts and projects). In return for material reward, clients mobilize political support and refer all decisions upward as a mark of deference to patrons.[19]

Van de Walle argued that neo-patrimonial governance was politically resilient but economically disastrous, dictating that governments supported inefficient clientelistic systems for reasons of regime survival.[20] This is surely correct. My concern here is different: to locate diverse and changing forms of neo-patrimonial governance within different political-economic circumstances. Thus, the wars of profit and predation and the 'warlord politics' that afflicted much of Africa from the 1980s to the early 2000s, described and analysed by Mark Duffield, David Keen and William Reno,[21] represent a specific conjuncture of factors, creating a particular historic variant of neo-patrimonialism. Since then, things have changed again: political markets have become more global, better funded and more complex.

I suggest that the framework of neo-patrimonialism, like that of kleptocracy, is relevant and useful but does not do full justice to the dynamism of political bargaining under the turbulent conditions of globalized political finance. Célestin Monga[22] argued that the neo-patrimonial paradigm was no longer operative: 'Even the most extreme forms of African patrimonialism have undergone revision. Far from being a system of mere privilege trafficking and influence peddling, patrimonialism is attuned to the social exigencies of the times and seeks to craft a type of power that is less direct and primi-tive, more equilibrated, and in a certain sense, interactive.' Monga writes in the tradition of Jean-François Bayart,[23] Christopher Clapham[24] and Patrick Chabal[25] who stress the continuities in forms of African governance, and their adaptability to circumstances. Much of this literature stresses the importance of factors rooted in culture, kinship organization and religion.[26] I prefer to focus on the material factors that drive change rather than the cultural factors that ensure continuities. Those cultural factors can be seen as elements that regu-late the hard facts of cash and coercion: my main concern is with those brute realities.

I also owe an intellectual debt to the Crisis States Research Centre,[27] which placed elite political settlements at the centre of analysis, and to the African Power and Politics Programme,[28] which focused on how the politics of development 'really' functions. Both these research programmes sought 'to open up the black box of political leadership and illuminate elite incentives'.[29] The political marketplace frame-work brings political finance, security and uncertainty to the centre of analysis, and emphasizes the contingent and open-ended nature of political bargaining.

In chapter 12 I will discuss how transformations in information systems, especially the capabilities for convening and communica-tion, have changed the nature of political power in north-east Africa. But I will not attempt a wider account of how charismatic poli-tics, the media and the political marketplace might drive a global de-institutionalization of political life.

The difference between a focus on systems and institutions, and concern with the individuals who manage them, also corresponds roughly to the distinction between different traditions of moral phi-losophy. The universalist theories of justice exemplified by John Rawls provide a philosophical grounding for state-building and institution-building. Concern for the virtuous or just individual, asso-ciated with Aristotle and modernized by Alastair MacIntyre, is a more relevant ethical guide for the real politics of societies in which individuals matter, and in which the idea of a wholly impersonal institutional functioning as the foundation of justice is a remote abstraction.[30]

A Story of Men

The political marketplace is gendered. The politicians in every chapter in this book are male. The social values and norms of a political marketplace are militarized and masculine. Those who rise in these political systems are those who can best mobilize money and deploy violence: not only men but men who are ruthless and inured to sentiment, who reduce human beings and human dignity to instruments and commodities. I do not develop a gender critique of the political marketplace in this book. However, the gendered nature of the business of power should be evident on every page.

3

The Horn of Africa
Subcontinental War in Three Acts

Visualizing the Horn of Africa

The 'Horn of Africa' consists of three countries that have become (de facto) six: Ethiopia plus Eritrea; Sudan plus South Sudan; Somalia plus Somaliland; as well as the enclave of Djibouti. Like a constellation of visible stars that rotate round a powerful but invisible black hole, the formal politics of boundaries, sovereign states, institutions and official budgets functions only within the gravitational field of the informal bargaining over power. It is remarkably hard to write an account of the Horn of Africa that does not over-privilege the formal, and I fear I have not succeeded – not least because (after trying many different formulations) I ended up writing a chapter on each recognized country, plus Somaliland and Darfur, minus Djibouti.

How would one visualize the Horn of Africa without using the conventional territorial map of the boundaries of nations, and the commensurate catalogue of internationally recognized states? One way is to think of the map as a woodland landscape seen from above. Each centre of power is a tree, with a trunk, branches and twigs. At the beginning of our story in the 1980s, this was a spare savannah landscape with thin and straggly trees. In some places there was open space between the trees; in others their branches met to form a canopy. As time passed, the trees grew, helped by better rainfall. Some grew strongly; others languished. Some had their branches cut back and saw vigorous new growth. The new growth led to thicker, bushier trees, which competed more vigorously for sunlight. A few bushes were content to grow in shadier spots, but the basic rule was: reach the sunlight or die.

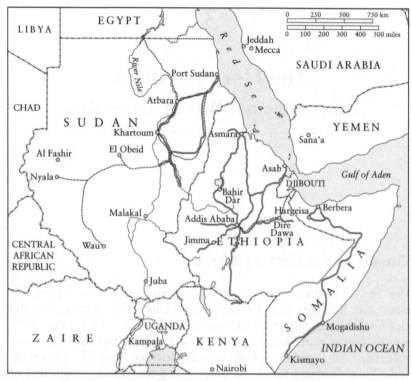

Map 3.1 The Horn of Africa, 1980

We begin with three trees, each of them ailing. The Khartoum tree
had spread furthest, its branches reaching as far as N'djaména and
northern Uganda, and – taking advantage of the savage pruning of
the Ethiopian tree, almost cut back to its roots – spreading into
Ethiopia too. The Somali tree was felled entirely and sprouted new
trunks. Throughout the 1990s, the Sudanese tree was sick, and the
newly invigorated Ethiopian and Eritrean trees became intense competitors, each extending branches into Sudan and into the near-empty
space of Somalia. Later, at Ethiopia's instigation, the international
community sawed off Eritrea's branch that reached into Somalia. In
the 2000s, the Chadian tree, newly nourished, challenged the Sudanese
one for parity, which it achieved. Planted in rich soil and tended by
international foresters, the South Sudanese sapling grew fast, and also
challenged the Sudanese for sunlight – but came crashing down
before it had grown strong roots.[1]

The image of the trees reminds us that political geography is like
a living entity, growing and competing. The design of a tree, with

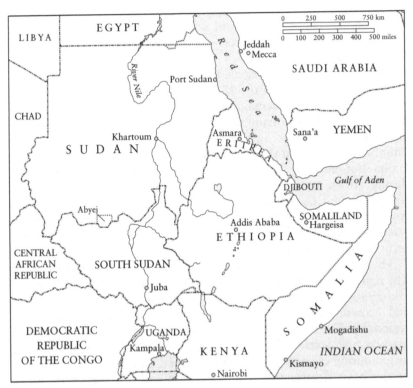

Map 3.2 The Horn of Africa, 2011

trunk, major limbs, and branches growing smaller and spreading, is also a fair metaphor for a patrimonial hierarchy, in which each patron has multiple clients, each of which is in turn a patron of others. This also signals the fractal characteristic of the political marketplace: the same patterns are reproduced at different levels.[2]

A Laboratory of Conflicts

For the student of war, the Horn of Africa offers a cornucopia of violence and destruction. It has interstate wars and civil wars; conventional wars fought in trenches with air-to-air combat overhead and irregular wars fought by jihadists and followers of a messianic cult; international military interventions and maritime piracy; genocidal massacres and non-violent popular uprisings. It has had three major territorial wars and three secessions. There are no purely internal wars: the neighbours are entangled in all. Making sense of these conflicts is not simple, but I will try, telling the story as a series of wars for regional dominance – territorial, ideological and, finally, business-political.[3]

This is a drama in three acts. But first is the prologue: the conflicts of the colonial period, of the 1880s when Africa was carved up, and in the 1940s when the remaining details were settled. Act One proper is the Cold War: involving the drama of the Ethiopian Revolution and the Ogaden War and ending with the violent concluding of unfinished business at the end of the 1980s, as the US and the Soviet Union lost interest. Act Two is the inter-imperium of the 1990s, during which Islamists and their left-wing revolutionary enemies fought an undeclared subcontinental war, which ended in a draw. And Act Three is the twenty-first century, an era of 'new rentierism' – funds from oil and counter-terrorism – and the African peace and security architecture.

This is also a story of economic and fiscal collapse and recovery. The region went through a collective near-death experience from the mid-1980s to the early 1990s. As it rebounded thereafter, its politics and economics were put back together in a different way: as a regional political marketplace. The contemporary form of political markets first developed in Sudan and Somalia in the 1980s, and some neighbouring countries, for example, Chad and Zaire, were also run on this basis. Transnational integration followed in the 1990s, intensified in the political wreckage that followed the collapse of the military-political axis of Eritrea, Ethiopia, Uganda and Rwanda – the liberators in power – in 1998.

In the earlier imperial era, the territorial carve-up of the Horn of Africa and the Nile Valley was determined by the politics of European conquest, and of control of the shipping lanes from Europe to Asia, through the Suez Canal and Red Sea. In the Cold War era, US and Soviet security rents and military assistance shaped the political logic of the coup d'état and indirectly shaped the coercion of state-building and of destabilization by proxy. The decline of superpower interest in the late 1980s lifted those external mechanisms for regulating political violence and what followed was the most destructive period in the region's recent history. Since the millennium, the logic of the political market has come to dominate the whole region, except Ethiopia. New patterns of violence have followed, notably the endemic turbulent violence of peripheral governance.

Here we have a paradox: *large-scale killing is declining but volatility is increasing.* The numbers of people killed in today's conflicts are considerably fewer than those in Acts One and Two. Military coups and large-scale wars are now rarer. But reduced violence does not mean greater political stability. More effort than ever is invested in peacemaking, and agreements are more elaborate than ever before, but they seem not to bring peace. One of the interesting and perhaps counter-intuitive outcomes of the political marketplace is that although violence is embedded in the system, very large-scale violence occurs when the system malfunctions – when senior politicians make mistakes. In a more perfect market, violence is pervasive but large-scale killing is rarer.

The Contested Political Geography of the Horn

Drawing the borders of Ethiopia is the prelude to our drama. In the 1880s, when the European colonial powers were dividing Africa, Emperor Menelik of Ethiopia succeeded in keeping his independence. He lost his ports on the Red Sea coast and part of the northern highlands to Italian annexation. But Menelik was able to carve out a hinterland in the east, taking part of the Somali peninsula, which was divided five ways: Italy took the largest share including Mogadishu on the Indian Ocean side, Britain took part for its Kenya colony and British Somaliland, opposite Aden, France took the port of Djibouti and its immediate vicinity, and Ethiopia took what became known as the Ogaden – a claim only fully confirmed in the post-Second World War consolidation of boundaries.

The Somali nationalists' emblem of the five-pointed star referred to the five parts of their country and, in 1960, when Italian and British Somaliland achieved independence within a few days of one another and united as the Republic of Somalia, the Somali government immediately claimed the remaining territories. Early attempts at instigating irredentist wars did not succeed, and there the matter rested. In 1969, General Mohammed Siyad Barre took power in a coup modelled on Gamal Abdel Nasser's in Egypt, and energetically set about modernizing the country. The Somali language was written down for the first time and an ambitious literacy programme was launched. Roads and factories were built and drought relief provided. With support from the Soviet Union, which coveted military bases on the Red Sea and Indian Ocean, Siyad also built a huge army.

Ethiopia escaped colonization until the Italian Fascists invaded in 1935. Mussolini's generals violated the precepts of the League of Nations, used mustard gas against Ethiopian troops and, after overrunning the country, massacred tens of thousands of Ethiopians. British imperial forces and Ethiopian partisans recaptured the country in 1941 and restored Haile Selassie I as emperor. Haile Selassie distrusted the British, whom he suspected of wanting him only as a titular figurehead, and sought allies across the globe. The US became his biggest patron, but he vested much diplomacy in multilateral organizations, including the UN and the Organisation of African Unity (OAU) – which he came to host.

Britain handed the question of Eritrea – also freed from Italian rule – over to the UN, which in 1952 decided that the territory should be federated under the imperial Crown. Although this shackled a relatively developed former colony with a parliamentary system together with a feudal monarchy, it might have been a workable arrangement. But in 1962 Haile Selassie succumbed to the temptation to swallow Eritrea entirely. An insurgency in the lowlands gradually spread to become the first nationalist movement, the Eritrean Liberation Front (ELF). In 1970 a more radical splinter of the ELF, the Eritrean People's Liberation Front (EPLF), was created, which in due course dislodged its older rival.

The Ethiopian emperor could annex Eritrea because he had American support, which was linked to the Kagnew airbase and intelligence station in Eritrea. We are now entering Act One of the modern drama: the Cold War.

A combination of the Eritrean insurgency, internal reform failures, discontent among army non-commissioned officers and the scandal of a famine contributed to a series of strikes and demonstrations in Addis Ababa in 1974. The army stepped in and deposed Haile Selassie, and a little-known major, Mengistu Haile Mariam, steeped the revolution in blood. The old feudal order was destroyed.

This was the era of African modernism: genuine faith in state-building and political transformation. States were capital cities plus a bit more. All roads and railways led to the capital or the port, a colonial inheritance. And, indeed, beneath the efforts at building national institutions, governance remained on the imperial model, with a metropolis, limited economically useful areas which were closely administered, and peripheries which were run with the utmost economy on the basis of tribal chiefs. When governments wanted to reach deep into the rural areas, the favoured means was a brief spurt of energy in the form of a mass campaign. Thus, the radical governments of the 1970s organized literacy campaigns, or sent students to the rural areas to enforce decrees on land tenure.

These regimes had small domestic tax bases but large budgets and coercive capacities, obtained from foreign sponsors. As David

Laitin observes, this made for a high-stakes political game of coup-making:

> From a domestic point of view, for a rival to challenge a post-coup leader – once he took control of the radio station, the presidential palace and the customhouse – would be foolhardy. The enormous military and surveillance power (the 'prize') garnered by the first entrant into the presidential palace after the incumbent was deposed gave that entrant excellent bargaining power. Usually a bandwagon followed, with sycophants from all tribal and clan groups seeking to curry favor with the new regime to get their 'fair' share.[4]

After the Congo crisis, in which each superpower had continued backing its Congolese client even when the outcome in the capital was decided, causing a major crisis that threatened geostrategic ramifications, the superpowers tacitly played by the rules that each would accept the other's domain. This rule was observed in Sudan and Somalia in 1969, but it went awry in Ethiopia after 1974.

Ethiopia had been aligned with the US since the 1950s and was the site of an important military station. The first entrant to the palace – General Aman Andoum – had no intent of changing that. But domestic events moved too fast, and Washington did not respond expeditiously and decisively. Andoum was gunned down and buried in the rubble of his house, succeeded by Brigadier Tafari Benti who was then murdered by Mengistu. The violence culminated in the Red Terror of 1977–8, when the soldiers turned on their fellow revolutionaries, and tens of thousands of young people were slaughtered.

The apparent disintegration of Ethiopia was too tempting for Siyad, who invaded Ethiopia. It is usually a mistake to attack a revolutionary regime and this was no exception. In this case, resurgent Ethiopian nationalism was conjoined with a Soviet decision to throw itself into an enthusiastic alliance with the revolutionary regime, which seemed to be reliving the October Revolution itself. A massive airlift of Soviet weaponry and Cuban combat troops turned the tide against the Somalis. Siyad turned to the US for assistance, which he received. It was the most remarkable switch in allegiances of the Cold War era. As US National Security Advisor Zbigniew Brzezinski said at the time, détente was buried in the sands of the Ogaden.[5] At this point, the US and the Soviet Union realized that neither was ready to risk a wider war over an African issue.

Thereafter, the logic of security patronage was to preserve the status quo. Each superpower would protect a client regime from collapse, but – in contrast to Afghanistan or Central America – neither would seek to roll back the other. Ideological and political antipathy to a regime did not translate into efforts to overthrow it. Throughout the late 1970s and 1980s, each government in the Horn supported rebels fighting its neighbour and rival, but none of these opposition movements received significant backing from the US or USSR.

Soviet support for Mengistu was not sufficient to defeat the Eritreans or the Tigray People's Liberation Front (TPLF). Nine massive conventional offensives forced the EPLF into a strategic withdrawal to the mountains of Sahel province, but no further. Between 1978 and 1991, the war zones of Eritrea and Tigray were lifeless during daylight, as airforce MiGs shot at anything that moved. The guerrillas dug in underground and moved only at night. Little by little, in a war of astonishing tenacity and organization, the fronts wore down the Ethiopian army, eventually defeating it utterly in 1991.

American, Italian and Arab support for Siyad was similarly not enough to defeat the Somali National Movement (SNM) and other rebellions. An early adopter of the marketplace principle of security politics, the Somali strongman could not afford the price of loyalty, and his government collapsed in 1991.

Like Somalia, Sudan defected from the eastern to the western bloc, albeit in stages. Sudan was the first sub-Saharan country to achieve independence after the Second World War, in 1956. But this achievement is neglected in African celebrations in favour of Ghana's 1957 independence. This is because a rebellion in southern Sudan was already under way, and the independence leader, Ismail al Azhari, promised that independence was a step towards unification with Egypt. Sudan's independent governments delivered neither on the 'unity of the Nile Valley' nor a federal system that would award southern Sudanese the equal political rights they demanded. From 1963 to 1972, a guerrilla movement known as Anyanya fought for an independent southern Sudan.

Power was seized in 1969 by Colonel Jaafar Nimeiri, a radical colonel putchist, also in the Nasserist mould. He started off on the far left, in alliance with the Sudanese Communist Party – the largest of its ilk in Africa. The cohabitation of colonels and comrades lasted just two years, before Nimeiri crushed the Communists after they tried to mount a coup. Having earlier turned on the old political establishment – sectarian Islamist parties – Nimeiri now embarked upon an accelerated modernization programme, including cutting a peace deal with the Anyanya in 1972. This agreement, signed in Addis Ababa, provided southern Sudan with an autonomous regional government, and ushered in a decade of peace. By the end of the

1970s, Nimeiri had embraced the Muslim Brothers (then seen by Saudi Arabia and the US as a friendly, pro-business and anti-Communist force), supported Egypt's Camp David accords with Israel, and was cooperating with the US in opposing Ethiopia and Libya. Nimeiri was favoured with military aid, with lenient treatment by the IMF and the Paris Club of creditor nations, and with only mild reprimands for instituting a crude and brutal version of Islamic law in September 1983, and abrogating key provisions of the Addis Ababa agreement. The latter provoked new rebellions in southern Sudan, from which emerged the SPLA led by John Garang. A combination of the war, Nimeiri's erratic repression, drought and famine, and austerity measures, contributed to a non-violent popular uprising that brought down Nimeiri in 1985.

But the euphoria of sudden political freedoms and free elections twelve months later brought no end to war and crisis. Overtures from the new government were summarily rejected by the SPLA. The IMF was unforgiving. What was, at the time, Africa's newest democracy, was mired in war and economic crisis. Prime Minister Sadiq al Mahdi could not pay for the war. With a tiny political budget, he could not put together a workable coalition. In 1989 the army stepped in again, this time led by an obscure Islamist, Brigadier Omar al Bashir.

By the early 1980s, mutual wars of destabilization were in high gear. The EPLF and TPLF, plus smaller Ethiopian insurgent groups, enjoyed safe passage and rear bases in Sudan and Somalia. Ethiopia hosted the Somali opposition (principally the SNM) and the SPLA. Both of the latter devoted part of their military effort to defeating insurgents inside Ethiopia, repaying their debt to Mengistu and also clearing the way to take the war inside their respective countries. This mutual destabilization by proxy intensified throughout the decade, until all three governments were at the point of military collapse. In Somalia and Ethiopia this duly occurred.

Sudan escaped, but only just. In November 1989, SPLA and Ethiopian troops crossed the border at Kurmuk and were poised to take the town of Damazin, and the nearby Blue Nile dam that generated Khartoum's electricity supply. The Sudanese army was helpless – and was saved only by a secret commando action by the EPLF, which defeated the SPLA and the Ethiopians in January 1990. In August that year, President Bashir's cautious alignment with Saudi Arabia was overruled by the leader of the Sudanese Islamists, Hassan al Turabi, who declared Sudan's support for the Iraqi invasion of Kuwait. This caused a deep financial crisis, and the Sudanese regime was saved only by the weakness of the SPLA – which collapsed after its sponsor, Mengistu, was overthrown – and by remarkably creative political-business management (detailed in chapter 5).

When Things Fell Apart

In the 1980s (the last scene of Act One), many African states went through near-death experiences: in the words of Robert Bates, quoting Chinua Achebe, 'things fell apart'. Those countries subsequently recovered, but that recovery did not put them back together as they were before. Africa's reconstituted governance systems carry with them the imprint of late-century state failure.

Following his participation in a World Bank mission to Uganda in 1982, Bates wrote of his 'palpable shock', both at the situation he encountered and its similarities to Thomas Hobbes's description of 'warre'.[6] In a later book, Bates expands his account to theorize the collapse of economic and political order in many African countries during the 1980s. He posits that 'the possibility of political order rests on the value of three variables: the level of public revenue, the rewards from predation [compared to taxation], and the specialist [in violence]'s rate of discount [i.e., time horizon].'[7] From this it follows that when the level of public revenues in African states descended to extremely low levels in the late 1970s and early 1980s because of domestic and international economic crisis, compounded by austerity measures required by international financial institutions, the rulers of those countries focused on their own short-term survival and primary accumulation. Thus they stayed in power by dint of generating divisions within their own societies and stripping the assets of their own economies. Bates writes:

> Posed dispassionately, Africa was subject to an experiment, as these forces pushed the value of key variables into ranges in which the possibility of political order became vanishingly small. It was the misfortune of Africa's peoples to be caught in a perfect storm – one in which political fundamentals were so altered that the foundations of the state lay nakedly revealed: a sight that was both horrible – and instructive.[8]

This budgetary crisis was accentuated as the Cold War thawed and superpower security rents were scaled back. Mikhail Gorbachev began this in 1985, and shortly afterwards Ethiopia lost its indefinite line of military credit. On the US side, change was marked by the indecision over the fate of Nimeiri. Secretary of State James Baker called time on Sudan's repeated debt bailouts in January 1985. Without these funds, Nimeiri would surely go, and both knew it. The US reversed course in April, but too late: Nimeiri was toppled hours after meeting President Ronald Reagan in the White House. The US extended only sufficient indulgences to his successors to prevent the government from collapsing entirely, and was not unhappy to see a military coup in 1989. In short, as superpower interest declined, the scope for the Horn's rulers to extract a commission from foreign patrons was squeezed.[9]

Three other developments changed the logic of violence. One was the opening of the arms markets. This began with Chadian resale of captured Libyan stocks in 1987, and intensified when the eastern bloc floodgates opened two years later: weapons, transport planes and men ready to use them became available to hire, and cheaply. Second, rulers could now negotiate with multiple alternative patrons, both commercial and political. Mengistu turned to Israel, trading the fate of the Falasha Jews of Ethiopia for armaments; Siyad called upon Italy, and Sudan called upon the Gulf States and Libya. Third, rulers 'coup-proofed' their regimes[10] by distributing armed capacity among different elements of the army and security forces, for example, by creating special presidential guard units and armed intelligence groups. These changes made elite politics a more open contest: central rents were reduced and the centralized means for allocating them weaker. The relative military power of the ruler – or successful coup-maker – was no longer much higher than other contenders.[11] This made coups less decisive and insurgencies more viable.

Thus, between 1985 and 1991, security rents were reduced but the political contests were unresolved, while the massive stocks of weaponry remained and further supplies were cheap to procure. The political leaders of the time were still intent on state power and convinced that normal business – state rents – would resume in due course. In addition, no regional mechanisms for managing conflict or mitigating its human toll existed. These instruments began to be improvised in 1989, with Operation Lifeline Sudan – the first internationally mandated relief operation to assist a civilian population under rebel control. But, mostly, the armies were simply left to fight it out. The Americans only convened peace talks on Ethiopia and Eritrea in 1991 when the outcome of the war was already decided.

A nadir of violence was reached in 1988, the Horn's sanguinary high-water mark. In Sudan, it was the height of the militia war in southern Sudan, of the ravaging of defenceless communities, and the zenith of mass killings of Nuba by Military Intelligence, as well as a nasty under-reported conflict in Darfur. In Ethiopia and Eritrea, vast battles were fought in which tens of thousands of soldiers died, and the Ethiopian airforce killed an estimated 1,800 people at the market town of Hausien in a single day – an atrocity that was only publicized some months later. The Somali army and airforce destroyed completely the towns of Hargaisa and Burao that same year and emptied north-western Somalia (now Somaliland) of most of its population, and armed land-grabbing escalated in the fertile south of the country.

Africa's Subcontinental War

The period from 1991 to 1998 was, in retrospect, an intriguing and anomalous period during which the Horn's conflicts were framed by two competing ideological projects. This is Act Two. On one side was a political Islamism, which under its Sudanese leaders sought to build an Islamic state and society, not just in Sudan but across north-east Africa as a whole. On the other side were the leaders of left-wing liberation struggles, who had taken power after long wars in Uganda, Eritrea, Ethiopia and – a latecomer to the club, outside our region but nonetheless influential – Rwanda. After the international withdrawal from Somalia in 1993–4, that country was neglected. The second war in the Democratic Republic of Congo (DRC) (1998–2003) has been described as 'Africa's Great War', but it was in fact an extension of a subcontinental war that had already begun in 1994, pitting Islamists against their enemies across the Horn, and extending through opportunistic alliances into central Africa, where the war and genocide in Rwanda unleashed another dynamic.[12]

The 1990s was an 'inter-rentier' period: Cold War security rents had gone, and the global War on Terror security rents had yet to begin. Governments that had borrowed lavishly were now ineligible for anything save bailouts and humanitarian aid, and Sudanese oil exports began only in 1999. The geopolitical order of the grudging US-Soviet condominium had dissolved, but the multilateral African peace and security architecture had yet to be designed.

For a moment, after the defeat of the military regime in Ethiopia in 1991, it seemed that there might be a new peaceful order in the Horn. The EPLF and EPRDF – close allies at the time – had come to power in Asmara and Addis Ababa. The new Ethiopian government accepted the independence of Eritrea, and began drafting a constitution that – uniquely – granted the right of self-determination to all Ethiopian nationalities. Both new governments had friendly relations with their erstwhile backer in Khartoum and all were ready to help Somalia find a way out of its quagmire. But the Sudanese leadership overreached: it wanted not just friendly neighbours, but ideological fellow travellers. It began exporting militant Islam.

The outbreak of a new regional war was heralded in January 1994 when Eritrean President Isaias Afeworki ordered out the Sudanese ambassador, handed over the embassy to the Sudanese opposition and announced that there would be a new government in Khartoum before the end of the year. The Ethiopians were more discreet but they began training and arming the SPLA, and drafted a declaration of principles for the Sudanese peace process that espoused national democracy and self-determination for southern Sudan. The next year, following an attempt by a Sudanese-backed jihadist group to assassinate the Egyptian President Husni Mubarak while he was attending an African summit in Addis Ababa, the hostility became public, even though Ethiopian military actions remained secret. Those included a mechanized invasion of Sudan (through Kurmuk) and the deployment of generals to direct SPLA operations. Sudan protested but, with Egyptian and US diplomatic support, nobody heard. This secret war does not show up on any database: the Uppsala Conflict Database reports just one internationalized intrastate conflict in 1994–5 and two in 1996–7: in the Horn of Africa alone there were between three and five in those years, each involving hundreds of fatalities. The war also included Ugandan operations to assist the SPLA, two Ethiopian military incursions into Somalia to destroy jihadist bases and Eritrean operations in eastern Sudan.

The admission of Rwanda to the club of 'frontline states' after the Rwandese Patriotic Front (RPF) defeated the genocidal government in Rwanda, and the threat to Rwanda from the reorganized génocidaires in eastern Zaire, broadened this war. Meeting in Uganda in August 1996, military chiefs from the four allies decided that – with the Sudanese regime contained – the most urgent threat was Zaire and the Rwandese and Ugandan opposition groups there. Two months later, the RPF opened its military offensive. It was supported by Uganda and Eritrea, and had the immediate aim of removing the former Rwandese army from eastern Zaire, then intended to march to Kinshasa and install a new government. Ethiopia's contribution was to organize an attack on the southern Sudanese town of Yei to prevent Sudanese reinforcements travelling overland to Zaire. (The operation was publicly attributed to the SPLA.)

By the end of 1997, the axis of liberators, from Asmara to Kinshasa via Addis Ababa, Kampala and Kigali, appeared triumphant. They had won in Zaire and were on the brink of victory in Sudan. Secretary of State Madeleine Albright had blessed the Sudanese opposition, led by Garang, as the next Sudanese government.[13] But the liberators also

overreached. Having installed Laurent Kabila in power in Zaire –
now renamed the Democratic Republic of Congo – they found their
client erratic, vain and capable of rebuffing his sponsors. But even
before the crisis that sparked the second Congolese war in August
1998, Eritrea and Ethiopia had gone to war. It was an unexpected
conflict, sparked by an apparently trivial dispute over local administrators moving boundary markers, and it unleashed the bloodiest
conventional war of modern African history. It was a war of conventional armies fighting for fixed positions. Both countries dug trenches,
deployed massive artillery barrages and dispatched third-generation
fighter-bombers in air-to-air combat. It cost tens of thousands of lives
of young soldiers on either side, before it was ended with a military
offensive by Ethiopia. As a side effect, it saved the Sudanese regime,
as Ethiopia and Eritrea withdrew their troops from Sudan and nor-
malized their relations with Khartoum. As another side effect, it
ignited a proxy war in Somalia, as the contenders backed different
factions there. Meanwhile, Rwanda and Ugandan forces came to
blows in the Congolese city of Kisangani. In that instance too, the
causes of the fighting appear trivial compared to the consequences,
though the Uganda–Rwanda dispute did not become a life-and-death
struggle, without compromise, as occurred between Asmara and
Addis Ababa.

Scholars of the region have speculated anxiously about the causes
of these two internecine wars. One explanation, however, stands out
clearly as soon as the narrative of the continental war is told. They
were fighting for who would be on top of the hierarchy. Eritrea's
Isaias was convinced of his military invincibility following his operations in Sudan and Zaire (as well as a short, victorious war with
Yemen over the disputed Hanish islands in the Red Sea), and was not
ready to continue to be an equal partner with Ethiopia, which he
considered too cautious, too concerned with political formalities –
and its economy deeply penetrated by Eritrean businesspeople. The
EPLF leader had long considered the TPLF as a younger brother, and
as a new leadership in Khartoum was imminent, now was the moment
to assert regional dominance. A tiny piece of land, scarcely big
enough to serve as a cemetery for the young men and women who
died in the Eritrean frontlines, was merely the symbol for Isaias's
belief in his limitless capacity for leadership through boldness, as
against Ethiopia's tiresome and timid proceduralism.

Rwanda's President Paul Kagame similarly felt that his display of
chutzpah in Congo warranted equal standing with his former patron,
Yoweri Museveni. The Kisangani fighting certainly showed that the
RPF was a disciplined and decisive combat force, while the Ugandan

army was close to shambolic. Ugandan commanders had stumbled across Congo's mineral wealth and were helping themselves, making the army into a commercial venture and a patronage vehicle. The RPF was also looting, but it was a centrally directed operation that efficiently translated the resources into the president's political and security budget.

When Eritrea and Ethiopia went to war, they abandoned their regime change agenda in Sudan, leaving Uganda, the SPLA and the US unable to accomplish the task – especially when, in 1999, Sudanese oil diplomacy started winning friends in the neighbourhood. Sudan was thereby saved the Zaire–Congo scenario. Instead, there was a truce: the CPA.

Act Two in the drama of the Horn concludes with the military campaigns ending in disarray. The liberators won in Zaire but could not manage the DRC. On the brink of triumph in Sudan, they could not agree on which country should be the senior partner. Both the liberators and their enemies had dissolved boundaries and torn up the previous governing order. What survived was the most elementary transnational political order: the marketplace. The leaders of Eritrea, Ethiopia, Rwanda and Uganda began their wars for political goals – including position in a continental hierarchy and state-building – but the result was that militarized political mercantilism triumphed. The political system of the defeated and discredited orders – Mobutu's kleptocracy in Zaire, the military-commercial oligarchy in Sudan – prevailed in the end.

The New Rentierism and the African Security Architecture

North-east Africa's political economy changed at the millennium. Sudanese political-business managers were now flush with money, their revenues growing tenfold in just seven years. Two events in the US heralded a new rentier era: Act Three of our drama. The first event was the National Energy Policy Development Group ('Cheney Report') in May 2001 that recommended that the US promote oil producers in Africa. The second was September 11. Although al-Qaeda was largely defeated in the Horn before 2001, a combination of local political factors, Saudi and Qatari sponsorship of Wahhabi groups, and the policies pursued by the US and its allies in the global War on Terror helped create conditions for a new militant jihadism. America's security strategy became entangled in regional power rivalries, including the contests between Saudi Arabia, Qatar, Iran and Israel.

The new rentierism is multifaceted and globalized. There are five principal sources of rent: minerals; aid (and related forms of humanitarian solidarity); security cooperation (counter-terrorism, peace-keeping and policing); political (sovereign and policy rent, including payoffs for cooperation); and crime (in our region, arms trafficking, human trafficking and maritime piracy). These rents drove an economic boom, and made mercantile short-term political management strategies very profitable. They not only funded the governance system, but changed its nature.

In the old-style, well-regulated patrimonial system during the Cold War, the ruler centralized his sources of external rent (loans and security assistance) and insulated them from his domestic political spending (local currency, favours and privileges). Beginning in the 1990s, the political marketplace dissolved these boundaries and deregulated the bargaining over access to rents. Rather than rentier *states*, a rentier *system* emerged.

Consider the political entrepreneur who succeeds in becoming the CEO of a country. What next? Given that formal territorial expansion by invasion or annexation is frowned upon, how does he pursue his ambition? The answer is by establishing a transnational patronage dominion, which can include provincial elites in neighbouring countries and eventually the rulers of those countries. Thus the ambitious and capable national political CEO can promote himself in the regional hierarchy. As he does so, his rivals lose market share and are demoted, and herein lie the seeds of transnational conflict. Countries on the geographical periphery of transnational patronage domains are invariably contested and therefore unstable: this has been the fate of Central African Republic (CAR), Somalia and South Sudan. In Somalia, the Ethiopians brought in the AU and international powers to make their domination more presentable and to share the costs. In South Sudan, the ascending powers (Ethiopia and Uganda) established a truce with the declining power (Sudan) and with one another – but this is unlikely to be a stable arrangement.

The other development at the turn of millennium was that African leaders began to build a regional political infrastructure, for the purposes of managing conflicts. The continent had been shamed by the Rwandese genocide and recognized that its political norms had to change. Isaias, who had despised the OAU and publicly condemned it, found that he had to turn to it for mediating an end to the war with Ethiopia. The opportunity for a thorough overhaul of the continental organization came by chance when, in September 1999,

Gaddafi announced his intention to set up a United States of Africa, immediately. Other African leaders quickly massaged this into something resembling a hybrid between the European Union and the UN Security Council, and over the following decade an elaborate peace and security architecture was designed. The real function of the African Union's meetings and procedures, however, was to provide a forum for the continent's leaders to meet and transact political business. The AU became both a convening mechanism and a broker in the regional marketplace. New models of peace-support operation took on a central role in political markets, as means for putting militaries on the international payroll, and for pursuing political-economic interests in contested peripheries.

As the region rebounded from the successive crises of the late twentieth century, its politics and economics were put back together in a different way: as a regional political marketplace, integrated horizontally (across borders) and vertically (with foreign sponsors).

4

Darfur
The Auction of Loyalties

___

A Near-Perfect Political Marketplace

During the twentieth century, Darfur and its neighbouring areas were governed with the utmost economy. The skeletal administration, formal or customary, was dictated by remoteness. This part of Africa is the furthest from any ocean and still has the poorest infrastructure. Local loyalties were rented cheaply on long-term contracts. Local leaders ably played for time against colonial officers – Sultan Idris Abubakr of the Gimir's fifty-six years in office earned the record for outlasting different administrations and prompted the Anglo-Sudanese coinage *tajility* – the skill of strategic delay.[1] The people who lived in this area were self-reliant and entrepreneurial, ready to travel vast distances to earn a livelihood. Governments were distant, services were few, and vast territories were written off by their rulers – known as *Tchad inutile* and, in Sudan, 'closed districts'.

In less than a generation this most neglected expanse has become perhaps the most efficient auction-room of loyalties in Africa. Across Darfur, Chad, the entire Sahara desert and the CAR there is a remarkably open, competitive and unregulated marketplace for allegiances. A political entrepreneur who has some money, guns, vehicles and communications, and who is skilled, bold and lucky, has opportunities to rise. Telling the story of contemporary Darfur brings the features of an advanced political marketplace into focus: its turbulence, its fractal and open-system nature, and the functions of violence and peacemaking.

The speed at which Darfurian politics became marketized caught political-business managers in faraway Khartoum by surprise. They assumed that the provincial aristocracy and armed malcontents were political marginalia who could be bought up for pocket money, the crumbs left over from the big spending items in their metropolitan political budget. This led Sudan's security chiefs and party bosses into a miscalculation with terrible consequences. As insurgency spread in 2002, they underbid for the loyalty of Darfurian insurgents, pitching them into a war for which neither was prepared. The war and massacres in turn drew interest in N'djaména, Tripoli and Washington, DC, and Darfur became a competitive rentier marketplace, in which the main form of rent was straightforward cash payment to do what the patron asked. The price of loyalty was bid up in a manner that resembled a speculative bubble, and in common with other such booms the ripple effects of price inflation were felt in nearby areas. Peace negotiations – ostensibly an attempt to resolve conflict – served perversely to increase political competition, lower the barriers for new entrepreneurs to enter the market, and (in the paradox of security markets) further inflate the price of loyalty. Following the logic of efficient political markets, violence in Darfur became less extreme but more widespread and intractable.

Closed Districts and the Thirty Years' War

In the eighteenth and nineteenth centuries, the sultanate of Dar Fur was as wealthy and powerful as its counterparts in the Nile Valley. It was shattered by decades of conquest, revolution, famine and bloodshed, between 1874 and 1917, culminating in Darfur's incorporation into the British Empire. Darfur never recovered from that calamity.

The next forty years of colonial rule left Darfur with the worst schools, hospitals and basic infrastructure of anywhere in Sudan.[2] Independence came with promises of better. Although the railway was extended to Nyala in 1960, Darfur remained the end of the line: the last place to receive its quota of grants in aid, and the first to suffer cuts. When I first travelled to Darfur in 1985, local government had been running on empty for half a decade. What little there had been, had fallen apart: police without petrol, clinics without roofs, schools without doors, windows or supplies.

Khartoum impoverished Darfur because of security fears and tight-fistedness. The British were worried that Darfurians would revive their militant Mahdism of the 1880s and ran the province through tribal chiefs[3] with a vested interest in the little parcels of dictatorial privilege handed down to them. This 'native administration' then aligned with Sudan's conservative sectarian parties after independence, and guarded the status quo. The sectarian parties, however, never established stable government, so provincial leaders had to polish the craft of political hedging, keeping their lines of communication open to other potential Khartoum patrons, including the army. A paramount chief might instruct his sons to enter political parties, the diplomatic service, the professions and the military. Darfur's younger politicians, such as Ahmed Diraige of the Darfur Development Front, tried to build a constituency for modernization, but they faced insurmountable problems of funds and organization, and ended up making deals with one or other of the central parties. Not much changed over forty years. In May 2000, Darfurian Islamists published *The Black Book: Imbalance of Power and Wealth in the Sudan*, documenting the region's marginalization by the Khartoum elite.[4]

Khartoum patrons dispensed just enough to keep the provincial squirearchy in place. Darfur was almost cashless. When a labour migrant returned home with savings, it was a windfall. What counted for local livelihoods was land, both farmland and pasture, including the wells and reservoirs required to make use of it. What mattered most politically were the administrative systems that exercised jurisdiction over land and the intertribal conferences intermittently convened to resolve major disputes.[5] Because all the channels for organizing patronage and resolving disputes were through tribal chiefs, politics and conflicts necessarily took on ethnic lines. Darfurians say that 'conflict defines origins', because when disputes come to be settled and compensation paid, everyone must identify with their tribal group which is responsible for paying blood-money.[6]

One of the authors of *The Black Book* was Khalil Ibrahim, who went on to found the Justice and Equality Movement (JEM). Khalil reports that, when Vice President Ali Osman Taha was warned of imminent revolt in Darfur, he contemptuously dismissed the possibility on the grounds that Darfurians were 'too hungry to stage an armed revolution'.[7]

Ali Osman was wrong, but his mistake tells us much. The twentieth century had shown that farming and herding did not generate enough political finance to fund a modest political party, let alone a full-scale rebellion. Darfur's wage earners were working on commercial farms and irrigation projects in central and eastern Sudan: some had become radicalized, but sending money home was difficult enough, and political organization at a distance was all but impossible. Trade had long been dominated by a class of merchants from the Nile, known colloquially as *jellaba*. They made money, but reinvested their profits in Khartoum.[8] The vice president should have been more attentive to the growing wealth of traders from the Zaghawa ethnic group, which spans the Darfur–Chad border. Zaghawa businessmen had rapidly come to dominate markets in Darfur and Chad, and one of their brethren – Idriss Déby Itno – was president of Chad. What Ali Osman missed was that the price of Darfurian loyalties was rising, an oversight that led his government into a disastrous blunder.

Darfur was already awash with guns and military entrepreneurs. This was a legacy of the Chadian civil wars and of the adventurism of the Libyan leader Muammar Gaddafi. Since nationalizing his country's oil industry in the early 1970s, Gaddafi's funds surpassed any good judgement he may have had. He became a compulsive shopper in the continental marketplace, often for vanity purchases,[9] though sometimes showing a Bedouin keenness for getting the best possible deal.

Gaddafi's poisonous gift to Darfur, by way of Chad, was weapons. He did not begin the 'thirty years' war'[10] that involved Chad, Sudan and Libya – it was the founders of the Chadian National Liberation Front (FROLINAT), meeting in Nyala in 1966, who did that. But Gaddafi turned it from a small war into a large one, by occupying the Aozou Strip in the north of Chad in 1973 and trying to annex the whole country in 1980. This led to civil war on the streets of the capital N'djaména. Chad was the first African country to earn the label 'failed state'; Chadian military entrepreneurs were the first to be called 'warlords'; and N'djaména was the site of the OAU's first peacekeeping mission (which failed). Gaddafi's ambitions provoked the largest 'contra' operation in Africa in which France, the US and Sudan backed his Chadian adversaries. The most effective of them was Hissène Habré, who invaded Chad from Sudan in 1983, took power, and waged a tactically brilliant military campaign that defeated a huge conventional Libyan army in the battle of Ouadi Doum in 1987. He then sold the captured weapons, turning N'djaména into Africa's biggest arms entrepôt. Habré did not value human lives: the Chadian commission of inquiry established after his overthrow counted 3,780 political murders and estimated that it had covered a tenth of the probable cases.[11]

Following Ouadi Doum, Chadian Arab militias that had served as Libyan proxies retreated to Darfur, where they were chased by Habré and French commandos. The penniless Sudanese government was nowhere to be seen in Darfur for the entire decade. This epilogue to the Libya–Chad war intersected with local Darfurian conflicts and ignited a war for land.[12] The Arab supremacism of the

Libyan-sponsored militia – the first *janjawiid* – collided with the 'African' consciousness of non-Arab Darfurians who had been listening to Radio SPLA.

The Islamist military government that took power in 1989 had little money, and its Arab and Islamist sponsors were uninterested in Darfur. The exception was Libya, but as soon as Bashir had helped install Idriss Déby in power in Chad, the following year, the three leaders made a de facto truce. It seemed that the thirty years' war had ended with a whimper.

Sudanese Islamists had a strong following in Darfur and an effective political apparatus. They knew the members of the small Darfurian elite one by one, and used a judicious combination of threat and co-option, and so did not need either large-scale coercion or political spending. The importance of this Islamist organization was demonstrated in 1991, when an SPLA incursion was defeated and the SPLA's political network quickly neutralized.[13] A few years later when Eritrean emissaries arrived in Chad to ask for help in provoking rebellion in Darfur, they were blocked by Déby. Local Darfurian conflicts rumbled on, mostly concerned with land, and a divided and distant government in Khartoum intervened rarely to stop them – sometimes one member of the ruling cabal would step in to support one side or the other, most often the Arabs against the non-Arabs. At the end of the 1990s, a dispute over the control of the local administration in Dar Masalit in the far west sparked conflict. In a rare show of force, Bashir sent a special envoy to play the role of Leviathan in khaki. This stopped the fighting, though the Masalit leaders justifiably complained that Khartoum was biased against them.[14]

The conflict that escalated in central Darfur in 2001–2 at first looked much the same: local disputes over land and local government boundaries. Khartoum's political-business managers discounted signs that Islamists such as Khalil would turn to rebellion, partly because intelligence operatives found them living in humble circumstances in N'djaména.[15] Khalil's own account suggests the security assessment not wholly wrong. Speaking to his biographer, he describes how when he first left Sudan to foment rebellion, his main task was raising money, from Chad and the diaspora. In 2002, Khalil called his network together for a conference in Vlotho, Germany. There was no shortage of antipathy to the government and sympathy for armed opposition, but '[f]inance remained the most daunting problem with which I left Vlotho'.[16] Delays in getting the needed money and careless handling of the funds they had delayed the start of military operations by six months. 'Part of my problem was lack of experience,' Khalil said. 'I would never handle scarce money in that way today.'[17]

Nonetheless, the price of loyalty was going up. Khalil was confident that he would find funds, not initially from Chad or Libya, but from the Zaghawa and Islamist businesspeople. Darfur was changing, and Sudan's political-business managers failed to see it. The then-governor of Northern Darfur, Ibrahim Suleiman, argued that it was possible to settle the problem using the newfound national oil wealth to fund development and services. But he was overruled.

Well-targeted political spending might have neutralized the Darfur rebellion at that early stage. The rebels were much harder to defeat on the battlefield. The fighters of JEM and the Sudan Liberation Army (SLA) introduced the tactical innovation of Landcruiser-based mobile warfare, something for which the Sudanese army had not been trained,[18] attacked al Fashir Airport in April 2003, destroying many aircraft, and won the great majority of battles during that year, causing panic in the army. They demobilized the government's Islamist political and intelligence apparatus in Darfur. Instead of the efficient retail politics of coercing and co-opting individuals one by one, Khartoum's intelligence officers had to work at a wholesale level, targeting or buying off entire constituencies. In the desperate early stages of the war, they tried both, and when the militia from non-Arab Darfurian communities went over to the rebels, they turned to the Arab militia, popularly known as *Janjawiid*, to destroy ethnically defined communities. Khalil called it 'genocide'.

The Auction of Loyalties

The logic of a rent-seeking rebellion is that the insurgent stakes a claim by attacking a government asset. The government, before opening negotiations, responds with a counter-attack on the rebels' asset base – the population – to convey its seriousness. This may continue for several rounds until a bargain is reached.

The Darfur war between the al Fashir airport attack of April 2003, and the end of mass burning of villages in January 2005, shows broadly the same pattern except on a much larger scale. The rebel attacks humbled the army. In three huge counter-offensives, the army and militia killed perhaps 30,000 civilians, caused a famine that killed several hundred thousand more, and displaced millions. At this scale, however, the logic of the contest changed. The atrocities dragged Chad (newly an oil state) into the war on the rebel side, brought major US attention including the Save Darfur campaign, and compelled the Sudanese government to submit to an African Union peace process and a peacekeeping mission. The marketplace was opened up to a host of new patrons, each with money to spend. A conflict that had begun with rudimentary and low-priced political bargaining became a fast-changing, integrated and high-priced auction room. The resources that came in were the purest form of rent: simple loyalty payments. The instruments for getting these payments were force, the threat of force, or the threat of third-party force (such as calling in international troops).

Any detailed narrative of the political and military alliances in Darfur since 2005 will quickly become confusing to all but the most knowledgeable observer, with literally dozens of different-named groups. A mapping of incidents of violence quickly becomes an apparently random splatter of marks, a war of all against all – except for the fact that most of the time there is no fighting, and yesterday's enemies are today's allies. There was no repeat of the extremes of massacre witnessed in 2003–4, but violence became locked into the marketplace. Between 2005 and 2011, about 1,500–2,000 civilians and fighters died violently each year. Tabulating violent incidents shows diverse kinds of combat, crime and attacks on civilians – including, most intriguingly, incidents in which government-armed paramilitaries fought against one another and against the army, police and security forces, and even different arms of the official security establishment fought one another.[19] The ethnic pattern of victimization changed from year to year: in 2007–9, for example, most of the fighting was among Arab tribes and paramilitaries,[20] so the dead were mostly Arabs; in 2011–12 there was an upsurge of targeting Zaghawa civilians. If this was war, it was fought at a low intensity. It resembled more Thomas Hobbes's description of 'warre' as generalized insecurity which he compared to inclement weather, when it is not necessarily raining all the time but one should not venture outside unprepared for the chance of rain.[21]

Ethnic labels played important roles in this turbulent 'warre'. Armed units were constituted around kinship, with tribal hierarchies transplanted on to military ones. (Indeed Khartoum's Islamization of chiefly titles had already merged them with military ranks.) Ethnic branding also signalled which patrons might be interested: 'African' rebel groups with English-language initials would draw the attention of regional and international sponsors, while Arabs – tarnished by the label *Janjawiid* – could deal only with the Sudanese. The Arab insurgencies are a neglected part of the wider history of the Darfur war, and they provide a particularly candid glimpse into how political bargaining works.

The Arab militia had been incentivized with loot and land, but the former soon ran out and the latter proved problematic. The costs of maintaining the vehicles and weapons needed for self-defence would be enough to bankrupt all but the wealthiest camel herder. The Arabs were denied humanitarian aid and were excluded from the AU-mediated peace talks in Abuja, on the grounds that the government spoke for them. The government rewarded Musa Hilal, the most prominent militia commander of the 2003–4 campaigns, with a position as commander of the Border Intelligence Brigade, a paramilitary group newly created to put his men on the payroll. For the Khartoum military chiefs it was also a means of exerting some control over Hilal, who had been wayward and independent before the 2003 war, and was to prove so again. Most militiamen felt defrauded and disavowed and, as soon as the intense fighting was over, a handful began defecting to the rebels. In 2007, a unit calling itself Jundi al Mazlum ('The Wronged Soldiers') rebelled and that name 'became a catch phrase for all mutinous groupings as the Arab mutiny gained momentum'.[22]

The most serious Arab mutineer was Mohamed Hamdan Hemeti, who took his forces into the mountains, opened talks on a possible alliance with the SLA and shot down an army helicopter. His approaches to Chad and Libya were rebuffed, he was ignored by the UN and AU (with the exception of some UN political affairs officers, of Somali origin, who quickly figured out what was happening), and found the SLA too divided and ineffective. Julie Flint writes:

> [Hemeti] stayed 'in the desert' for six months, supporting 4,000 men who began trickling back to their families, unopposed by him, as their isolation and lack of support became apparent. When his money ran out, Hemeti said, he had two choices: to rejoin the government, or become a 'Janjaweed' – in Arab parlance, a robber.

A journalist, Nima Elbagir, was in Hemeti's camp when the government made its offer. It was not only too little for Hemeti's taste but also the government had reneged on earlier offers. Hemeti sent a message back to the government, 'give me what I want or face the consequences... this is the second time that they haven't delivered and within the next 24 to 72 hours, we are going to make clear to the world what our position from them is [...] we will fight them til judgment day.'[23] Two days later, the government increased its offer and Hemeti accepted.

The Arab mutinies are a particularly clear-cut case of rent-seeking rebellion followed by a promotion-and-payroll agreement that also serves as a security pact. The political entrepreneurs and business managers spoke directly to one another, without international mediators, so there was no need to frame their cause as a struggle to put deep-seated wrongs to right, or to achieve justice, democracy and development. The only issue on the table was the price. Flint wrote:

> Uncertainty still surrounds the exact terms of the deal under which Khartoum brought Hemeti back. Unconfirmed reports said he demanded, in addition to development for the Um al Qora area, the position of lieutenant general in the army for himself, a nazirship for his uncle Juma Dogolo, the post of commissioner for his brother Abdel Rahim Hamdan Dogolo, a cash payment of SDP 1 billion (USD 440,000) for himself, and half that amount again for his brother, ostensibly to compensate fighters and their families. UN informants said 3,000 of his men were incorporated into the regular army, with army salaries, and 200–300 were promised officer training. Colleagues said the deal had two main components – 'money and weapons', including RPGs [rocket-propelled grenades] and machine guns.[24]

Hemeti remarked to a UN political officer that he expected the government to deliver on 40 per cent, and that would be sufficient for eighteen months.

Bargaining by non-Arab political entrepreneurs was more complicated: they had many more potential patrons. Khalil was particularly adventurous in this regard. His forces fought in defence of N'djaména against Sudanese-backed rebels and were later stationed in Libya (there is controversy over whether they fought in the Libyan civil war or not). Eritrea was another sponsor, though Khalil complained that Asmara was difficult to reach and had inordinately expensive telecoms. Khalil also struck deals with Uganda and South Sudan, and was leading his forces on a long drive from Tripoli to bases in South Sudan in December 2011, when he was killed by a Sudanese air strike. JEM was also good at private-sector fundraising and its campaign to label the governments' atrocities as 'genocide' succeeded beyond expectation[25] – though Khalil never made the error, committed by Abdel Wahid al Nur, of confusing tactical instruments with strategic goals.

As soon as the Darfur war erupted in 2003, mediators stepped in. The first was Déby, who correctly feared that he would be in danger if the war were not stopped. The US strong-armed both government and rebels into signing the April 2004 Humanitarian Ceasefire Agreement in N'djaména. The AU incrementally took over the mediation, and soon the peace conference became the main theatre for both formal negotiation and real bargaining. At the official sessions in

Nigerian hotel conference rooms, government and rebels faced each other on opposite sides of a square table, while the mediators framed an agenda around legalistic documents. In the rooms, curtains drawn, the government team compiled its files on each individual and discreetly made its offers one by one, and the rebels spent their time and effort with the international observers (especially the Americans) begging for financial, political and military help.[26]

The AU chief mediator, Salim Ahmed Salim, was a veteran of African liberation struggles and was painfully aware how a divided opposition would be picked off piecemeal. He tried to limit recognition at the peace talks to the government and the two rebel groups, SLM and JEM, and reluctantly recognized SLM-Abdel Wahid and SLM-Minawi as separate groups in late 2005, when the split between the two was irrevocable. Other splinter groups were denied a seat at the table. Even as the rebels fractured, pretence of unity was maintained at the talks. This changed after May 2006, once the peace talks ended, when Chad was fully involved in supporting the rebels and the international peacekeeping presence was scaled up. Buyer competition had increased, the regulatory mechanism of limiting seats at the peace talks was relaxed, and the peacekeepers had to deal with realities on the ground – whichever group was stopping trucks on the road or taking hostages. The barrier to entry for political entrepreneurs became very low indeed.[27]

After the failure of the 2006 Darfur Peace Agreement, the AU and UN chief mediators took the peace forum to Libya in 2007, in the hope that Gaddafi's blessing would encourage the diverse groups to come to a common position. That did not happen: and instead Gaddafi forfeited the hosting to one of his main Arab rivals, Qatar.

Agreement at this point was impossible because Sudan and Chad were deep into a proxy war, with Libya mostly on the Chadian side. Since December 2005, Chad had been actively supporting the rebels. Chadian supplies and troops regularly crossed the border, and in April 2006 JEM fighters fought in N'djaména against Chadian insurgents backed by Sudan. The contest escalated in February 2008, when a Chadian rebel force, armed by Sudan's National Intelligence and Security Service (NISS), fought its way to the gates of the presidential palace in N'djaména. As the French offered to evacuate Déby to safety (he refused), the rebels bickered over the spoils in their moment of apparent triumph – and Déby counter-attacked. Three months later, a JEM column, supplied by Gaddafi and assisted by Chad, mounted an even bolder attack on the Sudanese capital, repulsed only at the bridges across the Nile by Sudanese security forces. Déby was no longer a subordinate player in a Sudanese-run regional hierarchy: he was co-equal with Bashir.

Déby's rise from Sudanese client to challenger was fuelled by crude oil and expressed in an increase in his defence budget from $69 million in 2005 to $594 million in 2008.[28] Chad began to export oil in 2003. Three years before that, the Chad-Cameroon Petroleum Development and Pipeline Project was launched with ExxonMobil, Petronas (Malaysia) and Chevron, and the support of the World Bank. The pipeline through Cameroon was designed to minimize environmental damage. A substantial part of the revenue from Chad's oil production was to be invested in socio-economic development, thus minimizing the political and economic risks associated with the 'resource curse'. The project included an elaborate scheme whereby oil revenues were to be allocated by a Petroleum Revenue Oversight Committee to a Future Generations Fund, services and development projects, a fund to compensate the oil-producing regions, and the government. This was considered a model of its kind. As soon as the civil war began, Chad amended the Petroleum Revenue Management Law, increasing the share of revenues to the government's general fund from 15 per cent to 30 per cent. Then, Déby paid off the World Bank contributions ($66 million) and scrapped the scheme: he needed cash at once.

During 2009, the two sides spent hugely on renting proxies and arming them.[29] Déby had oil money and Gaddafi's support. Sudan's NISS organized and funded Chadian rebels. But, following the plunge in the oil price, both sides' budgets were squeezed. Bashir and Déby called a truce and resumed their former security pact, this time as equal partners. One consequence of the competition, and the price that Khartoum paid for settling the Arab mutinies, is that the Sudanese government became the guest of the Arab militias in Darfur.

Regulating the Market?

The March 2010 'Framework Agreement' between the government of Sudan and JEM was drawn up by Déby's staff in French, agreed with the Sudanese, and then presented to Khalil Ibrahim as a fait accompli. Finally, it was sent to the official mediation in Qatar to be signed, so that the internationally appointed Joint Chief Mediator, the Burkinabe business manager Djibril Bassolé, could claim some credit – and, more importantly, would not undermine it.[30] It was principally a security pact aimed at regulating (and reducing) the price of loyalty. It was consummated in a tangible and customary manner in 2012 when Déby took Amani Musa Hilal, daughter of the Darfurian Arab militia leader, as his junior wife.

When the UN and AU initially appointed Bassolé in 2008, they gave him a prefabricated office in the UNAMID compound in al Fashir and proposed that he be full-time there. Bassolé preferred Doha, and over the following three years this became the exclusive location for convening the Darfurian political elite. The Joint Chief Mediator showed little interest in the details of Darfur but had a sharp sense of political markets and the potential for Qatari money to be the determining factor at the talks.[31] Very little negotiation took place between government and rebels. Instead, the exercise took the form of UN experts drawing up a series of documents which were then approved by the government, selected Darfurian rebels and by Darfurian civil society representatives (who did not have the chance to read the documents before their endorsement was announced). There was a payoff for all concerned: the Qataris were generous hosts, and were inclined to give generous personal gifts at every Muslim holiday, and also covered many of the delegates' and mediation staff members' expenses. They also indicated that, once a deal was signed, Qatari money would ensure that it was implemented.

With the Darfur rebels unable to coordinate, and JEM increasingly unwilling to travel from Libya to Qatar, the mediators found themselves in the awkward position of not having a credible rebel intermediary. With the assistance of the US, they contrived one: the Liberation and Justice Movement (LJM), which comprised individuals from every group who were keen to see a deal done and development delivered – and also wanted to be part of this effort themselves. The LJM's leader was Tijani Sese, a prominent Darfurian economist who was, prior to his rather civil rebellion, a senior UN officer in Addis Ababa. Rather than an agreement among combatants, or a consensus position drawn from consulting Darfurians, the Doha Document for Peace in Darfur, adopted in 2011, is a blueprint for a technocratic governance of Darfur, made possible by Qatari patronage and legitimized by the UN.

Bashir and Déby hoped that their rapprochement would bring peace to the region. The Chadian leader did his part when he turned Khalil back from N'djaména Airport in March 2010. But Gaddafi took in Khalil and continued to support him. One reason he did this was that Qatar was hosting and funding the Darfur peace talks, which Gaddafi saw (correctly) as a rebuff and a challenge: a year later, Al Jazeera, the Muslim Brothers, Qatari arms and Sudan's NISS and military intelligence would all play roles in his downfall. Bashir and Déby differed on how to handle Libya. As the first Arab Spring protests in Tripoli began in February 2011, Déby warned against forcible regime change, telling fellow African leaders to 'beware of opening the Libyan Pandora's box'.[32] He saw Gaddafi as sitting at the apex of a political-criminal cartel, which, if decapitated, would leave the various transnational armed groups present in Libya to search for new sources of funds, at the same moment that the vast Libyan arsenals were opened to all comers. Déby stayed neutral in the Libyan war. His fears, as he later pointedly remarked, were not unfounded. The Sudanese, on the other hand, were early and aggressive intervenors in Libya, dispatching their own troops to capture the desert town of Kufra, and their own security operatives to help train and coordinate the rebels. Sudan also served as the overland arms supply route for Qatari arms destined for the rebels, and Sudanese intelligence officers and surveillance drones provided intelligence about the vast interior spaces of Libya for the coalition.

The fall of Gaddafi forced JEM to leave Libya. In a remarkable journey, JEM fighters crossed the Sahara, northern Chad, Darfur and Kordofan in Sudan, towards South Sudan. Khalil was killed in Kordofan and his brother Jibreel took over the leadership. In South Sudan they received support from President Museveni and SPLA Military Intelligence. This support was conditional on a political alignment with the SPLA-North, which was fighting an insurgency in Southern Kordofan and Blue Nile, inside (northern) Sudan but adjacent to South Sudan. Consequently the Sudan Revolutionary Forces (SRF) was formed as an umbrella for the Darfurian groups and SPLA-N.

But the hope that the SRF would impose some order on the Darfur insurgency did not last: Abdel Wahid was as feckless as ever, and Minni Minawi continued to display the political skills of a street gang leader. The Darfur talks that resumed in Addis Ababa in November 2014 were a farcical re-enactment of the last round in Abuja nine years earlier. The same 'rebel' leaders were there, with greyer hair, fatter waists and smarter suits; a near-identical government delegation came, dominated by army and intelligence generals. The rebels begged for money and the government was not ready to concede anything that might jeopardize Qatari pledges of money. Having been transformed from regional peacemaker to near-pariah over the previous two years, because of its links to the Muslim Brotherhood, Qatar was left holding on to the 2011 Doha Document for Peace in Darfur as a rare token of its diplomatic success, and insisted that its funds were dependent on no alterations to that agreement. The Darfur Arabs, who have the power to make or unmake any agreement, were not represented. Meanwhile the American representatives rather pathetically insisted, as they had nine years earlier, that Minni was a credible interlocutor who should be given another chance.

It is possible that the Chad-Sudan agreement, the relative centralization of the rebels, and Qatari funds, could provide the basis for a stable and affordable political market in Darfur. The architects of this formula are all accomplished practitioners of market politics. But each has pursued a short-term and narrow interest, and all have succumbed to the same error that prevented a timely resolution of the conflict in the early 2000s – they have underestimated the price to be paid. Aware of the probable perfidy of the external brokers, Darfurian political entrepreneurs will hedge their bets. Political spending will continue to crowd out development and services, leaving the ordinary people of Darfur no better off.

The Functions and Limits of Violence

There are three main forms of political violence in Darfur and its vicinity: the routine killing, burning and raping of the rent-seeking rebellion cycle and bargaining for position; fights for dominance or power between peers; and large-scale massacre.

For the political entrepreneur, inflicting damage and killing people is a routine way of signalling one's existence and claims. For the governmental political-business manager, violence is a way of denying or weakening those claims. The asymmetry of the bargaining is reflected in the different kinds of violence inflicted: the claimant attacks assets that are politically or commercially valuable, the business manager responds by attacking the human resources of the rebels. Atrocities serve insurgents as a signal of serious commitment to followers, rivals and would-be patrons, and serve rulers as an index of determination. But conspicuous atrocities may now involve international costs, as Bashir and Gaddafi discovered.

Fighting for power or dominance among peers involves fiercer battles, because the loser may lose all. Examples are the attacks on N'djaména in 2006 and 2008, on Omdurman in 2008, and the battles in Libya in 2011. These are not typically instances of the greatest violence against civilians: the purpose of attack is victory on the battlefield.

The very large-scale killings of civilians in Darfur in 2003–4 cannot be explained as the use of violence for bargaining, or because of peer rivalry, because Chadian involvement followed the atrocities rather than preceding them. The logic of massacre was habit, blunder and escalation. The habitual element was that for twenty years, Sudan's military had waged counter-insurgency by licensing militia to pillage, burn, rape and kill.[33] So they had in effect declared Darfur an 'ethics-free zone' in a similar way to their earlier abandonment of account-ability and humanity in southern Sudan and told the soldiers and militiamen to do what they could get away with and not report back. The motive was military victory and the intent was criminal.[34] Panicking because of the tempo of military defeats and the fear of an Islamist uprising within Khartoum, in the dark as to the rebels' support base, the ruling cabal used every means at their disposal, without putting a limit on how far their agents should go.

The element of blunder was a failure of military intelligence to understand the threat posed by the rebels' tactics, and of political business to make an offer when it would have been affordable: by the time the government was ready to bargain, the price demanded had increased far beyond what Khartoum's business managers had budgeted.

Violence, once inflicted at scale, brought its own logic of escala-tion. There were two unforeseen consequences of the 2003–4 atroci-ties: international sympathy for 'African' Darfurians as the victims of mass atrocity and the fact that Darfur's vast IDP camps became places outside government control. These bid up the price, but Darfurian rebel leaders missed their opportunity. They failed to use the high tide of international patronage at the time of the 2006 Darfur peace talks to float domestic political businesses. They also failed to take the opportunity of compensating for low levels of politi-cal finance and infrastructure by organizing a populist political plat-form in the IDP camps that could have delivered votes in the national elections. The escalation ended in the political dead end of the arrest warrant by the International Criminal Court (ICC) against Bashir, a hollow victory.

Implications: the Interwar

Darfurians in 2006 described the disappearance of institutionalized government as *fawdha* – anarchy – and feared that reverence for government had vanished forever.[35] Darfur may yet see a strongman, who can centralize control over rents and coerce his rivals, but the prospects of institutional government are close to zero. There is no state-building in Darfur.

In Chad, long definitive of absence of government, Déby is today a 'democratic dictator'.[36] His imitation of a state is plausible only to those professionally obliged to sustain the pretence. Déby rules over a contingent peace as a fragile Leviathan. Marielle Debos describes an enduring expectation among Chadian fighters, and its implications.

> [W]ar is not fought in a context of hatred or ideological polarization. It is thought of as a 'situation'. This 'situation' implies and justifies the recourse to arms and the (tragic but unavoidable) possibility of a violent encounter with a friend or a relative who was recruited to a competing faction. Dialogue and negotiation between warring parties are only interrupted during actual fighting. Faction leaders have friendly relations when they meet at the negotiating table. A rebel leader explained the pattern thus: 'The social and affective sides of things, the alliances among tribes are crucial. But when the war is on, you have to be ready to fight. When there is no fighting, we are brothers. That's the way it is.'[37]

Debos does away with the distinction between war and peace, preferring 'the situation of actual combat' and the 'interwar'. There is no 'pre-war normalcy' to which people can aspire, just a situation of less and more predictable violence. Peace negotiations are an instrument for both power-holders and insurgents for continuing the war, security pacts that enable them to position themselves better for the next round of fighting. Debos dispenses with the opposition between government and rebels, preferring the common *métier* (craft or profession) of those who make a living from their use of arms. Commanders and combatants in the various branches of the regular forces, and in other militia and rebel groups, are interchangeable and often interchanged. Taking up arms for rent-seeking rebellions is common, leading to negotiations over a better deal for leaders. Debos concludes, 'war belongs to politics, and violence derives from the situation rather than from radical enmity. War is not waged because there are enemies; there are enemies because a war is waged.'[38]

Debos's conclusions apply equally well to the advanced political market in Darfur: the best we can hope for is the 'interwar' in which the 'situation' makes a low level of violence optimal. A modestly encouraging conclusion follows, namely, that violence on the scale of the 2003–4 Darfur massacres is a bad political-business strategy. Not only were those atrocities an error, but the perpetrators recognized them to be so. Unfortunately, it is a mistake that Sudanese political-business managers have made, time and again, over thirty years. They recurrently reject the price of peace, hoping for a cheaper deal, only to find that they are compelled to pay an even higher price later on. Majzoub al Khalifa, the government's chief negotiator for the Darfur Peace Agreement, was correct that the rebels' price had been

68   *Darfur: The Auction of Loyalties*

inflated in a speculative bubble that would soon burst. But he short-changed them nonetheless. His priority was the metropolitan political marketplace, and he left the peripheries to collect the small change. Khartoum's political-business managers have continued to under-value Darfurians – including most dangerously the Arab militia leaders – since then.

Similarly, throughout the 1980s and 1990s, Khartoum could have accepted any one of a number of options for peace in southern Sudan, which would have kept the country united, but each time judged the price as too high. They paid pocket money to rent militia, and ended up losing the South altogether. How Sudanese regimes stayed in power, while the country crashed around them, is the challenge of the next chapter.

5

Sudan
Managing the Unmanageable

The Unexpected Survivor

On the morning of 1 July 1989, Sudanese awoke to martial music on Radio Omdurman and a new face as their head of state, Brigadier Omar Hassan al Bashir.[1] Few expected Bashir to stay long in the palace: he appeared clumsy and he and the other officers in the Revolutionary Command Council seemed out of their depth. They were Islamists. They had pulled off a trick to fool the Egyptians, who might have strangled their takeover at birth. The ruse was to dispatch their co-conspirators, notably Sheikh Hassan al Turabi and Ali Osman Mohamed Taha, to Kober Prison along with other parliamentarians and trade unionists, while the generals donned the garb of nationalism. It worked: Egyptian intelligence endorsed the coup. Still, even after the Islamists were out of prison and were running the executive from their private houses, the regime looked shaky. Just six months later, it was at the point of military collapse when the Ethiopian army and the SPLA moved into Blue Nile, and the Sudanese Armed Forces could not respond. (The Eritreans did the job.) After another seven months, Turabi overruled his president and declared for Saddam Hussein who had just invaded Kuwait, thereby definitively cutting off Sudan from its major economic and political lifelines: Saudi Arabia, Egypt and the US. Sudan was already bankrupt and panic buying of food set off hyperinflation and a nationwide famine.

Twenty-five years later, President Bashir had the choice of whether and how to stay in office. Even close members of Bashir's own entourage are puzzled as to how he managed to stay in power for so long.

He had survived intensified international sanctions, the fallout from hosting Osama bin Laden (which included an American cruise missile strike on Khartoum in 1998), and an arrest warrant from the ICC. Having seized power to pre-empt a peace agreement with the SPLA that would have involved suspending Islamic law and sharing power, Bashir seriously considered stepping down in 2014 after having presided over the separation of South Sudan. He decided to stay on because his anointed successor, General Bakri Hassan Saleh, did not appear capable of managing Sudan's political business.

The Financial Skeleton of Sudanese Politics

There are many entry points for the study of Sudan's ever-fascinating politics. My choice in this chapter is budgets: government budgets (for which we have data) and political budgets (for which we can make inferences). Sudanese budgets are works of wonder and sorcery and the fiscal sociology of Sudan is illuminating.

Between 1970 and 1978 there was a threefold increase in government spending, driven largely by borrowing. It is no accident that two nationwide peace agreements were reached in this period of expanding state and political budgets. It could not last: Sudan ran into arrears in 1978 and had to be bailed out. It had by 1985 achieved the largest number of official debt reschedulings in the world (eight) and the following year became the first country ever to be suspended from the IMF, for failing to pay the interest due on its debt to the fund itself. During the 1980s, Sudan's Minister of Finance and Central Bank administrators had to become fiscal jugglers to keep the government from crashing. During the 1990s, the government ran on an annual budget of under $1 billion and, following the export of oil, its spending increased tenfold between 1999 and 2008. It was again no accident that the negotiations leading to the Comprehensive Peace Agreement (CPA) were conducted in this boom period, followed by provincial peace agreements in southern Sudan, Darfur and eastern Sudan. From this, a simple observation is derived: the essential precondition for a peace agreement is an expanding budget, with most of it under the ruler's discretionary control. The key to a workable peace deal is an allocation of resources to the adversary sufficient for him to join the government.

In this account of Sudan's financial politics, I seek to show how the political marketplace emerged and how it functions, and how it has submerged the politics of institutions and ideas. The following chapter does the same for South Sudan.

This is not, of course, the dominant narrative of Sudanese history. The most common starting point for understanding Sudan is conflicts of identity and wars of vision. Is Sudan an Arab or an African country (or both)? Does it have an Islamic identity? Should it be one, two or several nations? The country's unresolved racial, religious and ethnic identities have been the subject of deep and sensitive analysis, with some of the most delicate insights expressed in fiction.[2] Identity markers, including skin colour, language and everyday cultural practices, define a hierarchy that every Sudanese knows and respects, or disputes. Successive attempts to forge a new Sudan along nationalist, socialist or Islamist lines have failed, each one failing to command consensus in society, and each falling prey to the short-term demands of political survival.

The topography of wealth and administration is another starting point. The inequalities of wealth between Khartoum and the nearby towns and agricultural schemes – a middle-income zone, even during the depths of austerity – and some of the provinces to the east, west and south, where human development indicators are among the lowest in the world, is compelling. Today, there are nine bridges across the Nile in the city of Khartoum, four in the rest of (northern) Sudan and just one in South Sudan. The world's largest irrigated farm in Gezira has a landscape not unlike the Netherlands, which would provide an appropriate cover for James Scott's book *Seeing Like a State*.[3] The hydraulics and finance of the scheme demand bureaucratic administration of the utmost attentiveness and rigour. By contrast, the remoter areas – what were called 'closed districts' in the colonial era – retain the decentralized despotisms of administrative tribalism, still called 'native administration'.[4] On the frontiers of governmentality, people practise 'the art of not being governed',[5] finding ways of subverting or escaping the intrusions of external power.

These elements will not be absent from my account. Indeed they interact with the fiscal sociology of political finance. An illustration of this is the thought and practice of Abdel Rahim Hamdi, an Islamist financier who served as Minister of Finance in the early 1990s, at the very depths of Sudan's financial meltdown. One of his decisions was to change the currency, from Sudanese pounds to dinars, an action that served several purposes: it struck many zeros off the denominations, making it psychologically easier to stabilize the currency after a period of hyperinflation, it gave an Islamic identity to the notes, and the process of exchanging banknotes provided a lot of information about the economy. Almost 90 per cent of the notes that were exchanged were in Khartoum and its immediate environs. Hamdi is infamous for having proposed that investment should be targeted to

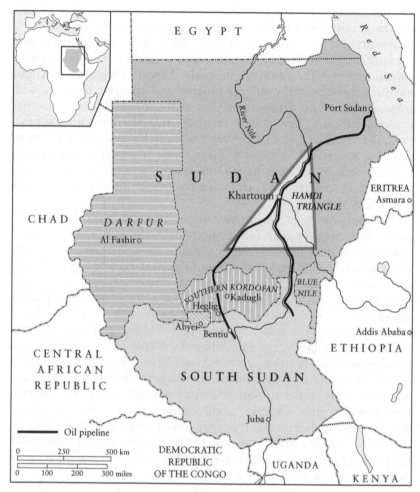

Map 5.1   Sudan and South Sudan

an area within a day's drive of the capital. 'Hamdi's Triangle', as it became known, is coterminous with that middle-income enclave. He was also architect of radical adjustment measures, including privatization of the remaining state-owned enterprises and a cash budget – every month, the money actually existing in the Central Bank of Sudan was counted and allocated according to defined criteria.

   A core principle of the Islamist revolution in Sudan was that 'sovereignty belongs to God'. States and their claims on authority are usurpers, and territorial boundaries are infringements on the fundamental unity of the Muslim community (*umma*). The intersection of Islamist principle, neo-liberal economics and extreme austerity created a situation in which the economic frontiers of Sudan were drawn very differently from its formal state boundaries. The Hamdi Triangle, plus Port Sudan, constituted an economic core, a viable putative future Islamic state. The outlying provinces constituted a burden: a welfare bill and a security threat, but a source of natural resources and trading profits. The distant frontiers of the Sudanese economic space stretched further still, as far as the trading networks of the Jellaba merchants, originating from Khartoum and the riverian provinces to the north, had penetrated. Therefore Chad, CAR and parts of northern Uganda and north-eastern DRC, plus the western lowlands of Ethiopia and Eritrea, should be included in this domain.

Whatever the ideological basis for Hamdi's political geography, or the Islamist thinking that underpinned the contemporaneous experiment in dissolving a state into the operations of a broader transnational Islamist movement with its commercial, philanthropic and military components, the character and fate of such political projects ultimately became determined by the mercantile logic of the political marketplace.

Nimeiri's Chameleon Dictatorship 1969–85

Colonel Jaafar Nimeiri began as a free officer in the Nasserist tradition. He seized power in May 1969 in alliance with the Communists and fought the traditional parties and Islamists. He then fell out with the Communists (1971) and tried to build a secular, modernist, developmental state in alliance with southern Sudanese and technocrats, borrowing extensively. He signed the Addis Ababa Agreement with Joseph Lagu, leader of the southern Anyanya movement, in January 1972, and the 'National Reconciliation' that brought his sectarian and Islamist adversaries back into the political fold in 1977. From the viewpoint of fiscal sociology, the key element here is borrowing. Nimeiri was able to borrow from the World Bank, western governments and Arab oil producers. Senior members of the government authorized about $8 billion in borrowing over the period 1971–7. Only a quarter of the loans were actually spent on their intended purposes: corruption became 'the fifth factor of production' in the country.[6] Borrowing gave Nimeiri a political budget to secure elite loyalty.

When the debts became due, Sudan could not pay. If the 1970s were a party, the 1980s were a long hangover. Nimeiri needed political funds somehow, and each of the medicines he took had side effects, as bad as the headache itself. One was a series of debt reschedulings, an endless exercise in financial juggling to remain politically solvent. He performed political-financial acrobatics to secure other funds, such as permitting Israel to airlift the Falasha Jews from refugee camps. Nimeiri's aim was to stay in power long enough for Chevron to start pumping oil, scheduled for 2 April 1986.[7]

Nimeiri took two other prescriptions, both of which proved addictive. One was modelled on Egypt: giving the army ownership of commercial companies, in an attempt to buy the loyalty of its officers. Commanders in the field and military intelligence officers were also given the latitude to strike deals with local traders or foreign investors to mount operations or provide security for facilities.

The second was opening his government to the Muslim Brothers and the economy to Islamic banks. The Faisal Islamic Bank of Sudan (FIBS) was the first, incorporated in 1978, with Saudi capital and Islamist management. It funded the Muslim Brothers – directly through contributions to the organization and its affiliates, and indirectly by extending loans to people who would become an Islamist constituency. Identifying a big unmet need for financial services to small businesses (which, under the Islamic system, took the form of commercial partnerships and profit-sharing, not interest-bearing loans), the FIBS and other Islamic banks rapidly increased their equity. As noted by Endre Stiansen, 'A striking feature of the formative phase of Islamic finance in the Sudan was how closely the different banks were associated with different political groups... The FIBS was the political bank par excellence.'[8] As a result, the Islamists' 'operational budget rocketed from a few tens of thousands of pounds to millions, and many members became CEOs or senior executives in banks and corporations, or directors of multi-million dollar international [Islamic] NGOs.'[9] In line with Turabi's 'jurisprudence of necessity', the Islamists were ready to cut deals on all sides to achieve their objective of hegemony. In the words of Abdullahi Gallab, these strands 'connected the operation of these financial institutions to the party's mode of operation and situated al-Turabi as the CEO of this corporation.'[10]

In early 1985, Nimeiri ran out of time and money. The US reversed its imposed austerity measures and mounted a huge USAID-funded famine-relief effort, but too late. Figure 5.1 shows what happened to three key indicators of the regime's political-financial health: government current spending, aid receipts, and payments on foreign debts (both official and private). The boom years of the 1970s are clearly

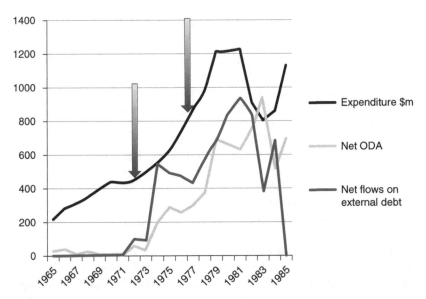

Figure 5.1 Sudanese government finances and peace agreements, 1965–84

Source: World Bank datasets, showing general government final consumption expenditure, net official development assistance and net flows on total debt stock in current US dollars (millions). Note that the famine-relief programme mounted by USAID and the World Food Programme in 1984–5 has been excluded.

seen, and the crisis of 1983, then the too-late recovery in foreign aid in 1985, accompanied by a crash on net flows of debt (which turned negative in 1985). Peace agreements are marked by vertical arrows.

In March 1985 a well-orchestrated campaign of civil disobedience showed that Sudanese civil society, led by the trade unions, still possessed the cohesion and discipline to pose a political challenge to the regime. Nimeiri's last-minute dash to Washington, DC, to secure funds was too late, and he was overthrown. He had inherited a government with strong institutions at the centre and a light, patrimonial administration in the provinces, and left it with a deeply corrupted central government and no administration at all in the remoter areas. His successor was General Abdel Rahman Suwar al Dahab, who ran a transitional government and kept his promise of free elections exactly a year later. He was probably grateful to hand over, leaving his successor with insoluble problems.

Sadiq al Mahdi's Impossible Balancing Act

Sadiq al Mahdi was elected prime minister of Africa's newest democracy in April 1986. He faced two major challenges: finding money to run his government and making a peace agreement in southern Sudan. The two contradicted each other: Sadiq's political funds came from people who did not want peace.

The IMF was unforgiving: just two months before the election, it suspended Sudan for non-payment of arrears. But it had no plan for what to do next, and the fund and the US government improvised arrangements whereby they could continue to do informal business with Sudan, propping up the government at moments of extremis, while encouraging economic reform. Sadiq's biggest economic task involved meeting the austerity conditions required by the IMF. Central to this was lifting the subsidy on bread, which consumed 7 per cent of government revenue. Townspeople regarded cheap bread as an entitlement and forced him to back down.[11] Sadiq's capitulation happened at exactly the same time that the famine in southern Sudan was costing tens of thousands of lives, and desperate and starving southerners were arriving in Khartoum, to be met with complete indifference by the government.

A peace agreement with the SPLA required compromising on Islamic law. Sadiq himself had sharply criticized Nimeiri's Sharia code – known as the 'September Laws' – and consistently said that citizenship should be the sole basis for rights. But when in government, he needed money. Although government spending was increasing, it was locked in by interest groups and tied to subsidies on fuel, sugar and bread, salaries and the army. Sudan was a democracy and Sadiq needed a political budget for election expenses and parliamentarians' demands, and the Islamists were ready to provide – or put together an alternative coalition to unseat him. So Sadiq prevaricated and manoeuvred, trying to buy time until a better political configuration came his way.

In the meantime, the government privatized the war. The key step was taken in July 1985, during Suwar al Dahab's transitional government. Faced with an SPLA incursion into northern Sudan, the Minister of Defence, General Fadallah Burma Nasir (a member of Sadiq's Umma Party), accompanied military intelligence chiefs on a helicopter tour of Southern Kordofan and Southern Darfur. They met with army officers, tribal chiefs from the Baggara Arabs, and former commanders of the sectarian parties' guerrilla forces who had been demobilized after the 1977 National Reconciliation and sent home. The arrangement was simple: the government would provide guns and help with military coordination, and the Baggara would form militias that would fight the SPLA. In return, the Baggara militia would help themselves to whatever they could find south of the internal boundary.

The militia strategy was counter-insurgency on the cheap. The militia – known locally as *murahaliin* ('nomads') or *fursan* ('horsemen') – looted, burned, killed and raped their way across a swathe of southern Sudan from 1985 until 1989, at which point they had so exhaustively pillaged the accessible areas that there was little left there of value, and SPLA units made it dangerous to go any further. Not only did they steal hundreds of thousands of cattle, but they also stole people. Abduction and enslavement in modern Sudan dates from this place and this time.

Under the parliamentary government, the processes of political marketization under way since the late 1970s were accelerated. Institutions decayed. One marker of this is the decline in the value of the salary paid to civil servants. By 1986, the official minimum wage was just 16 per cent of its level in 1970, and by 1988 it could cover only 6.5 per cent of basic living expenses.[12] In outlying areas, such as Darfur, not even that basic salary was paid regularly or in full. Civil servants had to moonlight or take bribes to get by. Official positions became prebends for extracting funds from the public. Sudan Railways literally ground to a halt.

The formal processes of budgeting and spending were inoperable. Officials from provincial governments camped out in Khartoum, visiting ministries each morning to see if there was any money to be had that day, and begging for a cheque to cover basic salaries – and hoping the cheque would be honoured at the bank. The prime minister was feverishly searching for short-term funds of any kind, and therefore unable to put together a strategy of any kind. At the end, he seemed resigned to a coup, even welcoming it. The Muslim Brothers, having bought up Sudan's political machinery, decided this was the time to abandon democratic practice and seize power, under the camouflage of a nationalist coup.

The 1990s: Survival Against the Odds

President Bashir has been lucky: his adversaries at home and abroad have fallen out among each other or pursued self-defeating strategies. But the political-business model adopted by Bashir and Turabi, and their key lieutenants including Taha and Hamdi, had much to do with it. The model was a cartel with distributed responsibilities. The civilian Islamists were tasked with implementing political and economic programmes, and Bashir's job was to keep the regime in power. For ten years they managed to cohabit.

A Country Memorandum by the World Bank documents their extraordinary efforts at fiscal stabilization. Unable to raise revenues or borrow, the government restricted its spending:

> Under the cash budget system, prescribed under the government's Comprehensive National Strategy (1992–2002), public disbursements is [*sic*] restricted to take place only when liquidity is available. A monthly reporting system was introduced in order to closely monitor government accounts and to avoid overspending. A new approval system was put in place. All cash releases had to be approved by a centralized Cash Committee who approved disbursements based on available liquidity and a broad system of prioritized budget items. The cash budget system curbed effectively expenditures, especially non-wage-recurrent expenditures such as transfers to the states, debt service payments, O&M [operations and maintenance], and development expenditures.[13]

The IMF economists were impressed: nowhere else was austerity taken so seriously.

It worked. The government's budget deficit fell from 13 per cent of GDP during 1985–90 to less than 1 per cent after 1996. Total government spending was cut in half, to just 9.4 per cent of GDP. Everything was cut, with salaries the last to go – but still, in the Bank's words, 'formal salaries to civil servants have eroded and are far below the level needed to operate an effective public administration'.[14] Development spending and local government were the lowest priorities and these sectors were stripped of almost all funds. With so little spending, domestic tax collection also suffered: the capacity was not there and people were unwilling to pay, and able to avoid paying. Tax revenue fell to just 8 per cent of GDP.

Military spending was protected and remained by far the biggest government outlay. But it was still extremely modest compared to the demands of running a war in Africa's largest country.

From where did the ruling cartel obtain its political finance? It helped that, by ruthlessly suppressing the opposition at the outset, their party did not need much money. In fact, the Islamist party, the National Islamic Front, was dissolved into the regime and its networks, ceasing to exist as such. It helped too that the regime's immediate enemies (the SPLA and its sponsors in Eritrea, Ethiopia and Uganda) were themselves cash-strapped and fought on the battlefield, rather than bidding for the allegiances of members of the Sudanese provincial elite.

One channel of funds was provided by international Islamist philanthropic organizations. The second most prominent Islamist, Taha, took the post of Minister of Social Planning and launched a series of initiatives, such as the 'Comprehensive Call to God', and 'Return to the Roots', which channelled international Islamist funds to social programmes, and used voluntary mechanisms and local NGOs for mobilization. The Islamist agencies also trained the Popular Defence Forces and found food and fuel for military operations. The revival of the 'native administration' system of administrative tribalism was local government on the cheap.

The military-commercial complex was another channel. The international Islamist network, which included such diverse members as Osama bin Laden, the Iranian government and its political-charitable foundations, and Malaysia, invested in military industries. The army's trading activities in the war zones, and over Sudan's borders, continued, making the war largely a self-sustaining venture. Whenever the army mounted an operation, the order would be bargained at each level in the command structure, with officers deciding how to interpret the instruction in line with their capacities and preferences, as well as the priorities of local businessmen who provided cash, fuel and food. Throughout the decade, the SPLA was so deeply fractured that dissident commanders could be rented cheaply to pursue internecine mayhem.

The most important financially stabilizing factor, however, involved the 'hidden adjustments' that had taken place in the wider economy over the previous fifteen years. The migration of several hundred thousand skilled Sudanese, including most of the professional class, to Arab countries, where they earned many times their Sudanese salaries, generated a vast offshore economy. This was not just earnings (equivalent to 40 per cent of GDP) but also assets (larger overall than Sudan's official debt). As Richard Brown notes,

> alongside the formal economy there is a thriving underground economy that should not be treated as simply the 'side-show' in the overall functioning of Sudan's economy – it has become its central feature, apparently awash in both savings and foreign exchange surpluses.[15]

This 'central feature' of the Sudanese economy was also central to its political economy. Although the Islamists did not control the diaspora, their corporate investments in Islamic finance, and in the economic sectors that continued to profit during the country's crisis, kept them politically solvent, albeit at the expense of wider society.[16]

This source of revenue is intriguingly different from almost every other kind of political finance in recent Sudanese history, in that it is not pure rent. These are funds from wages and business activities, through a cartel of 'grey companies', including parastatals, military-owned businesses and philanthropic organizations that also ran commercial activities.[17] Sudan's political-business managers had to bargain with those who provided equity, and this made their system more resilient and stable. And indeed, despite its external challenges and internal rifts, the alliance of security cabal, Muslim Brothers and merchants remained intact almost until the end of the decade. The members of the coalition were in constant rotation, round the twin suns of a solar system, like a complex gyroscope that appeared never in balance, but never actually fell over. One centre of gravity was Turabi: his assets were his Islamist credentials and connections, which made him the dominant figure in a restricted market of dedicated Islamists. The other was Bashir. His particular assets were that he carefully husbanded his authority, using it only sparingly when the regime as a whole was jeopardized, and he never threw a member of the wider group out of orbit entirely. Even when his close comrades were caught red-handed trying to assassinate President Mubarak in 1995, Bashir only demoted them temporarily. In a system characterized by pervasive suspicion, Bashir earned that rarest of commodities, trust.

Relations among the members of the ruling cartel were acrimonious. By the end of the decade, several camps were bitterly divided. The key struggle was between Turabi, who felt it was time for him to assume the leadership and move towards a truly Islamic state, and Bashir, who wanted a more conventional authoritarian government. This contest paralysed the regime, until – at the moment at which Turabi appeared to have won the contest – Bashir played his last card, declaring a state of emergency and dismissing his rival from all official positions. Even then, the contest continued throughout the following year before Bashir could consolidate power, and one of the outcomes of the fracture was the creation of a dissident Islamist faction led by Darfurians.

The Turabi–Bashir contest was fought out within government and using the procedures of drafting a new constitution, adopting it and then filling its key positions. The rhetoric was fidelity to the principles of the Islamist revolution. Beneath this, the struggle had two other elements: oil, which sharpened the contest, and an elite political culture, which softened it.

The prize of the contest was oil rent. The government had bought up Chevron's long-abandoned oil concessions and brought in Chinese companies to develop the oilfields and build a pipeline. It was a risky deal on all sides, but as soon as the military threat to the oil-producing areas was lifted in 1998, the ruling group knew that their financial straitjacket would be loosened. Sudan's first oil was pumped in August 1999. As anticipated, revenues from oil not only dwarfed all other sources of rent, but attracted secondary investment too. Turabi wanted this prize for the Islamic movement and its institutions. Bashir wanted it for those loyal to him. The early phase of the struggle was played out in the financial arena, with the central bank moving against Islamic banks, exploiting their financial weaknesses and driving them into bankruptcy. Still, in order to bring sufficient members of the ruling cartel on side, Bashir could not wholly centralize control over oil rents: the army, security services and key Islamists had to have their fiefdoms and the access to the money, through a network of 'grey' companies, many of them incorporated in the Gulf or Malaysia.[18]

It was a contest for political life and death, and Bashir imposed a state of emergency and then had Turabi arrested, while there were rumours of an Islamist mutiny within the armed forces. However, the power struggle was conducted without resort to violence. The fissure within the Islamists translated into war in the periphery (Darfur), but it did not do so in Khartoum because conflict was moderated by the societal-political norms of the ruling elite.

Although the formal institutions of government had long since been eviscerated in the provinces, their basis remained in metropolitan Sudan. Despite the fact that it was thirty years since civil servants were last paid a living wage, a societal norm of respect for government office remained. This was more than just a cultural relic. It was sustained by the code of the Khartoum elite, which regulated the patronage system to produce semi-public goods, that is, goods shared among a restricted but nonetheless substantial metropolitan class. Most of the ruling group came from families associated with the Khatmiyya Sufi sect and although they had abandoned Sufi-ism for modern Islamism, one of those Khatmiyya principles remained embedded, which was that any member of the group who wandered away was considered a prodigal son who would in due course return. Personal civility across the sharpest political divides remained the norm in metropolitan Sudan during the 1990s.

The characteristics of turbulence and indeterminacy in political affairs – found in all political marketplace systems, and pronounced in Sudan – mean that there is a low level of trust. Today's friend can be tomorrow's adversary. But by the same token, today's rival may be tomorrow's ally. The Sudanese political elites may not have confidence in one another's good intentions, but they trust that the system of constant bargaining will generate certain outcomes.

The sociability of the Sudanese elite means that there is a very high density of interpersonal interactions and a high sharing of knowledge about one another's dealings. This intense transmission of information allows the marketplace to operate more efficiently. Members of this elite pride themselves on their hospitality, civility and tolerance to those they consider their peers, and in turn this cluster of norms reinforces the behaviour that enables the bargaining to proceed smoothly. In turn, this has made possible the emergence of significant semi-public goods. Thus, Khartoum is a safe city, with publicly funded infrastructure and functioning institutions. Individuals and offices are respected, learning is prized and open debate takes place. Wherever members of the political elite meet – in provincial towns, in foreign hotels – they are cordial irrespective of political difference. But when political bargaining is transferred to a different context – such as rural Darfur – they instruct their subordinates to act savagely.

The Oil Boom and Rentier Peace

For the following ten years, until the separation of South Sudan in 2011, Sudan was a rentier political marketplace funded by oil. Oil revenues provided more than half of the revenue, and associated infrastructural spending a big part of the balance. Oil income had a political significance beyond its size:[19] it came in hard currency and could be used directly for political spending, and Sudan could trade petroleum for political cooperation with Eritrea and Ethiopia. Figure 5.2 shows the dramatic increase in Sudanese government spending and revenue that followed oil exports in 1999 (and the income volatility as the oil price rose and fell). Peace agreements are marked by vertical arrows.

Sudan's chief executives were very happy to have Chinese investment, but did not want to rely exclusively on one oil company that would be in a position to dictate terms. So they carefully and deliberately diversified, inviting in Indian and Malaysian oil companies, among others.[20]

Sudan's rentier political marketplace in the 2000s had the following features. First, the rents were centralized within a small group that controlled the executive. It was a smaller clique than before, and

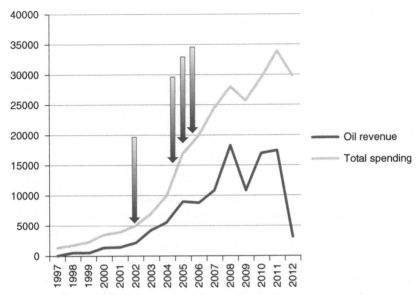

Figure 5.2 Sudanese government finances and peace agreements, 1997–2012
Source: IMF data, in millions of Sudanese pounds.

Bashir was the undisputed centre of power and hence more powerful, but it was nonetheless a version of the previous oligarchic system, subject to continuous haggling among its members.

Second, metropolitan Sudanese had the leverage to insist on a high level of public spending in their neighbourhoods. Almost all capital expenditure was within the Hamdi Triangle, to the extent that one merchant called the area 'like a miniature country'.[21] The biggest project was the Merowe Dam in Northern State. An opportunity for enormous graft in construction contracts that funded the ruling National Congress Party (NCP), this one dam consumed more than a third of Sudan's development budget in the mid-2000s.[22] The most visible signs of prosperity were in Khartoum. The boom generated its own class of nouveau riche and its own stories of corruption, further feeding a sense of resentment in the provinces.

Third, public-sector and security-sector employment were used as a massive patronage mechanism, reaching deeply into society. Oil financed salaries, bonuses, official cars, office buildings and furniture.

This contributed the fourth feature, a dominant party system and elections that resembled a form of 'competitive clientelism' in which electors, knowing that the ruling party would be returned, voted for the candidate most likely to be close to the ruler who would therefore attract jobs, investment and services to his constituency.

Oil plus other circumstances made the CPA possible. After 1998, without Ethiopian military support, the SPLA could not mount military operations capable of taking and holding large towns, and could not halt the government's oil extraction. Facing the prospect of vastly increased government military capacity, it might in fact lose. In January 2001, the incoming administration of President George W. Bush promptly abandoned its predecessor's policy of regime change by proxy. The Cheney Report on US energy dependence prompted American interest in Sudanese oil, while the Sudanese were keen for a major American oil company to bring technology that would enable them to extract Sudan's heavy crude oil much more efficiently. If US economic sanctions were to be lifted, the already fast-expanding economy might grow even more. To swing the American religious constituencies behind a policy of making peace with an Islamist government, Bush asked former Senator Jack Danforth, an ordained priest, to serve as his special envoy for Sudan. Danforth was appointed on 6 September 2001. Five days later, Sudan and the US had another incentive for cooperating: the government of Sudan feared it would be in line for US counter-terrorist retaliation (as in 1998), and the US knew that Sudanese intelligence officers had some of the best information about al-Qaeda, and were ready to share it.

The negotiations leading to the signing of the CPA in January 2005 were, in large part, to design a rent allocation formula that would satisfy both the NCP and the SPLA and its affiliate Movement (SPLM). The arithmetic was possible because the fast-expanding budget meant that Khartoum's ruling cartel could offer a generous incentive without hardship to itself.

On the basis that the CPA promised peace, national unity and normalization of relations with the US, Bashir agreed to sign. In a moment of characteristic humour, he waved the document in public and said, 'La illahi illa Allah,' paused for a moment, and continued, 'Hallelujah!' He hailed the CPA as 'Sudan's second independence'. The core provisions of the CPA were a Government of National Unity (NCP plus SPLM with other parties given a minor role), an autonomous government of Southern Sudan with the SPLA forming its army and the Sudanese army withdrawing from the south, a six-year interim period leading to a vote on self-determination for southern Sudan, and mid-term elections halfway through that period.

The peace that followed was an extension and intensification of the rentier political marketplace. The recently established patterns of spending hardly changed. One of the provisions of the CPA was that half the revenue from southern Sudan's oil would be retained by the federal government for national spending. In practice this money was spent entirely in northern Sudan, so that southern Sudanese felt that these funds were a northern share of their rents, rather than a national fund. The decentralization provisions meant that more funds were allocated to states, and most of state spending was on salaries. Most striking was security spending. The SPLM/A strategy was to *increase* its military payroll (see chapter 6): the north had the same approach. Between 2000 and 2005 – while the war in the south was still not concluded and Darfur was raging – spending on the army, police and security services remained constant in real terms, falling from about 30 per cent of federal government expenditure in 2000 to 10 per cent. However, after 2006 – with peace in the south and relative quiet in Darfur – it expanded, regaining its share of 25–30 per cent of federal spending, at a much higher level than before.[23] The number of men on the army and security payroll in (northern) Sudan by 2009 was estimated at 369,500.[24]

Democratization during the CPA interim period should be understood in this light. The stated intent of the CPA drafters was that elections would broaden representation in the governments in Khartoum and Juba, and legitimize those governments in advance of the vote on self-determination. However, the outcome was the opposite. While the parliament designated in the CPA allocated 80 per cent of the seats to the NCP and SPLM and 20 per cent to other parties, the parliament elected in 2010 had a proportion of 95 per cent of seats for the two ruling parties and just 5 per cent for the rest.

Voters understood early on that the NCP and SPLM were certain to win, and preferred candidates whom they expected to be close to the seat of power, and so able to bring jobs, resources and services to their constituencies. The principal opposition parties also understood this and realized they would be better served by the status quo, or by a negotiated broadening of the government, and thus pressed for the postponement or cancellation of the elections. Opposition miscalculations, especially in failing to encourage their supporters to register to vote, contributed to the landslide. The NCP may have rigged the election to secure its victory, but it hardly needed to do so.[25] Sudanese called it the 'ugly election': a reverse beauty parade in which candidates competed to display their proximity to the president, which entailed not outshining him in physical appearance. While Bashir's campaign posters airbrushed him into a younger self, his party faithful scowled from their election posters.[26]

Hence the 2005–11 Interim Period saw two parallel and competing patronage systems in Sudan. The NCP ran a complex rentier political marketplace. Lacking institutions to regulate nationwide political competition, and determined to remain in power, its party managers and security chiefs inadvertently contributed to price inflation in the cost of loyalty, so that even though revenues increased geometrically, they were always outrun by spending. Government deficits caused concern at the World Bank, which noted the political pressures on provincial administrations to spend more, particularly on salaries, and to inflate expected state revenues to match the projected spending.[27]

In the south, the system was cruder: the SPLA had an expensive security strategy and the southern elite rushed to emulate their northern peers' self-enrichment. By the time the northern political managers realized that the SPLM/A had deliberately inflated the price of loyalty in southern Sudan, such that the northerners could no longer compete, it was too late. The two ruling elites were jointly in danger of pricing themselves out of their own political marketplace.[28] This is what transpired in South Sudan after independence. Bashir was cannier: he knew when to pull back. In northern Sudan, despite the bitter recriminations and austerities that followed the loss of the south, and a collapse in oil rents, he survived.

Post-Separation Sudan

In a preparatory study for the economic impact of the separation of southern Sudan on Sudan, the IMF estimated that it would take three and a half years for Sudan to absorb the economic shock. The loss of the south would entail the loss of three-quarters of Sudan's oil production, half of the national budget and 90 per cent of its hard currency. The finance gap was estimated at just over $9 billion over the three and a half years. The government of Sudan and the SPLM agreed that this gap should be filled in a three-way split: Sudanese austerity measures, foreign aid and 'transitional financial arrangements' to be paid to Sudan from South Sudanese oil revenues (in addition to transit fees for using the pipeline).

None of the three transpired as hoped. Sudan's rulers were in denial about the separation and so paralysed by internal division that although the need for expenditure cuts was recognized in 2010, it was not until 2012 that a reduced budget was introduced, and not until late 2013 that key subsidies were cut (sparking street demonstrations). The US continued adding more preconditions for lifting its economic and financial sanctions and, debarred from the IMF, Sudan received no cushion of concessionary finance. Worse, agreement was not reached on the oil transit fees and transitional financial arrangements, and in January 2012 South Sudan shut down its oil production entirely. The first payments began only in 2013 and, because of disruption to oil production, the amounts have been well below expectations.

With the remaining oil in northern Sudan sufficient only for domestic consumption, Bashir needed cash. He looked abroad. Sudanese investment in the overthrow of Gaddafi did not bring material reward because Libya plunged into crisis. For a while a better option was Qatar, regional sponsor of the Muslim Brothers and also patron of the Darfur peace process. However, in early 2014, Saudi Arabia and Egypt pressed Qatar into scaling back its support for the Muslim Brothers, and Saudi Arabia briefly froze banking transactions with Sudan, sending the Sudanese pound briefly into free fall.

Artisanal gold was found in Northern Darfur and several other places. Initially, smugglers traded most of the gold out of the country. However, the government adopted a policy of setting the price of gold at a level, in local currency, above the international rate. Prospectors then switched to selling gold to Sudanese official buyers so the government obtained the hard currency. The Bank of Sudan squared the circle by printing money, using inflationary financing to postpone the reckoning. Nonetheless, the gold mines sparked fierce local contests over which authorities would control and benefit from them.

More broadly, Bashir's cabal returned to a version of its distributed financial strategy of the 1990s, which is based on allowing sections of the governing coalition to pursue their separate political, military and commercial policies, with coordination limited to ensuring that they do not directly threaten the regime itself.

The price of this was the encouragement of corruption among the political, security and military leadership, allowing them to pursue policies that (at best) prevent the president from making the sacrifices necessary for peace, and (at worst) promote conflict. One example of this was the emergence of a new paramilitary force, the Rapid Response Force, commanded by the former mutineer Mohamed Hemeti, which had a separate financial and command structure to the army and national security. Another outcome was that provincial governments were starved of funds, contributing to instability (notably in Darfur) and the reversion of paramilitaries to looting.

With the political budget dwindling and distributed among different components of the military-commercial-Islamist elite, the kinds of

rent-allocation share-out and spending on public goods that were possible in the early 2000s became impossible, as the funds were insufficient and the veto-holders too many. Having given up on US
normalization, there was little financial incentive for the government
to enter serious peace talks. To the contrary, the financial interests of
the army leadership were more closely bound up with high defence
spending and new procurement contracts, and these narrow interests
overruled the wider interests of peace. In this context, the civil political
norms of the metropolitan elite became critically important. Even the
government's harshest critics, such as al Mahdi and Turabi, were aware
from long experience of the constraints under which the government
was operating, and the impossibility of overcoming those constraints
through simply changing the leadership. The National Dialogue, heralded as a mechanism for democratizing and transforming Sudan,
became by tacit consensus a mechanism for maintaining a working
government and avoiding collapse, until another option arose.

Separation did not resolve the political competition between
Khartoum and Juba. As part of that competition, South Sudan sponsored the SPLM/A-North in a full-blown insurrection in the 'Two
Areas' of Southern Kordofan and Blue Nile, where the SPLM
had strong constituencies, including two capable army divisions.
Khartoum's political-business managers made a characteristic miscalculation: they were confident that, if they could humble Juba and buy
off a sufficient quota of the local elites in the 'Two Areas', they would
resolve the problem. They were wrong.[29]

The Nuba people of Southern Kordofan had long been exposed to
the racism of northern Sudanese society and, at the height of their
ideological hubris in the early 1990s, the Islamists had mounted a
campaign against the SPLA in the Nuba Mountains, under the flag
of *jihad*, which sparked fear among the Nuba of collective annihila-
tion.[30] That onslaught, and the local people's successful resistance to
it, strengthened Nuba demands for a peace deal on the same terms
as southern Sudan – that is, including self-determination. The CPA
denied them this, giving them only a 'popular consultation' of uncertain value, which was not even properly implemented. A political deal
was possible in the first half of 2011, up to the day on which hostilities broke out in Kadugli on 5 June. Three weeks later, a 'Framework
Agreement' to end the war was negotiated under AU auspices, but
its Khartoum signatory, Nafie Ali Nafie, was pre-empted by his rivals
who persuaded Bashir to repudiate the deal before Nafie could sell
it internally.

Violence is a routine element in political bargaining, deployed by
the government to bring down the price of a settlement. But war can

also be driven by its own logic of escalation, and this is what happened in the 'Two Areas'. Over the following years, during nine rounds of talks facilitated by the AUHIP, government negotiators made no concessions. The former security chief Salah Gosh explained the preferred strategy: 'If we can address the people of these two regions, bypassing the SPLM-North we can resolve these issues. However, we are devoted to finding solutions with the leadership of the movement, and this is one of the mistakes we are committing.'[31] Gosh was actually unfair to his colleagues: they were trying the 'divide-and-rent' strategy as best they could, but it was not working. The price demanded by the SPLM-North had risen so that even when the government delegation discreetly offered the same deal that had been on the table in June 2011, it was no longer a viable option. The Nuba rebels had shown that they would not be defeated, despite the travails of their South Sudanese sponsor, and the record of government perfidy meant that Khartoum's offers were heavily discounted. As a result, for example, the SPLM-North leaders refused to consider relinquishing their army at an early stage of implementing any future peace agreement, because they did not trust the government to honour its side of the bargain.

Something else was also at work: a political agenda of ethnic-territorial localism that defied the logic of the political marketplace. Sudanese provincial movements historically display two contradictory features. One of them is the familiar readiness of members of the provincial elite to succumb to material reward. But the other is an anti-materialist and populist logic of ethnic particularism. The Nuba anthropologist Guma Kunda Komey has described how this emerges:

Four common features characterize the various ethno-political movements in Sudan. First, they arose in the regions whose populations are largely of African origin in response to persistent exclusion and marginalization by the central state. Second, in pursuing their political endeavours, these regions form a loose political solidarity in some national issues of common interest, particularly in their demand for a federal system. Third, these movements pursue their demands to the central government on the basis of their ethno-territorial affiliations, with each region progressively becoming a spatial expression of belonging and attachment, a source of economic livelihood, and an icon for socio-cultural identification. Finally...these regional movements gradually shifted from peaceful and political to armed movements coupled with a change of loyalties from national to regional levels, with each region (land) being concretized as a political category with a specific character, image and status in the minds of its inhabitants.[32]

Political settlements such as the CPA bring these movements' leaders into government, where they (mostly) adopt political-business models that conform to the dominant marketplace logic. But prolonged war, such as that in the Nuba Mountains since 2011, and the social isolation of the enclave population in the war zones, feeds different values and logics and thereby confounds the calculations of political-business managers. The errors made by Khartoum's security and political bosses may end in further fragmentation of Sudan.

Implications

For a succession of Sudanese rulers, the strategic priority has been managing the politics of Khartoum and the surrounding areas – the 'miniature country'. Throughout the twists and turns of political financing, repression and liberalization, austerity and boom, there has been sufficient cohesion and agreement on political rules within this domain, that government – in the broadest sense – has survived. The vast peripheries to south, west and east have been governed differently, through militarized patronage that has turned into a violent political marketplace. Political-business managers have always assumed that the provincial elites were disorganized and lacked alternatives and that, at the end of the day, they would settle on an affordable price, regardless of the rulers' political colours. In Darfur and the Nuba Mountains, they miscalculated the price; in the South, they underbid even more seriously.

Despite the near-catastrophic loss of the South, there is no indication that the prevailing business model of Bashir, and indeed the wider Khartoum political elite, has fundamentally changed. Their priority is the costly and mostly civil political market of the metropolis, and if Darfur and Southern Kordofan remain mired in turmoil and bloodshed, so be it.

6

South Sudan
The Boom and Bust of a Kleptocracy

The Price of Independence

The real politics of north-east Africa's ruling elites operates on a different moral register to the lives of their citizens. South Sudan is a particularly shocking example. In July 2011, for the first time in its history, South Sudanese constituted a sovereign government for themselves.[1] In January 2012, the military-political aristocrats[2] of the ruling SPLM and SPLA,[3] who had obtained fabulous wealth by any standards, decided to shut down their country's oil production and thereby eliminate 98 per cent of government revenue. They explained away the impact this might have on the desperately poor citizens with the remark that the South Sudanese had suffered and survived before, and could do so again.[4] Among other things, this overlooked the fact that at a least a million southern Sudanese had died during the long war of 1983–2005, most of them from famine and disease.[5]

In December 2013, a political dispute within the highest echelons of the SPLM and SPLA led to civil war and ethnic mass killing. Commentators on South Sudan's civil war have attributed this to political and personal rivalries, ethnic animosities between the Dinka tribe[6] of President Salva Kiir Mayardit and the Nuer of Riek Machar Teny Dhurgon, and the unresolved grievances from the internecine wars among southern Sudanese factions in the 1990s.[7] These factors are real, but the framework of the political marketplace suggests that they are secondary to the elemental contest over buying loyalties.

What happened in South Sudan was that, in 2005, Salva adopted a political-business plan of massive purchase of loyalty using oil money. He did this because the SPLM/A had neither the political nor military strength to dominate southern Sudan, and to secure independence in the referendum scheduled for 2011. It was similar to northern Sudanese retail politics: Salva wanted to price Khartoum out of the market. The former head of NISS, Salah Gosh, complained about this overpricing shortly before the referendum. His former southern Sudanese deputy, General Majak D'Agoot, described it from the southern viewpoint to the BBC's James Copnall: 'You have to buy in warlords, some political leaders who may destabilize the country. We have been doing this for the last seven, eight years. Khartoum has been making things difficult, they are on the other side of the option market.'[8]

The price, Gosh said, would come down in due course but, for Bashir, it was too late. Two weeks later, in December 2010, Bashir abruptly closed a meeting of the Shura (consultative council) of the NCP after just half the business, in order to pre-empt a challenge to the decision to permit the referendum to proceed. On 4 January 2011, Bashir flew to Juba and, speaking from a script he had prepared himself, spoke of his commitment to unity: 'But I will be happy if, after the referendum and the creation of the two states, we achieve the final and real peace.' He delighted southerners by promising, 'The leadership of this country will stand and salute the wish of the citizens in the south.'[9]

At this point, the outcome of the referendum on self-determination was a foregone conclusion. The SPLM/A had done everything it could to exclude constituencies that might be influenced by Khartoum, for example, debarring southerners whose native language was Arabic from being eligible to vote. The official figure was 99.83 per cent from a turnout of 97.58 per cent.[10] It was a competition among constituencies to register the highest vote for independence, and thereby proclaim their loyalty.[11]

A majority of this size implies that independence itself was inevitable. For sure, South Sudanese nationalist sentiment, nourished by the previous two centuries' experience, is likely to have outweighed attachment to a government in Khartoum that had delivered at best neglect and at worst horrible suffering. But the southern rulers' assumption that the vote needed to be secured through a huge exercise in militarized patrimonialism suggests that, under different political management, the outcome could have been different.

Garang's Challenges

John Garang's successors in the leadership of the SPLM/A have made him posthumously into the founding father of the Republic of South

Sudan. This is a travesty: he would be better remembered as the leader of a leftist military revolution, as the visionary of the 'New Sudan' – a unified, secular, African state.

Garang was a unionist and proudly repeated that the SPLA's first battles were against the secessionists of the Anyanya II guerrillas. Throughout the war, this brought tactical advantages, notably support from Ethiopia (which was fighting its own wars for national unity) and from northern Sudanese opposition parties. Garang's unionist position also persuaded Ali Osman Taha that he was a credible partner in the CPA. But Garang was also a *convinced* unionist: he believed that southern Sudanese should not be content with only governing the South, but should also lay claim to their fair share of the power and wealth at the centre. Most southerners were convinced by their leader's tactical position but not by his goal of a united Sudan – the real programme of the fighting men was reflected in the Dinka saying popular among fighters: '*Ke tharku, angicku,*' 'What we are fighting for, we know.'[12]

In a famous 1961 essay, 'The Dilemma of the Southern Intellectual', the Communist Joseph Ukel Garang[13] foresaw that an independent South Sudan would be a pawn of the colonial powers. He subordinated the north–south contradiction to the struggle against imperialism. John Garang reframed the internal contradiction as between centre and periphery and made an explicit appeal to the 'African' majority in western and eastern as well as southern Sudan.

For the two Garangs – one an orthodox and the other a flexible Marxist – southern Sudan was an inauspicious place to achieve social transformation. During colonial days just a handful of British officers presided over an ethnographic museum with a 'care and maintenance' administration pared to the absolute minimum. In the 1970s the regional government relied on subventions from Khartoum that covered 85 per cent of budgeted expenditures, with the result that when money ran short (as it usually did) southern leaders congregated in Khartoum and spent their time petitioning for handouts.[14] Southern Sudanese decried the method of individual patronage, but their politicians emulated their northern peers in trying to acquire wealth as quickly as possible,[15] and allocated the jobs and project funds that they had to their clients and constituents. International NGOs such as Norwegian Church Aid dispensed bigger budgets than the regional government, and provided most of the basic services.[16]

Garang did not start the rebellion in southern Sudan: his first challenge was 'reforming the mob' that had rushed to arms to fight Khartoum.[17] Among them, he feared, were 'bourgoisiefied southern elites' who were intent on grasping personal positions.[18] Garang's approach was straightforward: force.[19] He centralized politics in the military command, and the military command in himself. He financed his army by foreign sponsorship, living off the land and aid. International relief efforts were sporadic but had a deep impact on southern Sudanese, generating something akin to a veritable cargo cult: some southern Sudanese children surmised that every white person owned his or her own airplane, and community leaders built airstrips as if buying lottery tickets for a chance of these bizarre winnings.[20] It was a long, hungry war, and Garang promised 'payback' for the sufferings when it was over.

The SPLA never recovered from its split in 1991. From a maximum strength of over 100,000, it was reduced to a fighting force of perhaps 10,000. Garang's rivals put self-determination – by which they meant secession – on the political agenda, after which it never went away.[21] The SPLA commanders forced a 'national convention' on their reluctant chairman, and passed resolutions promising to build institutions and civilianize the movement.[22] Garang tried to evade the implications of both these steps, and cleverly leveraged his international status to secure his position and keep his unionist agenda intact. He kept personal political control, so that his critics accused him of carrying the movement 'in his briefcase'.[23] Until the CPA, Garang and the southern political elites danced around each other: each knew that they needed the other to survive, but none trusted the other. Garang was compelled to listen to popular demands, while the separatist majority was compelled to accept that without Garang their cause would be lost.

The former US Presidential Envoy to Sudan, Andrew Natsios, tells a story of when Garang challenged his deputy, Salva Kiir, 'to a contest during a commander's conference as to which of them could remember the full names of the sixty individual commanders as they shook hands with them. Kiir was able to remember each one flawlessly, while Garang could not and conceded the contest to Kiir.'[24] However, if the challenge had been to name regional and international leaders, and northern Sudanese political figures, there is no question that Garang would have won. Natsios's anecdote reflects not only the personal orientations of the two leaders, but their particular skills and goals. Garang's goal was to seize the rents accessed in and through Khartoum to restructure the Sudanese political system. His strategy for doing so was to use his foreign backers to bring him to power. For Salva, the aim was to control southern Sudan, and the means was unifying its domestic constituencies.

When the peace talks with Khartoum began in earnest in 2002, Garang explained that he had three parallel strategies, of which a negotiated settlement between the SPLM/A and the government was just one. The other two were the military overthrow of the government – with neighbourly assistance and new insurrections in eastern and western Sudan – and a 'protected uprising' in which a coalition of northern civilian political parties and trade unions staged non-violent protest while the SPLA and other armed units of the opposition National Democratic Alliance rushed to Khartoum to secure their triumph. The foreign backers of the peace process briefly considered more inclusive peace negotiations, but fell in behind Garang's insistence that the SPLM/A should be Khartoum's sole partner in the peace talks, held in Kenya (mostly in the town of Naivasha), and should also be the government-in-waiting for southern Sudan on signature of the CPA in January 2005.

Having been schooled at the University of Dar es Salaam and having initially intended to build the SPLM/A as a vanguardist revolutionary front, Garang was obliged by the demands of the Sudanese political marketplace to learn a different set of skills. Just because Garang became a political-business manager, focusing most of his energy on tactical manoeuvre, did not mean that he abandoned a substantive political vision. For sure, he intended to use the power and resources of the state as the engine for transformation. Garang's '180 day programme' for accelerated change following his appointment as First Vice President, laid out in spreadsheets like a high-powered management consultancy plan, is a blueprint for such socio-political engineering.[25]

We can only speculate about Garang's plans for the SPLM after the CPA. But there are indications that he intended to jettison the 'southern sector' of the SPLM/A in favour of a new national political venture centred on Khartoum. This was one of the reasons why senior commanders called a meeting in Rumbek in November 2004, where they challenged Garang over the way in which he had led the SPLM/A, and in particular the secrecy with which he had conducted the talks with Khartoum. Garang responded that, in the middle of difficult negotiations, this was not the time for reform. Salva rejected this, accusing Garang of having 'already crossed to the other side of the river' and then refusing to return the boat so that his comrades in arms could cross too.[26]

Salva's Business Plan

On 30 July 2005, Garang died in a helicopter crash. Salva Kiir became President of the Government of Southern Sudan (GoSS). Over the next six years, he and the SPLM/A leadership developed a

remarkably pure example of a rentier militarized political marketplace, animated by the agenda of separation, with just enough con-
cealment of its true nature and intention to keep Khartoum and
international sponsors onside. The GoSS did one big thing only: it
turned oil rents into patrimonial militarized tribalism with the aim
of making it too expensive for Khartoum to interfere with secession.
Based on Khartoum's deplorable record of dishonouring agreements,[27]
Salva had justifiable fears that the Sudanese government would derail
or manipulate the referendum on self-determination in January 2011
or fail to respect its outcome. Over the previous half-century,
Khartoum had created a market of allegiances in southern Sudan and
had rented enough members of the southern elite to make the region
ungovernable if it so wished. To secede, the SPLM/A needed to outbid
Bashir. It did.

Salva's immediate problem was that the SPLA was a minority force
in southern Sudan, heavily outnumbered by the southern Sudanese
troops serving in SAF, the militia forces aligned with the government,
and other freelance militia. The SPLA had recently grown to about
50,000 troops, while the numbers of 'other armed groups' and southern Sudanese on the SAF payroll were about three times higher. The
CPA had no provision for these men: they had to disarm or be disarmed. Garang had threatened to fight the other armed groups; Salva
decided to absorb them. The SPLA tried just one serious effort at
forcible disarmament, a campaign against the 'White Army' of Jonglei
in 2006. More than 2,000 people died.[28] It did not repeat the exercise:
subsequent disarmament, demobilization and reintegration programmes sponsored by foreign donors were a modest means for the
SPLA to replenish its forces by discharging women and the unfit.[29]

The foundational agreement for the future of southern Sudan was
signed in Juba on 8 January 2006, between Salva and General Paulino
Matiep, commander of the South Sudan Defence Force (SSDF), the
largest and best-armed of the militia. Paulino became Deputy Chief
of Staff in the SPLA, his generals were absorbed at their existing
ranks, and about 50,000 soldiers were put on the SPLA payroll. The
Juba Declaration was 'short, easily understood, without legal jargon',
and was respected.[30]

To match the flood of new ex-SSDF generals, Salva promoted
hundreds of SPLA officers. By independence, the SPLA had 745 generals. In 2006, Southern Sudanese legislators also voted to double the
base pay of an infantryman from the equivalent of $75 a month (the
standard rate for SAF) to $150 a month. The officers became the best
paid in Africa, also enjoying a personal retinue, bodyguards and cars.
Commanders had licence to recruit, and they did, putting their

kinsmen on the payroll. As a result, in 2006, the SPLA salaries budget had overspent by 363 per cent, so that more than 80 per cent of defence spending was on wages and allowances,[31] a proportion that remained unchanged up to 2011.[32] Salaries were doubled again on the eve of independence.[33]

The SPLA payroll was over 230,000 in 2012,[34] plus an additional 84,000–90,000 police, prison warders and wildlife forces.[35] The real fighting strength was much less: generals were pocketing the wages of tens of thousands of ghost soldiers. With no centralized register of soldiers, payday consisted of handing bags filled with banknotes to commanders.

Despite these enormous numbers, the SPLA was unable to contain the threat to civilians posed by a few hundred bush guerrillas of the Lord's Resistance Army in Western Equatoria, and the government responded to that problem by providing $2 million to train and arm additional village militia, known as 'Arrow Bows'.[36]

The SPLA also bought weapons, both for conventional military deterrence and because of the bribes that went along with defence procurement deals. In 2006–7, southern Sudan purchased 110 T72 tanks from Ukraine and numerous other weapons.[37] The procurement was concealed and did not appear in the budget, not because it was illegal, but because of the kickbacks. Official figures for defence

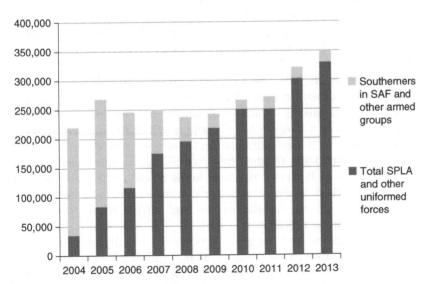

Figure 6.1 South Sudan's military payroll
Sources: Small Arms Survey and SPLA estimates.

spending rose from $586 million in 2006 to over $1 billion in 2011, averaging 5.5 per cent of GDP. With the inclusion of spending on paramilitaries, national security and off-budget arms procurement, the amount probably reached $1.6 billion in 2011.[38] An Ethiopian advisor to the SPLA commented, 'these are war budgets, they are preparing for war'.[39]

Fraud and theft undermined the SPLA's military effectiveness and some senior officers tried hard to build a more professional army. But the central logic of this expenditure was to bribe the southern military-political elite. It was payback time. The SPLA did not need to *fight* the north, but instead to *outbid* Khartoum in the militia commanders' auction of loyalties. Edward Lino, a senior SPLM member, complained: 'In reality, there was nothing called "SPLA"! It was divided and shredded into tribal formations adhering to individual commanders, based on localized tribal understanding.'[40] He also pointed out that most of the absorbed militia were from Greater Upper Nile and were Nuer.

Rent-seeking rebellion followed by payroll peace pushed up these numbers. The cycle is similar to that seen in Darfur. It begins with a provincial political entrepreneur who, dissatisfied with the resources allocated to him, seeks a better deal. He organizes a mutiny and mounts an armed attack to advertise his claim. Because the mutinous forces are tribally constituted, and because all government facilities are identified with the group that controls them, the attack takes on the character of a tribal raid and the conflict that follows resembles an intertribal war. Insofar as tribal authorities have been called upon, the issues they hold dear – such as grievances over land or past conflicts – also become relevant. However, the key function of the raids and counter-raids, and the casualties given and endured, is as an index of the determination of the protagonists. While fighting, the rebel leader is talking to the government and, in due course, they negotiate openly and reach a settlement in which the former mutineer is promoted (or a new administrative unit is created for him), his troops are put (back) on the army payroll and an intertribal conference is held which gives status and funds to the respective chiefs on both sides. Most likely, monies for compensation, awarded collectively, will benefit the families of the dead little if at all.

A rent-seeking rebellion is a stylized if bloody confrontation in which the fighting and the peace process are equally part of a cycle that validates militarized ethnicity as the building blocks of governance. The rules and expectations on all sides may not be precise, but the cycle of fighting and peacemaking follows rules that the protagonists understand and (mostly) follow. The cycle is inherently inflationary: each payoff creates incentives for others to rebel. David Yauyau is an example of a political-military entrepreneur who mastered this business plan, and went round the cycle twice; Peter Gatdet has mastered defection as a means of advancing his political career.

Tribal chiefs – politicized from their formalization in the colonial era, militarized by both Khartoum and the SPLA in the 1990s – also made their claims, both in parallel to the generals and as their hand-maidens. In Central Equatoria State alone, the number of officially recognized tribal chiefs rose from seventeen prior to the war to over 400.[41]

The members of the SPLM/A elite in Juba were closer to the spigot of money and did not need to use violence to claim their share. Massive corruption in South Sudan was not an error, but rather Salva's means of keeping the mob that was the SPLM/A leadership within a single camp. In 2012, in response to public outcry against a series of corruption scandals, Salva named seventy-five senior politi-cians alleged to have stolen $4 billion. An additional list of fifty generals was never made public after the officers went to meet the president.

After the CPA, the SPLM was a nationwide party formally com-mitted to the shared goal of 'making unity attractive'. This was the official reason why the Juba leadership took no steps to dissociate the wings of the party in the north and south, and to prepare the 30,000 SPLA soldiers from northern Sudan – most of them in the Ninth and Tenth Divisions – for a future within the north. An unstated reason for retaining a unified political and military command was that the leaders expected a new war. In April–May 2011, after the referendum result was announced but before the independence of South Sudan, the SPLM still campaigned in the state elections in Southern Kordofan as a united party. When the SPLA's Ninth Division (in Southern Kordofan) went to war with Khartoum the next month, its troops were still on Juba's payroll and carried the flag of Republic of South Sudan (the SPLM/A emblem) on their uniforms. The pro-war group in SPLA headquarters had argued that, when the inevitable war came, they were better off fighting with their northern comrades in the SPLA-North on their side.

Fear of war also contributed to electoral fraud because Salva wanted to ensure that all state governors, who have important secu-rity powers, were loyal to the president. In the 2010 elections, loyalist candidates were selected to run under the SPLM banner in each state, sometimes by manipulation of party selection procedures, and all of them won. The stolen elections did not lead straight away to rebel-lions, however, because southern Sudanese politicians did not want to disturb the fragile cohesion of the nascent country just a few months before the referendum.

The Skeleton of the South Sudanese State

It is rare for a review of public spending to make riveting reading. The World Bank's 2013 assessment of South Sudan's finance is an exception.[42] The first point to note is that South Sudan is rich compared to its neighbours. Oil revenues provided for public spending equivalent to $340 per capita in 2011, eight times that of Ethiopia, five times that of Uganda. South Sudan also received generous foreign assistance at over $100 per capita. Although South Sudan was starting from near zero, the country was born with a silver spoon in its mouth.

However, a second point to note is that, after a sharp early increase (from a near-zero baseline), education indicators deteriorated over the subsequent years. The education budget, which was just 5 per cent of total spending, was underspent most years, and the country was not making progress towards the Millennium Development Goals, or even towards the East Africa average.[43] Health was doing somewhat better, due to foreign aid. Half of total spending was on the army and security.

A third point is a 'cash-in-hand' approach to public spending. Despite the efforts of South Sudanese technocrats in the Ministry of Finance and foreign advisors, official budgets remained pieces of paper exchanged between technical staff. A donor official said, 'The technical advisors help prepare budget allocations, but then the army generals wheel into the minister's office, and they make the real allocations.'[44]

Fourth, formal budgetary management actually *declined* over the period 2007–12. There was a transient improvement in budgetary discipline in 2009, when the price of oil dropped dramatically and caused a fiscal crisis in Juba. However, as soon as the oil price rebounded, the previous pattern resumed.[45]

These are the symptoms of *political* budgeting. In southern Sudan, the political budget *is* the national budget, almost entirely. Any bubbles of technocratic integrity that might exist, here and there within the system, depend entirely on the goodwill and political clout of their individual mentors. When those individuals move, or political circumstances change, those bubbles are pricked. Foreign technical advisors and other well-wishers made the error of assuming that the cash-in-hand and kleptocratic system of government, and the failures

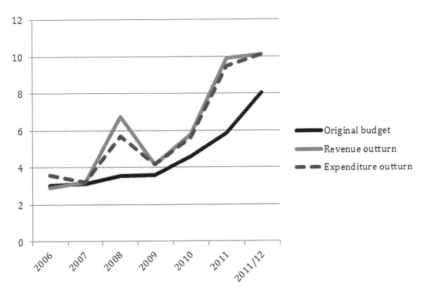

Figure 6.2 South Sudan's expenditures driven by revenues, not approved budget
Source: World Bank 2013: 4. Amounts in billions of Sudanese/South Sudanese pounds.

to reform and professionalize the armed forces, were a *failure* of government that could be remedied by advice and resources. This is not the case: these were elements of a *successful* political strategy. The South Sudanese were perfectly capable of running institutions and developing their country. But Salva and the leadership had other priorities.

A fifth point is implicit in this analysis: the viability of the system depends entirely on the inflow of resources. For South Sudan, this means oil. Figure 6.3 shows South Sudanese oil production. This figure also tells us much. First, the key peace agreements between north and south were signed between 2002 and 2006, at a time when funds were increasing and it was elementary for those in government to bring others into a rent-sharing deal without losing out. Second, in 2009, oil production peaked. But the small decline soon was offset by doubling of the amount of revenue allocated to Juba: between 2005 and 2011, southern Sudan received half of the revenue; from 2011 it got it all. But the 2011 revenue peak was also destined to drop, causing problems as the supply of funds dwindled but demand for payouts did not. Third, we can see the spectacular fall in revenue,

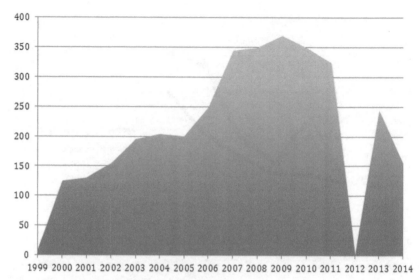

Figure 6.3   South Sudan's oil production
Sources: 1999–2012: Republic of South Sudan, Ministry of Finance and Economic Development, April 2013; 2012–13: estimates from press reports. Amounts in thousand barrels per day.

to zero, in 2012. This happened when South Sudan shut down its entire oil production. Production restarted in April 2013, but was cut again after the outbreak of the civil war.

The oil shutdown is an astonishing episode. As the talks between Sudan and South Sudan over financial arrangements for oil unfolded in December 2011 and January 2012, it appeared to be a game of chicken. Successful brinkmanship requires a central command with absolute authority, but in South Sudan there were too many hands on the steering wheel. Among those hands were two groups within the SPLM/A. One group was waiting for a war, expecting that the only way to settle territorial disputes with Sudan – especially over the disputed area of Abyei – would be fighting. Another wanted a war, calculating that Bashir was weak and discredited and would be overthrown quickly by a combination of military onslaught by the SPLA-North and JEM, and economic crisis. If there were a chance of a short victorious war with Sudan, then Juba could set the terms of its relations with the north and reverse the hierarchy: Khartoum would become subordinate to the SPLM/A (both south and north).

The financial calculation was as follows. South Sudan had deep pockets. It was debt-free and its income had doubled in July 2011. Sudan and South Sudan had agreed in principle to a 'transitional financial arrangement' that involved a transfer from South Sudan to Sudan of just over $3 billion over three and a half years, in addition to transit fees and tariffs. However, despite more than a year's negotiation, the two sides had failed to translate this principle into a fully fledged agreement. This meant that South Sudan was receiving all the revenue from oil sales and Sudan was receiving nothing. In December 2010, Sudan acted unilaterally by stealing oil, diverting it to its refineries and to ships it had illegally chartered. This threatened Juba's cashflow and required an immediate decision on war or peace. The SPLM Secretary General, Pagan Amum, was confident that South Sudan had cash reserves to last eight months, which would outlast Khartoum's.[46] Victory would mean, at minimum, keeping the $3 billion. A low-intensity war was already under way, and the attack on Sudan's main oilfield at Heglig in April was simply an escalation.

If South Sudan's leaders were aware of the domestic economic consequences of the oil shutdown, they did not appear to care. A World Bank mission depicted a scenario of near-complete collapse.[47] In the event, the impacts were less dire than feared, possibly because rural livelihoods were insulated from the cash-rich elite economy, just as the SPLM leaders had argued. The government instituted harsh austerity measures but exempted the army, which meant in reality the cuts were modest indeed. The financial gap was filled by drawing down all the reserves and borrowing, at undisclosed commercial rates, from oil companies.

If Pagan and Salva had counted on Sudan's collapse, they miscalculated. South Sudan was closer to the precipice than was Sudan. They also misjudged the international mood. The Americans did not endorse their war, and the AU and UN Security Council condemned the April 2012 attack. Although Sudan squandered its diplomatic advantage – its generals wanted to press home their financial advantage and extract more concessions from the South by obstructing an agreement – Juba had lost its international lustre.

New War, Old Peace

Salva's political-business plan was workable only while income kept increasing and while the South Sudanese elites stayed within a single camp because of the shared agenda of secession. When independence had been achieved, their plans diverged, and the groups that wanted war with Sudan prevailed. When that gambit failed, South Sudan was left without oil income. The president's political wallet was empty. This day was always sure to come, but the oil shutdown brought forward the day of reckoning. Salva had neither the political skills nor the means of coercion to manage the claims. He had no option but to negotiate with President Bashir. Both were weakened, but Salva was more so.

The two presidents signed a series of cooperation agreements to normalize relations in September 2012, but each had then to sell the compromises to his own constituents and in the process renegotiate key parts of the deal. Only in April 2013 did oil production restart, and it was lower than before because of damage to facilities and the fact that some wells were reaching the end of their lives and restarting them was not commercially viable.

Even a talented business manager would have struggled with this adversity, and Salva was neither skilled nor energetic. His government became paralysed when rivals declared their candidatures for the presidency in the elections scheduled for 2015. Salva's response was, naturally enough, to dismiss the challengers from the government. But while he gave some attention to smartening up the image of the administration – for example, by demanding that officials turn up for work on time – he inexplicably left his opponents free to mobilize. His challengers – Riek Machar, Pagan Amum, Rebecca Nyandeng (widow of Garang) and Deng Alor, among others – were divided and he could easily have picked them off one by one (buying off some, sending some abroad as ambassadors, intimidating others). Instead, Salva dismissed them en masse, thereby herding them into a single camp, united solely by their challenge to him. He then showed a fatal combination of hesitation and authoritarianism, allowing them to organize against him – and potentially assemble a majority in the SPLM politbureau. On both sides, there was no debate about policies or political choices, only about who would be in and who would be out. The opposition leaders did not want to abandon their claims to the label 'SPLM' as that was their ticket back to power.

To the extent that Salva had a political-business plan, it was crude: he would plough on and enforce his will. Salva dissolved party institutions and organized a committee of his closest allies to organize support, and he consolidated his 'presidential guard' (named the Tiger Battalion after his first SPLA command), and recruited a militia from his home area. He was not only dismantling the SPLM mechanisms but also circumventing the SPLA General Headquarters.

Salva's shoddy political management stumbled into a messy confrontation on 15–16 December 2013. It began when the SPLM's National Liberation Council finally met – a procedure grudgingly conceded by Salva – and concluded without a clear outcome, and escalated when shots were fired at SPLA headquarters. Immediately after that, loyalist units began selective killing of alleged opposition supporters – all of them ethnic Nuer – in Juba. Salva claimed he was forestalling a coup attempt, convincing nobody.

Peter Gatdet, an SPLA divisional commander, immediately mutinied.[48] He and Riek Machar mobilized a Nuer youth militia known as the 'White Army' to march on the Jonglei state capital, Bor, and then towards Juba. Reciprocal massacres followed as the towns of Bor, Bentiu and Malakal changed hands. It was not, initially, an ethnic divide: senior Nuer remained in the government camp and important Dinka political figures were with the opposition. But those who might have managed an accommodation in the first days were marginalized: the SPLA Chief of Staff, James Hoth Mai (himself a Nuer), and his deputy, Mac Paul Kuol, were left powerless, while most of the leading opposition figures (several of them Dinka) were arrested.

Beyond immediate personal security and the attendant organizational tasks, the priorities for Salva and Riek were finding money. Riek's strategy of a cheap insurgency fell into the ethnic trap: the White Army paid itself in booty and immediately branded its leaders as tribal chauvinists and war criminals. For a few weeks it appeared that Riek might actually attack Juba and seize power, but when he did not do that, he needed to find a strategic position in the regional political marketplace. His best source of funds was a protection racket with Sudan, which would pay him not to attack and disable the oilfields. Salva was in a stronger martial funding position: he could trade his alignment with Museveni for Ugandan troops and borrow from the oil companies. But counter-insurgency is more expensive than rebellion. The president borrowed at least $1.6 billion from the oil companies, at commercial rates, until they refused to lend him any more after six months.[49] Salva's inability to pay army salaries led to a series of mutinies, including among ethnic Dinka troops that should, according to a simple tribal calculus, have been his most loyal.[50] By the end of 2014, with lower oil production, government revenue scarcely covered the $1.6 billion official defence budget, let alone the political budget. As global oil prices fell because of the discount on South Sudan's waxy crude, payments to Sudan for use of the pipeline, and the oil companies' own repayments, the country was receiving as little as

$20–25 per barrel, the lowest in the world, on its much-reduced production.[51]

As soon as the shots were fired, mediators rushed to the scene. Within days, the foreign ministers of the InterGovernmental Authority on Development (IGAD) countries were in Juba, supported by the UN, African Union and the US. The subsequent history of the IGAD mediators illustrates the political integration of north-east Africa, and the way in which the mediation forum is an instrument for pursuing political-business interests.

At the outset, the region's leaders concurred that the war was a blunder in no one's interest. But the moment for decisive action to prevent escalation – the first week of fighting – passed. By the time of the IGAD summit meeting on 27 December, there was a new dynamic. In line with their experience of the CPA and the Juba Agreement, the South Sudanese political elite saw the peace forum as a new opportunity for maximizing rent – both during the process and in its outcome. For the mediators it was also a chance to improve their positions in the regional hierarchy. Uganda had already dispatched troops to South Sudan, and Museveni intervened occasionally but strategically in the process in favour of Salva. Ethiopia and Kenya were keen to put their troops on the peacekeeping payroll, and to assert their dominance vis-à-vis Uganda and one another. Sudan discreetly backed both sides: it maintained the flow of oil from South Sudan's oilfields, thereby a flow of funds to Juba, while giving money and arms to Riek to keep away from the oilfields and pipeline.

The model of a rent-sharing formula, drawn from the previous decades when southern Sudanese budgets were expanding, was guaranteed not to achieve its stated goal during a period of austerity. Unsurprisingly, the South Sudanese participants used the peace talks for purposes other than negotiating peace. Meanwhile, atrocities and starvation meant that the option of talking while fighting, with the protagonists sharing the spoils at the end, was not acceptable to the international sponsors of the talks.

The IGAD heads of state met seven times in the twelve months after the outbreak of the war. At these summits, regional power games were played out. With US support, Ethiopia usurped Kenya in providing the chief mediator, and Ethiopians also took the posts of force commander of UNMISS and head of the IGAD protection and deterrent force within UNMISS.[52] Museveni intervened directly in the talks to overrule a power-sharing formula that would have granted wide executive powers to a prime minister (implicitly, Riek), restoring all the power to the president (Salva). When the mediation stalled,

IGAD heads of state issued resolutions that included threat of asset freezes, travel bans and an arms embargo, and went even further: 'The IGAD region shall, without further reference to the warring Parties, take the necessary measures to directly intervene to protect life and to restore peace and stability.'[53] The enforcement arm of this threat consisted of the newly deployed battalions of the 'protection and deterrent force' from Ethiopia, Kenya and Rwanda. This was not mediation understood as assisting the warring parties to come to agreement, but rather the imposition of a new level of militarized regional governance on South Sudan.

An Alternative Ethic?

Immediately after the outbreak of war, Salva ordered the arrest of those political opponents who had challenged him. Riek had escaped, but the president's security men found eleven opposition leaders at home and imprisoned them. After intense African and international pressure, Salva handed seven over to the safekeeping of the Kenyans. The remaining four – Pagan Amum, former SPLA Chief of Staff Oyai Deng Ajak, former Deputy Defence Minister Majak D'Agoot and former Envoy to Washington Ezekiel Gatkuoth – were charged with treason and brought to court. Most expected a show trial, in which the testimony of security officers would ensure a conviction. It did not work out that way. Commenting on the judges chosen, my colleague Yoanes Ajawin observed that they were 'men of integrity' who might not be swayed by inducements or threat. Yoanes was right: the judges opened the court to the press, insisted that prosecution witnesses show up on time and that the defence have the chance to cross-examine them. This reached an apogee when Chief of Military Intelligence General Mac Paul took the stand and admitted there was no evidence that the four were involved in a coup plot. Rather than face the embarrassment of an acquittal, Salva suspended the trial and ordered the four to be released.

Of necessity, a judge in South Sudan must possess political intelligence as well as knowledge of the law. The treason trial judges may have calculated that the accused were favoured by the international community as potential future leaders of South Sudan, and that it would be unwise to bend to immediate political pressures. But nonetheless those pressures were severe, and their decisions were brave. It is interesting that, after the trial was suspended, South Sudanese credited the judges' personal integrity, rather than the judiciary as an institution. People's experience of the judicial system gave them deep cause for cynicism. Their faith was vested in individuals not institutions.

The judges' principled action was rare but not exceptional. Throughout the war and during the post-CPA scramble for money, land and position, some individuals in positions of public authority, such as chiefs, priests, journalists, teachers, health workers and judges, displayed personal integrity. Some of these individuals have been lauded as individual heroes, and indeed they have shown courage and commitment in the face of great adversity and threat. Some also succumbed to pressures, or displayed virtue in some circumstances and not in others. But the phenomenon of individuals of recognized integrity is sufficiently widespread, that personal heroism is not a sufficient explanation.

A more complete hypothesis hinges on reputation and ethics. Personal reputation is important for the efficient functioning of transactions in a deregulated political marketplace. Any political-business manager faces the challenge of how to ensure a deal is respected where there is no institutional enforcement. For the patron, a reputation for ruthlessness or unforgiving vengeance is useful. For the client, a record of reliability is useful. But for those who cannot call upon money or arms, there is an alternative. This is social respect, based on a known and reliable disposition to fairness: what we might call honour. The judges in the treason trial displayed this, and others in society have done so too. Possibly, the challenge to the arbitrary, militarized kleptocracy in South Sudan will come not from international peacemakers and their troops, nor from impersonal institutions for administration and justice, but from the societal recognition and reward of men and women of personal integrity.

7

Somalia
A Post-Apocalypse Workshop

Mogadishu 1992

Returning from Somalia as the 1991–2 civil war reached its depths, I wrote, 'Where will you get your car serviced after the apocalypse? If Somalia, 1992, is a contemporary definition of the apocalypse, the answer is simple: in a garage, of course.'[1] Things fell apart – but some things worked.

Among them were car mechanics. General Mohamed Farah Aidiid, the most resolute and ambitious political entrepreneur in Mogadishu, employed dozens of them in a vast workshop. His favoured specialists were members of the Somali Bantu minority, persecuted to the point of genocide elsewhere in the country, but protected in this engine room of military mechanics because of their special skills, not only patching up his Toyota 'technicals' but also, among other things, fitting air-to-air missiles taken from grounded MiG fighter-bombers and refitting them on to trucks to fire them down Mogadishu's boulevards into the opposing faction's vehicles. The missiles made a strange whooshing sound unlike any other. The stock of such improvisable weaponry was quickly used up. But Aidiid and his rivals also pressed a number of well-used socio-political technologies, salvaged from the wreckage of the regime of President Mohamed Siyad Barre, into service in their political-business models. These have proved more durable but no less destructive.

Analyses of Somalia routinely make the elementary and irritating error of dating the onset of the crisis, or even the war, to the overthrow of Siyad in January 1991, ignoring the reasons why the country reached this position. Examples include the UN Mission in Somalia: 'Following the downfall of President Siyad in 1991, a civil war broke out in Somalia,'[2] and the *New York Times*: 'Somalia has lurched from crisis to crisis since 1991 when the central government imploded.'[3] This is not just a lazy simplification of press officers and journalists, it is a fundamental misdiagnosis made by those who should know better. The implication is that the principal challenge facing Somalia is to reconstruct a government, following which the country's other problems can be addressed.[4] In this chapter I argue that, to the contrary, the persistent international effort to re-establish a government based on external rents is the central *problem* of contemporary Somalia: it is a futile enterprise that has condemned the country to endless turmoil. Some countries can be run as centralized rentier systems. Somalia is not one of them.

The Somali Nation and State

At no point in its history has Somali political life been governed by formal institutions. It was a neo-patrimonial system from independence on. But it has been regulated by elements of societal consensus, which include (transiently) the vision of a united and modern Somali nation-state, and (more enduringly) kinship and Islam.

The Somali state was at its zenith in the immediate aftermath of the 1969 coup, when Siyad's new revolutionary government mobilized Somali society in pursuit of nationalist and modernizing ideals. The idea of Somalia transcended clan and was associated with the unification of the Somali peoples, divided five ways by colonial conquest and post-colonial borders. Somali statehood was also linked with ambitious modernizing, including the adoption of a script for the Somali language and an accelerated effort to promote literacy. Other components of modernization included building infrastructure and providing relief to the victims of the 1975 drought. The Somali army, disproportionately large and well-equipped for a small country, was a source of national pride. In the 1970s, Somalia appeared set on the path of state-building. The common expectation among the people – at least among those in the vanguard of engaging with state institutions, including students – was that Somalia had a future as a modern state.

Somali society is organized around patrilineal segmentary lineage. Every Somali child is taught his or her patrilineage back to the ancestors who founded the main clan families, in an increasingly fictive line, and even further back to the common ancestor of all Somalis and to Adam and Eve. Lineage provides as many potential levels of social organization and relationship as there are known generations, though in practice the number of options is limited to a dozen, from clan family at the highest level of aggregation to father and grandfather at the lowest. Clans are not entities. Rather, lineage provides multiple potential scripts that can be utilized depending on circumstance and initiative. As Ioan Lewis puts it, 'Somali kinship, although ideologically endowed with supreme moral force and conceived of as a "natural fact" (blood), is, as elsewhere, deployed tactically as a multipurpose, culturally constructed resource.'[5] In pre-colonial days, the salient levels of lineage organization were at local and intermediate levels, what ethnographers came to call by convention clan and sub-clan.[6] In the heyday of nationalist mobilization, the promise of a nation-state made it possible for all Somalis to identify as Somalis. At the nadir of the civil war, the contest for central state power and the capabilities of the national media made it possible and relevant for people to identify with the highest level of clan aggregation, pitting Darood against Hawiye and Isaaq. In the normal turbulence of local politics, lower levels of identification become relevant again. The capacity of Somali political actors to realign their coalitions, within and across lineage lines, shows that clan animosities tend to be transient and circumstantial: they are a product of organization for conflict, not its cause.

Lineage is also the basis for patronage politics, because a high-level political leader will build a coalition by picking members of the political elite that represent a cross-section of different clans, thereby giving an impression of inclusivity, demonstrating that he can make a bargain regardless of clan identity, and thereby playing the game of divide and rule, also known as spreading one's investment in political clientage.[7]

Siyad Barre's Security Rentier Kleptocracy

In 1977, Siyad foolishly invaded Ethiopia in the throes of revolution and lost. According to the precepts of politics, Siyad should have been removed after that, especially as GDP contracted by a third following the defeat while inflation shot up. The first coup plotters duly tried their luck a few months later. For the next twelve years the question was, how long will Siyad last? For survival, he cut one of the more cynical bargains of the age of realpolitik and begged for US aid.[8] His new western patrons, of course, had no trust in this military adventurer and former socialist, but they were confident that in his predicament he would rent them his strategically placed real estate, which he did. Both parties to this bargain knew its terms.

Siyad's business plan was short-term survival using guns and dollars, spun out indefinitely. The World Bank reported in 1989, 'For all practical purposes in recent years, the ordinary budget finances only defense and general services.'[9] Foreign military assistance was important, but most aid came from concessionary loans, development assistance and relief for refugees, all of which were stolen or used as political reward.[10] Aid contracts for infrastructure were awarded to government cronies, and shamelessly overpriced and under-implemented. Food aid was a racket. At least 75 per cent of about $200 million per year in refugee relief was diverted,[11] some of it used to feed the army and militia.[12] Loans for agricultural development became a mechanism for land-grabbing, as government officials and military officers got land title by paying bribes at the relevant offices, often without even having seen the land in question, and then used the leasehold documents to obtain loans which they used for consumption or trade.[13] Tens of thousands of farmers, many of them from disadvantaged minority clans, were robbed of their land and livelihood.

Civil servants gained lucrative positions by bidding for them. Officials at Mogadishu Port Authority demanded deposits into foreign accounts before ships could dock. Government offices tolerated absenteeism so that staff could take other jobs, and no certificate or licence could be obtained without a bribe. The government sold state assets at discounted rates to well-connected members of the political elite, in the form of one-shot privatizations of government enterprises. These generated rent income in the same way that a real-estate broker gets income from deals[14] – creating a demand for more sales to keep up income.

Licensing corruption is ultimately a self-defeating strategy, but clever tyrants have managed to use it to stay in power for long periods. The obvious explanation for Siyad's failure is that the Cold War began to thaw, Somalia's strategic value went down, and the money dried up. Outraged at the wanton destruction of the cities of Hargaisa and Burao, the US Congress demanded a suspension of US arms shipments. Some years later, Ambassador Frank Crigler blamed Siyad's fall on that cutback in US assistance: 'We took away one of [his] most important tools, his repressive abilities. We did much the same on the economic side. We pulled both those legs out from under him.'[15] The problem with this claim is that US arms shipments continued until 1989, and at their peak the Americans provided only 22 per cent of all arms delivered to the country.[16] Siyad had sensibly diversified his suppliers (to include Italy – the biggest – but also Libya and Saudi Arabia), and overall levels of economic aid remained steady, averaging $450 million over 1988–90.

Another explanation is not that Siyad's budget went down but that his political-business plan was to deregulate the market in loyalties, and for reasons beyond his control – and perhaps his understanding – the price of loyalty went up. This warrants closer examination.

Somalia's economy was a paradox: formally bankrupt and informally thriving. In a fascinating analysis of the real economy, Vali Jamal observed:

> The official [1979] figures put the GDP per capita at...less than half the income one estimated necessary for bare essentials, yet all the evidence indicated that people were well fed, shops were full of goods, tailors were making stylish clothes, and a housing boom was in full swing, Toyota truck-taxis had more than doubled in the previous year and all kinds of imports were arriving through various channels.[17]

For ten years thereafter, macro indicators indicated a crash yet the real boom continued. The biggest element in resolving the puzzle was the remittances of over 150,000 Somalis working in the Gulf and earning five to six times the average Somali wage, who were repatriating funds that constituted two thirds of urban GDP, fifteen times the annual Somalia-based wage bill and fully 40 per cent of the adjusted (properly counted) GDP, giving Somalia a higher GDP per capita than Kenya. These hidden adjustments allowed Somalis to survive, and even prosper. The fact that these funds were highly dispersed and were transmitted in large numbers of small transactions, almost always evading official channels, not only placed the most dynamic sector of the economy outside official control but also helped generate a new class of entrepreneurs, making money in import–export businesses, construction and services. Somalia was far richer than the official data showed, especially in hard currency – but Siyad had less and less control over the incoming money, while businessmen, insurgents and officers in his own army had more and more leverage.

Foreign economists did not understand this at the time. Some individual World Bank staff developed an astute analysis,[18] but the bank as an institution could not absorb these insights and was compelled to publish such false platitudes as: 'The Government has become aware of some of the deficiencies, and has repeatedly expressed its desire to address them,'[19] even as the government collapsed. This was worse than just wishful thinking: international donors diagnosed the problem as excessive spending and inflationary monetary policies, and demanded austerity measures.[20] But these reforms only deepened the corrupt patrimonialism, for example, by enabling Siyad to sell state assets and create new government departments that bypassed existing bureaucracies. Meanwhile, the erosion of the value of public-sector salaries made it necessary for public servants to take bribes or second jobs in order to make a living, and therefore legitimized corruption throughout government.

This model of kleptocracy was politically inefficient. Converting foreign aid into political reward was hard to control and involved a hefty discount rate. Asset sales were also hard to regulate and had diminishing returns, while the associated loyalty payments to the patron became harder to enforce. Public officials, army officers and local notables interpreted their being licensed to steal as an entitlement rather than a favour bestowed by the ruler.

Meanwhile, Siyad's coup-proofing plan was to reconstitute the professional army on the basis of crony command. Senior officers were given authority to recruit their own soldiers and raise money, and were allocated hardware with lax terms on which it could be used. They of course used their payroll as reward and used operational autonomy for extortion and pillage. Siyad replaced the threat of a coup within the army with political-military entrepreneurs who had their own provincial power bases.

These are well-established strategies for staying in power. Siyad's problem was that he underestimated the price of loyalty. Like the World Bank, he saw the problem – a huge informal economy that overshadowed the formal one, with money pouring in along the circuits of trade and kinship – but he could neither capture nor block the informal transfers. He tried: he abolished the system whereby traders could use their foreign currency held abroad to buy and import goods (*franco valuta*) and squeezed the livestock export trade, but these tactics did not work. Other stratagems he might have tried would have been setting up his own shadow foreign-exchange system, parallel to the official one, to fund his own political budget, or authorizing Islamic banking – but his reliance on the Bretton Woods institutions and his resolute secularism precluded these.[21] Somalia was a middle-income country[22] but its ruler had a low-income country political budget. In these circumstances, licensing corruption and military entrepreneurism did not buy loyalty, but instead enabled his rivals to tap the money in the informal economy for their own political purposes.

Siyad was priced out of the political marketplace that he created, and was compelled to operate with shorter and shorter payoff periods and greater resort to roving banditry.[23] I saw this graphically in the

Jubba Valley, in 1989, where an armed land-grab was in full swing. I asked a local community leader in Luuq what kinds of conflicts he resolved, and he answered, 'None: it is total war.' By the end of Siyad's rule, 'The state was literally and shamelessly consuming itself.'[24]

Commerce without a State

Since 1991, Somalia has been famous for its state failure, but it could equally be lauded for its economic success. On both income and human development indicators, Somalia has done better since 1991 than before.[25] The economy is based on foreign wages (remittances from the global Somali workforce), trade and services (especially the telecom sector). Rents from aid and military assistance sustain a class of military-political entrepreneurs, but those rents are neither centralized nor large enough to dominate the political marketplace.

After 1991, the livestock export trade was the first to rebound. Bokhara market in Mogadishu continued to function throughout the battles of the early 1990s, as merchants and shopkeepers cooperated to provide security irrespective of clan. Somalia developed private airlines, with more than 400 flights in and out of the country by 2001. In 2004, Somali businessmen opened a Coca Cola plant in Mogadishu with investment of $8.3 million.[26]

A specialized financial sector replaced the collapsed old banks. The modus operandi of businesses such as Dahabshiil builds upon the strength of the kinship system and the ability to use relatives to locate individuals, confirm transactions and settle disputes. In the early 2000s, remittances amounted to about $1 billion per annum, which is over 70 per cent of GNP.[27] According to the UK Somali remittances survey, an estimated 40 per cent of Somali households, and more in urban areas, receive money from the diaspora. Remitters are wage earners and small business owners, redistributing funds to their families. About 14 per cent of remitted funds are invested, financing 80 per cent of business start-ups.[28]

Telecoms is the most remarkable of the success stories of Somali business.[29] From start-up in 1995 to 2004, $117.5 million was invested,[30] and Somalia's telecommunications were among the cheapest and most efficient in the world. Telecoms became the lead sector in the economic boom and this business was a key facilitator of the rapid and reliable transmission of remittances. Somali telecoms benefited from the unusual structure of the international telecommunications accounting and settlement rates regime.[31] Originally developed

in the nineteenth century by European carriers as a formula for dividing the revenues generated from international telegraph services
between originating and destination countries, this system means that
developing countries, which receive more calls than they originate,
receive net payments on this system. Hence, unlike almost every other
industry, there is a systemic bias in favour of the developing world,
which works to the particular advantage of a country like Somalia
which has a large migrant population in developed countries. Somali
entrepreneurs were aware of the potential rental income from this
disparity, and negotiated advantageous accounting rate agreements
with European and American carriers, which have provided their
main source of revenue.

Greg Collins has investigated how Somalia's telecom firms were
able to protect private property, enforce contracts and resolve disputes in the absence of state institutions.[32] Although they were the
wealthiest businesses with assets that would appear tempting to
looters, telecoms companies hired few armed guards. The guards
were there to deter opportunistic thieves but would never have been
able to resist a determined attack by a militia. Nonetheless, telecom
property, including such eminently lootable commodities as copper
wire, was respected. Telecoms providers had succeeded in making
their services into a public good: their protection did not lie in private
armies but in financial power. Somali society is exceptionally open:
there is no anonymity (every individual can be identified and traced
through name alone because the name is the patriliny), the diaspora
is global and connected, and information circulates rapidly. For
remittance providers, the clan system with its identification and guarantee system serves as a substitute for state-based rules and regulations.[33] Violating the norms of clan and business carries a reputational
cost.

Some business profits, however, derived from rent, in a rather
literal manner. During 1991, Aidiid's United Somali Congress (USC)
'cleansed' Mogadishu and the Shebelle Valley of members of the
Darood clan family, on the pretext that they were supporters of the
former dictatorship.[34] Their houses, businesses and land were seized
by the 'liberators' – USC commanders and associated businessmen.
Irrigated farms that produced, among other things, bananas for
export were profitable. Businesspeople became entangled in the military politics of territorial control, both of farmland and of export
routes. In 1995–6, Somalia saw its first 'banana war' in which export-
ers funded militia to secure their exports.[35] In Mogadishu itself the
stakes are higher. Real estate seized in 1991 is now worth billions of
dollars, and property developers are ready to invest even though

ownership is rarely possible to prove. Any comprehensive political reconciliation would involve property restitution and reignite land title disputes. For these reasons, some businesses are tied to the continuing territorial control of a particular faction.

Political Rentierism without a State

From the last offensives of the USC and its allies towards Mogadishu, in late 1990, until today, political-military entrepreneurs have financed their operations through a combination of looting and extortion, foreign patronage and political credit – offers of future positions to be repaid in anticipated rents. Instead of seeking to upend Siyad's business model and obtain political finance from the business sector as a whole, they have pursued variants of militarized rentierism.[36]

The first battle for Mogadishu, to overthrow Siyad, quickly turned into a contest between the two rival leaders of the USC, General Aidiid and Ali Mahdi Mohamed. The two began with different political finances: Aidiid mostly through seizing assets; Ali Mahdi through established businesses. But, when neither was able to claim the prize of the state, they converged on the same method: loot. The first targets were high-value electronic goods – televisions, videos, fridges, air conditioners, word processors, generators. Traders from Kenya, Sudan and the Gulf converged on Mogadishu with ships and light aircraft to take industrial machinery, furniture and then other goods with a resale value, such as light fittings, window frames, copper wiring and aluminium sheets. In markets on the Kenyan border, all could be bought for cash. This was the country's biggest forcible transfer of assets, and the unresolved and unforgotten violations, and land-grabbing, cast a shadow more than twenty years on.

The factions fought for control of ports and airports, checkpoints, food shipments and finally even kitchens – Somali relief workers had hoped that distributing cooked food would lessen the chance of looting.

In parallel, Ali Mahdi and Aidiid fought over the privileges of future government. Two of the fiercest clashes of Mogadishu in 1991–2 were sparked by attempts by Ali Mahdi to bring in planeloads of banknotes and, in one shipment, police uniforms. Ali Mahdi's huge number of ministerial appointments (over eighty) owed as much to the need to offer the prospect of future economic rewards to his allies as the need to build clan alliances.[37] Just as the prospect of an externally validated and funded government began to slip away, the US Operation Restore Hope restored hopes of US strategic rents. In turn, major issues such as land ownership could not be settled because, once there was a government, they would surely be re-opened to the advantage of those newly in office.

Every subsequent initiative from outside has nursed that hope, writing the same script over and over again. Since 1991, there have been six major Somali peace conferences. Experts on Somalia have dutifully recorded the desultory details of this parade of near-identical failures.[38] All have adopted the same formula: that a government should first be constituted, drawn from the leaders of political-military factions assembled around clan patronage, which would then share out rents. An agreement is also a security pact that channels foreign military patronage in pursuit of the interests of neighbours and the international community. Ken Menkhaus writes of the Transitional National Government (TNG) set up through negotiations in the Djibouti town of Arta in 2000:

> Nearly all energy invested in the Arta process (which culminated in the creation of the TNG) focused on the division of anticipated spoils; namely, the share of seats in the parliament and cabinet by clan. And once the TNG was established, virtually all its energy was geared to soliciting foreign aid. Very little attention was paid to actual administration for the country, or more precisely the portions of Mogadishu which the TNG controlled...the TNG was in essence a piece of paper on a fish hook, thrown into international waters to lure foreign aid which could then be diverted into appropriate pockets.[39]

Ethiopia vetoed the TNG, not because it was a rent-seekers' charter, but because of fears that it was a vehicle for Egyptian and Eritrean interests. As early as 1994, in discussions with this writer, Prime Minister Meles Zenawi recognized the cogency of the political-economic analysis of Somalia that placed political finance at the centre, and agreed that it made sense to focus first on a chamber of commerce and only later on a government. But, in 2000, Meles's antipathy to rent-seeking did not overrule his perception of an Eritrean threat incubating in Somalia. Another round of conferencing followed, this time with Ethiopian support, in the Kenyan towns of Eldoret and Mbagathi, from 2002–4. The meetings began with 300 delegates, rising to approximately 1,000 before stabilizing at 800. At times, the conference itself appeared itself to be a vehicle for the Somali elite to conduct every conceivable business and charge the costs of hotels, per diems, transport and security to the hosts and donors.[40] The Transitional Federal Government (TFG) was the outcome in 2004.

The TFG did not begin a system of public accounts until 2009, and a subsequent internal report into its finances found widespread failure to account for funds, with political leaders using foreign aid and port revenues as personal cash dispensers.[41] Between 2000 and 2011, successive governments raised $53 million from domestic sources (principally port and customs dues) and received $304 million in bilateral aid from Arab countries, of which only $124 million could be accounted for.

The Communications Revolution

The instruments of rentier-patronage are good enough to carve out a fiefdom, not rule Somalia. The old instrument of political communication, the national radio station, is now completely redundant, and the favoured means of political convening – the national conference – has questionable value.

In January 1991, the most strategic asset in the country – along with Villa Somalia, the seat of the presidency – was Radio Mogadishu. Aidiid intended to take the radio and make the standard coup maker's broadcast, announcing military rule and a new government. Normally decisive, he hesitated on 26 January 1991 when he learned that a militia loyal to Ali Mahdi had taken control of the radio station, allowing Mahdi to declare himself interim president. Aidiid missed his best chance.

This was the first of three confrontations at Radio Mogadishu during 1991–3, each of which set Somalia's political trajectory. In November 1991, when the Salebaan militia controlling the radio station switched sides, Aidiid announced the formation of a new interim administration, denounced Mahdi's government as illegal, and sent his forces to overrun Mahdi's headquarters. His attack failed and four months of intense and bloody urban war followed, infamous for artillery exchanges in which soldiers adopted the maxim of 'to whom it may concern' for targeting their shells. And, in June 1993, the UN foolishly sent a contingent of Pakistani soldiers to inspect Aidiid's arms depot at the radio, disregarding the frank statement of Abdi Qabdiid, one of Aidiid's aides, who said, 'this means war'.[42] Twenty-three peacekeepers were killed in the firefight, which led to four months of urban warfare, the humiliation of the US and the end of the international mission.

Political bargaining requires an infrastructure of convening: the political elite needs to meet. It needs mechanisms of communication: they need to talk with one another and the populace. Under Siyad, there was no freedom of speech or assembly, and the only open political meetings were held abroad, while the BBC Somali service was the most valued news provider. Without a functioning telephone system (landlines were scarce and mobile phones did not exist), reliable local news was circulated in person.[43] When Siyad was driven from power, the ongoing war meant that there was still no place in which the political entrepreneurs and brokers could gather. Radio Mogadishu remained the authoritative voice of government and the means whereby a politician could claim the presidency.

Just a few years later, communication was revolutionized by the rapid emergence of the Somali telecoms industry. Telecoms were profitable and politically important because Somalia is a transnational wage-earning and trading economy, and its financial and kinship circuitry are one and the same – close kin are the guarantors of creditworthiness. The local, person-to-person information networks that had been so crucial to survival suddenly became ubiquitous, near-instantaneous and the basis of financial transactions. Businesspeople cashed in, and in doing so also transformed political bargaining.

The national conference was a mechanism from the old era of regulated political bargaining. Participants to the national conferences held in 1991–3 represented the entire national political community, and all the knowledge necessary for reaching a settlement existed in the room. The conferences in Djibouti and Ethiopia failed for other reasons – and in Somaliland they succeeded (see the next chapter). Just a few years later, one fundamental variable had changed. Political negotiations among the selected elite were now transparent to all Somalis. Those following from afar would call and intervene. Delegates to a conference would leave the room and contact sponsors or financiers, and return to renegotiate a deal that had just been provisionally agreed. Faraway commanders would recalculate and recalibrate their strategies instantly. Efficient communication quickened the pace of bargaining and re-bargaining, increasing the leverage of provincial commanders and the price they could extract.

One of the reasons for the disorder of the Arta and Eldoret-Mbagathi processes was that a closed, rent-based negotiating formula could not match the open, business- and kinship-based political economy. The more the mediators tried to be inclusive the more the limits of the process were revealed. The Somali political entrepreneurs knew that there was more political finance outside the process than was on the table in the conference room. So they treated the outcome as a temporary bargain, to be exploited while it lasted and renegotiated when conditions changed, rather than a solemn and binding proto-constitution.

Islamist Challenges

Siyad shut out Islamists from politics and Aidiid and his rivals were uninterested in political Islam. In the 1990s, Islamists tried a succession of diverse political-business plans. They began modestly with al Ittihad al Islaami (the Islamic Union). Al-Qaeda despatched an active unit in the mid-1990s. In the 2000s, the Islamic Courts were important. Most recently, Harakat al Shabaab al Mujaheddin ('Movement of Young Holy Warriors', widely known as al Shabaab) has been Islamism's dominant face. Islamists face much the same problems as their international adversaries and their basic failure was the same: to underestimate the price of loyalty in Somalia, and underbudget for the operating costs of their political project.

Al Ittihad al Islaami's first venture – a military operation to capture Bosaso in 1992 – failed badly, and instead it focused on minority groups that did not have clan-based militia, especially the Benadir people of the port towns of Merca and Brava, south of Mogadishu, and the Gabwing minority group in Luuq in the Jubba River valley. Their hold on both was tenuous as they possessed neither the money nor the armaments to be major players. Following bin Laden's relocation to Sudan in 1991, and especially after Aidiid's militia humbled the Americans in 1993, al-Qaeda took an interest. It established a base in Luuq, which was attacked and destroyed by the Ethiopians in 1996, effectively ending al-Qaeda's presence in Somalia for the next five years.[44] When they overran Luuq, the Ethiopians found the bodies of more than a dozen foreign jihadis and a trove of documents. The latter they passed to the CIA, which began translating and analysing them in late 2001.

The Harmony Project, based at the US army's Combating Terrorism Center at West Point Military Academy, has analysed al-Qaeda's internal documents.[45] These reveal the political, financial and operational difficulties faced by al-Qaeda in trying to function without the protection of a government, such as it had enjoyed in Sudan or Afghanistan. Among their problems were trying to enforce discipline when members could mutiny or defect (for example, taking advantage of the US witness protection programme to inform on their superiors), and vulnerability to cross-border attacks from Ethiopia. The costs of transport, supplies and protection were high, and financial services were weak and unreliable.[46] The counter-terrorist analysts then provide a fascinating account of the jihadist business model at that time, and why – according to its own protagonists – it failed:

> While the costs for operating in Somalia were greater than expected, the value of al-Qa'ida's compensation package to the locals was much lower than expected. The two major practical benefits al-Qa'ida offered to local allies were money for tribes and military training.

The correspondence among al-Qaeda's political-business managers describes in detail how 'pecuniary benefits were the anchor for gaining support with the locals'.

> Al-Qa'ida expected it to be quite easy to win the locals with money; after all, their country was poverty-stricken. However, once on the ground, al-Qa'ida's leaders realized that they had competition in Somalia. Their offer of pecuniary benefits bought only temporary commitments from the Somali clans. Even in the unstable environment of early-1990s Somalia, businessmen were a threat to al-Qa'ida's ability to recruit.[47]

The jihadists' response was to turn against its political-business rivals. The documents quote an al-Qaeda member who proposed a strategy of 'draining an area of all outside financial support'. He saw this

> as a way to increase al-Qa'ida's leverage in recruiting individual terrorists and co-opting other groups to their cause. However, the group clearly recognized that to maintain the loyalty of the people, such a strategy must be followed by 'supervision of liberated areas and securing of lives, funds, and property of all members of the populace'.[48]

The counter-terrorist analysts concluded that the al-Qaeda intervention in Somalia in 1993–4 failed for much the same reasons that western intervention failed: they did not understand the social and political dynamics of the country. We can expand on this: both western intervenors and the jihadists underestimated the price of loyalty in Somalia. The Harmony Project account suggests that the Islamists were, at least, closer to the mark in their evaluation of how they went wrong.

Non-militant Islamists meanwhile were working with, not against, the financial circuitry of Somalia. Telecoms and remittance companies had solved one of the basic problems of enforcing contracts in a society without functioning courts: using the power of shared reputation among close kin. Islam provided a second set of societally validated norms and, in the late 1990s, the first experimental Islamic courts were set up, leading to an organized confederation of these courts in 2000, which were then folded into the TNG set up in the Arta Conference. These early Islamic courts were then swamped in the TNG's corruption.[49]

Somalia's communications and remittance system is global and transparent, and its business runs on societal reputation. Therefore, a few weeks after September 11, 2001, when the US administration – not ready to take military action in Somalia – decided to publish the names of individuals suspected of links to al-Qaeda, it had unwittingly stumbled upon a remarkably effective tool. Somali businessmen and politicians cannot function if they are financially ostracized. The US then misread Somalia (again) and froze the assets of the largest Somali transfer company, Al-Barakat, on the grounds that it was facilitating terrorist-related financial transfers. This was akin to financial carpet-bombing,[50] although in the longer term it served as a form of anti-trust action that liberalized the sector just as Al-Barakat was moving towards a quasi-monopoly.[51]

During 2004–5, a new round of local courts was established. Somali businessmen, notably telecoms companies, began to regulate violence in Mogadishu with a combination of appeal to Islam and judicious cash payments. They coalesced to become the Union of Islamic Courts (UIC). This was an experiment in regulating the political marketplace, using Islam as not only the normative code but also the enforcement mechanism.

Islamists asked for the courts' permission to set up a training camp to establish a new autonomous militia, which became the courts' enforcement arm but also something more.[52] The Ethiopians espied the presence of Eritrean agents within the militia, and the US administration was ready to use force against any suspected Islamist militants. Their initial response was to create the Alliance for Restoration of Peace and Counter-Terrorism, a group that consisted of men of such reputation for violence and corruption that it backfired at once. Mogadishu's businessmen and local people rallied in support of the UIC, enabling it to take over the city in June 2006.

Within a few months, the UIC delivered stability and the rule of law for the first time since the 1980s. The courts demonstrated that there is a non-rentier formula for regulating violence. However, success was too rapid for the UIC leadership, which was not able to consolidate business control over the militia. A minority group of armed men, al Shabaab, took a prominent role in dictating the UIC strategy, including draconian implementation of neo-fundamentalist reading of Islamic law and assassination of opponents. Influenced by

Eritrea, al Shabaab declared war on Ethiopia, which duly invaded and inflicted crushing military defeats. The US followed with drone strikes against al Shabaab leaders. The UIC's erstwhile financiers pressed for compromise,[53] while the combination of anti-Ethiopian nationalism and anti-American militancy drew more jihadis to al Shabaab.[54] The TFG was restored, and Ethiopian troops ensured that Somalia stayed within its security perimeter. It achieved this not only by expelling the Eritreans by military action, but also through UN Security Council sanctions which put the entire structure of Eritrea's state finance under unfriendly international scrutiny.

Globalized Somalia

The TFG's successor, the Somali Federal Government (SFG), is an internationally sponsored plan for a vertically integrated cartel to manage the Somali political marketplace. For thirty years, Somalia's donors treated governance as a project, subject to technical design and to be implemented according to plan. The London conference of February 2012 had one singular difference, symbolized by its location: it made no pretence that power was vested anywhere but with the internationals, who provided the money, along with the African 'frontline states', which provided the soldiers. The SFG started at the top: a donor-security cartel to minimize regional and international patronage competition, and an African coalition to enforce this oligopoly, with UN sanctions imposed on violators. The federal system is designed to distribute rents broadly enough – and reduce Mogadishu's role – to buy in everyone except those designated as terrorists or pirates.

Historians will recognize this as a contemporary hybrid of protectorate and native administration. But, unlike in the colonial era, the Somali economy is open and dynamic. Even if the SFG's patrons are successful in minimizing external patronage competition – which is not certain – they will face the same challenges as their predecessors in terms of controlling or co-opting the even larger but more distributed political finance in Somalia's business-societal circuits. They also need to convince sceptical political elites that they are here to stay. In the meantime, for political entrepreneurs it is a market rich with opportunity, but also with commensurate risks. It has a high price of loyalty, short time horizons, pervasive rent-seeking and tactical use of violence.

The African Union Mission in Somalia (AMISOM) was authorized in 2007. Its stated intent was to replace the Ethiopian army with troops from other African countries (Burundi and Uganda), but, when it became clear that this was not feasible, it became a supplement to the Ethiopians.[55] In 2011, following al Shabaab's kidnapping of Spanish aid workers in Kenya and other terrorist acts, the Kenyan army also invaded Somalia. The invasion and the conduct of Kenyan troops sparked an escalation of terrorist attacks inside Kenya, including the assault on the Westgate Mall in Nairobi in September 2013, which left sixty-seven people dead.

Rather than a peace mission, AMISOM is a security pact with the SFG and a combat operation intended to defeat al Shabaab. Its definition of success is based on counter-insurgency metrics that include the conquest ('liberation') of territory. In alliance with the Somali national army, it has captured a number of towns, but as the SFG extends its authority from Mogadishu outward, disputes over land and urban real estate, and contention over who is to control state governments (and their budgets) come to the surface. The Somali national army functions as a coalition of militia, each of which can operate in its own clan area but not outside it. Without AMISOM it would not exist. The National Intelligence and Security Agency, which obtains direct assistance from the US, has powers and capabilities beyond the oversight of any minister in the government and even the president himself.

The SFG's spending is handled by the Joint Financial Management Board, which gives power over key spending decisions to international donors. Somalia's government has almost no existence independent of its foreign sponsors. However, senior officials also face the demands of their constituents for payouts, and they must balance the formal and informal demands of their positions. They must also hedge their bets, as few expect their positions – or indeed the SFG itself – to last longer than its transient predecessors.

There is money to be made in the Mogadishu boom: real estate, services and contracts for the SFG and its patrons. In the short term, the profits match or exceed those of the remittance and telecoms sectors, and so the balance of political finance shifts accordingly for as long as the boom lasts.

Cut off from its business base in 2007, al Shabaab turned initially to taxing trade (especially charcoal) in the areas it controlled. By virtue of controlling ports and its tighter organizational structure – including foreign management – it could outperform the TFG financially as well as on the battlefield. Bin Laden advised Mukhtar Abu al Zubayr, the then leader of al Shabaab, to keep his ties to al-Qaeda a secret, partly so as not to incite more opposition, but also so that it would be easier to solicit monetary support from Arab businessmen, including for humanitarian aid.[56] Al Shabaab's use of conspicuous violence showed its commitment to staying the course, so people paid their taxes to al Shabaab dutifully, even those who were formally in government service. Roland Marchal observed, 'The bureaucratic structure of al-Shabaab has to be taken more seriously than the TFG State apparatus.'[57] Due to its effective control of internal corruption, Marchal drew the conclusion that 'the running costs of al-Shabaab are much less than if this organization were the usual Somali armed movement'.[58]

However, Mogadishu is the economic hub of Somalia and, deprived of access to the city, al Shabaab lost its biggest financiers. The movement was also hard-pressed by the 2011 famine, its own plight and that of ordinary Somalis worsened by its own distrust of foreign humanitarians and by US legal restrictions on aid agencies that prevented them from operating in areas controlled by a terrorist-designated entity. As many as 250,000 people, mostly children, died of hunger and disease in the worst famine of the twenty-first century thus far.[59] An internal power struggle over whether al Shabaab should negotiate with its adversaries[60] was resolved in February 2012 when – following an internal purge of rivals – Ahmed Abdi Godane openly declared affiliation with al-Qaeda. This ruled out negotiations with the US or any country linked to the US, thereby killing off the prospect of more inclusive negotiations, which had been discussed at the London Conference on Somalia the previous month.[61]

Godane's announcement definitively sealed off al Shabaab from the internationally sponsored Somali political market, and embedded it within the international jihadist market. His business strategy shifted accordingly, to attracting money and recruits by spectacular terrorist actions such as the Westgate Mall attack in Nairobi. This was risky, and a US drone strike killed Godane in September 2014.

Al Shabaab may wither, as al-Qaeda did in the Horn twenty years earlier. Somalia is an expensive and exposed place for international jihadists to operate, despite the political cards of nationalism, Islam and anti-corruption that they can play. Many in the jihadist camp will probably find it more profitable to switch to the counter-terror business, and will find that they can organize an optimal level of terrorist threat such that US counter-terror aid continues.

Piracy and Counter-Piracy

A readily available model for how political entrepreneurs can prosper in this kind of market can be seen in the recent history of piracy and anti-piracy in Somalia. Maritime piracy was, for a brief but spectacular period, a huge source of income. The number of attacks escalated in 2005, peaking in 2008–9, and falling away as international anti-piracy measures began to work. Although credit for the security of the shipping lanes is usually given to the forcible enforcement measures, such as the multinational Combined Task Force, a marketplace analysis would suggest that the financial incentives for pirates to cooperate with anti-piracy efforts would be just as important. In short, when counter-piracy becomes more profitable than piracy, armed entrepreneurs will change their business plans.

The July 2012 Report of the UN Monitoring Group on Somalia and Eritrea (UNMG) for Somalia provides detailed analysis of how the transition from piracy to counter-piracy occurred.

> Although pirates have been more active than ever in 2011, the adoption of best management practices by the shipping industry, more effective international counter-piracy naval operations and the increasing use of private maritime security companies have substantially lowered the number of vessels successfully hijacked. As a result, pirates have to adapt and diversify, engaging in kidnap for ransom on land, and marketing their services as 'counter-piracy' experts and 'consultants' in ransom negotiations. This evolution of the piracy business model is being driven largely by members of the Somali diaspora, whose foreign language skills, passports and bank accounts are all valuable assets. But the Monitoring Group has also been able to confirm the collusion of senior Transitional Federal Government officials in shielding a notorious pirate kingpin from prosecution, providing him with a diplomatic passport and describing him as a 'counter-piracy' envoy.[62]

A persistent theme in analyses of piracy is that the individuals who organize and profit from piracy are closely connected to those who organize and benefit from counter-piracy.

> Pirate negotiators have begun marketing their services as 'consultants' and 'experts' on piracy and 'consultants', while exploring new types of criminal activity. A growing proportion of Somalis involved in piracy are members of the diaspora who hold dual nationality, and the Monitoring Group has identified several such individuals involved with pirate militia based near Harardheere. Some may also have ties to Al-Shabaab militants, Somali officials and private security companies involved in the counter-piracy business.[63]

The counter-piracy business also provided opportunities for political-security entrepreneurs to pursue other agendas. A fine example is the Puntland Maritime Police Force (PMPF), which was set up in 2010. According to the UNMG, its actual function was as an elite force, answerable to the Puntland president and outside the Puntland Constitution, for internal security operations. It was funded by private individuals from the United Arab Emirates and rented the services of South African mercenaries under Saracen International, under the overall direction of Erik Prince, formerly head of Blackwater USA. Shortly afterwards Saracen International was taken over by, or rebranded as, Sterling Corporate Services (SCS). The PMPF/SCS base became the biggest and best-equipped military establishment in Somalia outside AMISOM headquarters. The UNMG noted that 'Although described as a counter-piracy initiative, the PMPF, formerly known as "Puntland Marine Force", has yet to be deployed as part of a comprehensive strategy to fight piracy in Puntland in cooperation with international partners',[64] and '[p]irate groups remain active in Puntland, where they appear to face no serious threat from the Puntland administration'.[65]

Conclusion

Somalia's current crisis began in the 1980s. The overthrow of Mohamed Siyad Barre did not change its main challenge, which is not to establish a state but to regulate a violent political marketplace. This can be done, but not with the kinds of measures adopted by African and international actors.

The crisis of the 1980s arose from an attempt to create a rentier political marketplace in a middle-income political economy, in which the population and local businesses enjoyed autonomy from that rentier system. The military dictatorship simply could not afford to pay the going rate for loyalty, and its efforts to do so – by deregulating corruption, especially in the military – just inflated the price further. Subsequent Somali and international efforts to build a government using money and guns have run into the same problem, and each failure has undermined Somalis' confidence in the likelihood that the next effort will last any longer. For any politician, short-term opportunist rentierism makes sense.

At particular times and places, it appeared as though non-rentier business finance might provide a basis for an alternative political order. The UIC was an experiment in this direction. But a combination of divisions within the business class (related to unresolved land disputes), the Islamist businesses' own rentier temptations, and the intersection of a jihadist business model, made that unsustainable.

Pursuing this alternative model to a successful outcome is not simple, as shown by the fortuitous circumstances and bitter contestation involved in creating Somaliland, described in the next chapter.

The current experiment in vertically integrated international governance may be sustained for longer, especially if it regulates external flows of political finance and generates confidence that there is no alternative power structure. The best prospect for the SFG and AMISOM would then be a hybrid cartel of Somali political-business managers, African troop contributors, and European and American patrons, collusively managing a rentier political marketplace. Such a system would retain the perverse incentives for corruption, instability and rebellion inherent in rentierism. It would be violent and turbulent and the internationals would need to stay indefinitely. The alternative of a governance system financed and regulated by the Somali business sector remains far off the policy agenda.

8

Somaliland
A Business-Social Contract

Somaliland Exceptionalism

Somaliland unilaterally declared independence from Somalia in May 1991 and set up a government that, more than two decades on, is functional but not internationally recognized. It has held a succession of competitive elections in which the loser has gracefully accepted his loss – including a presidential election in April 2003 that was decided by just eighty votes out of 675,000. The second-placed candidate, Ahmed Silanyo, gracefully ceded defeat to Dahir Kayin. Silanyo went on to win the 2010 elections by a handsome margin, and Kayin duly handed over power. Somaliland's political stability is an exception not only in Somalia but more widely in the region, and this small country of 3.5 million – a third of whom live in the capital Hargaisa – has become the focus of a small but fascinating branch of comparative political science.

From the beginning, accounts of Somaliland's emergence as a de facto state have focused on the role of clan elders and consultative processes.[1] These writings served to rebut cultural determinist theories of Somalis' statelessness, demonstrating that working government was possible in a clan-based society. Writers also delighted in criticizing the international agenda of top-down state-building exemplified by the UN Operation in Somalia (UNOSOM). Such writings were part analysis and part advocacy – intended among other things to deter the UN from dismantling Somaliland's experiment in locally driven problem-solving. At the time, Somaliland appeared workable only by comparison with the disaster in Mogadishu, but in all other respects it was a violent, unstable and contested place.[2] The details of this difficult birth are frankly documented by Mark Bradbury.[3] Other writers have addressed the analytical puzzle of Somaliland's stability, focusing on the organization of violence[4] and the contests between government and business.[5] Dominik Balthasar argues that war-making was a central component of Somaliland's state-building.[6]

In this chapter I analyse Somaliland as a well-regulated political marketplace. I suggest that the source of its stability lies in a lucky combination of circumstances in convening Somaliland's foundational conferences, and its sources of political finance – the domestic business community. It is unlikely that these elements will align again in the Horn, but there are important lessons to be drawn nonetheless. The account draws on unpublished research to chart a political ethnography of the early 1990s. It involves three elements: the process of regulating political bargaining; the source and organization of the political budget; and the organization of violence.

Convening Somaliland

Somaliland was created by the Somali National Movement (SNM). The SNM began – as its name suggests – as a resistance movement, aiming to build a nationwide constituency and take power in Mogadishu. Its name was a deliberate echo of the Somali National Army, which had been, until defeat in Ethiopia, the most prestigious institution in the country. Most of its leaders, including Abdurahmaan Tuur, the man who presided over the unilateral declaration of independence in 1991, believed in a united Somalia. The fact that a decision as momentous as declaring independence could be made, by popular acclaim, overruling the ostensible political leadership, gives us a clue as to why Somaliland has followed a different trajectory from elsewhere.

The origins of this decision lie in the politics of the SNM and in particular the aftermath of the 1988 attack on the cities of Hargaisa and Burao. Despite its national agenda, the SNM was overwhelmingly drawn from members of the Isaaq clan family of north-western Somalia. The SNM's commanders planned the attack at very short notice, after they were told by their Ethiopian hosts that Ethiopia was signing a peace deal with Somalia, which entailed closing down opposition bases. The SNM at the time comprised 3,000 men, and they decided not to go quietly, but instead to storm their home towns. The fighting force was shattered in those battles – losing as much as

40 per cent of its men – and Siyad unleashed a reign of terror in the north-west, destroying the cities and forcing most of the population to flee.[7]

Hartisheik in Ethiopia rapidly became the world's largest refugee camp, with more than 250,000 inhabitants. There, tens of thousands of young men demanded to join the fight. With little training and discipline, motivated chiefly by hatred for Siyad, they constituted a clan militia. Over the next two years, as the amalgam of veterans and clan militia overran the ruined land that was to become Somaliland, they formed what the veteran fighters colloquially called 'SNM-Two'. Thus, a national movement became an Isaaq clan-family movement and then a coalition of clan militia. The original veterans, who had a national vision and bonds of solidarity regardless of clan, were killed, demobilized or simply outnumbered.

The popular sentiment in Hartisheik was separatist. People demanded that as soon as Siyad was driven from power, the north-west should restore the state that existed, briefly in June 1960, within the boundaries of the former British Somaliland. (In a flush of nationalist passion, the territory's leaders had joined former Italian Somaliland following its independence just four days later.)

Three months after the SNM occupied Hargaisa, and with Mogadishu in turmoil, the SNM leaders, responding to popular clamour, declared the independent Republic of Somaliland. They went through a period of intense civil war, which during 1992 threatened to bring Somaliland to disintegration even faster than (southern) Somalia. There were three peace conferences, all locally organized. The first, in Sheekh, brought to an end the fighting in the port city of Berbera, which made possible the resumption of livestock exports and made Somaliland economically viable. The second, in Burao, formed the council of elders, known as the *guurti*. This superseded the former SNM council, which had been established during the war, and which had served among other things to mobilize fighters. The legitimation of the *guurti* was significant in part because it overshadowed the central committee of the SNM, the *beylaha*. In other cases of liberation movements in power, the ruling party has drawn on a combination of popular legitimacy derived from its standing as liberator and Leninist democratic centralism, to continue in power to the detriment of democracy.[8] The SNM did not have this capacity. Military commanders had lost the bonds of discipline, and the *beylaha* did not meet, so there was no prospect of them asserting military control. Theft and harassment by SNM militiamen, and their involvement in internecine conflicts, discredited them. Instead, the more powerful commanders – known colloquially as the *calan cas* – had to bargain to win power. Political order was created from the fact that the contending forces – military, civilian, commercial – were evenly matched, and through the well-regulated forum in which they were convened.

The third meeting was the four-month-long Boroma Conference, from January to May 1993, in which Somaliland's new political order was hammered out. The technology of convening was rudimentary, and that of communication and recording was even more basic. These constraints were important: they imposed discipline on the proceedings. Twenty years later, with mobile phones and internet platforms, the bargaining would have been open-ended and it would have been easier for dissenters to challenge the process and opt out.

Hamish Wilson was the only outsider present during the Boroma Conference and his unpublished notes provide an important testament to the contested, fractious nature of the process whereby the first leader of Somaliland, Abdurahmaan Tuur, was removed and Mohamed Ibrahim Egal was chosen as president.[9]

> Initially, Abdurahmaan Tuur had been a strong supporter of the Guurti, believing them to be readily manipulated through the influence of his own clan elders and the liberal application of money... Tuur was able to undermine the authority of the SNM central committee, whose power to question and challenge his decisions he feared, by by-passing them in favour of what he believed to be the more malleable Guurti.

However, Tuur's failures in 1991–2 encouraged the Guurti to take on more administrative responsibilities, and to convene peace conferences, notably the Sheekh meeting. A rift developed between Tuur, who was showing clear dictatorial tendencies, and the Guurti. The Guurti called the Boroma Conference, which opened on 24 January 1993. It comprised 150 participants from all parts of Somaliland, plus guests and observers, and was chaired by the eight senior members of the Guurti in rotation. As well as the formal daytime sessions, the participants talked long into the night, chewing qat. Wilson's account of the conference is worth quoting at some length, because of its insights into this seminal process.

> Tuur addressed the conference towards the end of February. Putting misplaced trust in the support he could expect from the Guurti and in the belief they would re-elect him as President, he announced to the conference that he was 'giving authority to the Guurti and the 150 representatives to solve the problems of Somaliland.' 'Whatever they decided, I shall accept,' he declared to popular applause.

Tuur did not try to manipulate the conference. But as the meeting approached its conclusion, the Guurti members suspected that he was going to renege on his promise. In early May, as the date of the elections neared, four candidates put their names forward. Egal was emerging as clear favourite. A second, Ahmed Hala, was a founder of the SNM but, following many years in solitary confinement in Siyad's prison, had been left physically and mentally scarred. Omaar Arteh had been a minister in Siyad's government and subsequently under Ali Mahdi, and had recently returned to Hargaisa. Despite having publicly opposed the independence of Somaliland, Arteh hoped that his financial resources, including funds from Saudi businessmen and a senior Saudi security officer, would buy him support. There was wild speculation about Saudi intentions. Wilson wrote:

> Whatever the imagined motives, the money was real. In the run up to the election, Omaar Arteh commissioned the construction of a vast villa in Hargeysa containing numerous guest suites, reception rooms, staff quarters and a satellite communications office, and for the Booraama meeting he and his party rented the largest house in town. On at least one occasion a party of three Saudi Arabian men arrived in Booraama to observe the meeting's proceedings and for those who were unable to visit, a video was made, carefully edited to show Arteh as the popular candidate for election to President. Local charities and hospitals were showered with gifts and in Booraama the impact of Arteh's distribution of wealth was widely felt. The abandon with which US dollars were being handed out by Arteh in return for pledges of support in the election was the subject of much jocular comment in the town's tea shops and in the mosques and qat houses elders and sheekhs debated the lawfulness of accepting the gifts of money. Pragmatically they concluded that being in receipt of the money was permitted as it did after all belong to the Saudi Arabians and not to Arteh himself. Therefore by accepting the money no debt would be incurred in consequence. The situation reached a dizzying peak in the days immediately prior to the election [with] the return of Arteh's son, Mahamed, from Riyad with fresh supplies of cash.

The election was scheduled for 15 May. The conference was convened that morning, every participant's credentials checked by the secretariat, and the room was sealed. Egal was widely recognized as the front-runner, a fact that disturbed Arteh and Tuur, who demanded that the chair of the conference for that day, Sheekh Muusa, permit them to speak. Muusa refused, saying that the day was set aside solely for elections. First Tuur and then Arteh appealed to the participants to overrule the chair, but did not convince them.

Angry at the further delay being caused to the elections, they called for [Arteh] to shut up and be seated. At this, Omaar Arteh turned to Tuur, Hala and others in his group and urged them to join him in leaving the hall. 'This is injustice!' he shouted, waving his finger angrily at the Guurti before storming angrily towards the locked doors of the hall. The meeting erupted into chaos. Everyone rose to their feet. The secretariat tried to restrain Arteh whilst the representatives and the Guurti called for all candidates to return to their seats. It was to no avail. Omaar Arteh, closely followed by Abdurahmaan Tuur and then Ahmed Hala, Hassan Issa Jama, their advisors and 26 out of the 150 representatives left the hall.

Sensing a deliberate plot to disrupt and delay the election, Sheekh Muusa wasted no time in calling the meeting to order. 'This is not the day for the chairman of a meeting such as this to be a coward,' he told them. 'Those who have left have the right to do so. It is their decision alone. We request that they now return as we have no disrespect for them or ill feelings towards them.' His message was passed to those who had walked out, but when they failed to heed his call, Sheekh Muusa ordered the doors to the hall to be re-sealed and the elections to commence.

Egal won with ninety-nine votes. This was greeted with acclaim inside the hall. Boroma and Somaliland were not, however, completely disconnected from the rest of the world. Somalis are avid followers of news, and the BBC Somali service was – especially during the years of conflict – as close as there was to a national media. Arteh and Tuur called a press conference and denounced the process as illegal, and despatched one of their group to speak to the BBC to claim that war was breaking out as a result of a fraudulent election.

For Omaar Arteh ... his ignorance of Somaliland and its ways had been dramatically demonstrated by his inability to woo the electorate with both promises and money. To many it appeared that he was even somewhat mystified as to why the formula of sophisticated seduction and bribery which was so much part of Mogadishu politics had failed so completely in Somaliland. Arteh went as far as to question some of those whom he had given gifts of money and was shocked by their replies. The most famous retort came from the venerable elder, Hajo Abdi Warabe... 'We stole your money, but you did not steal our minds.'

After four days of pressure and representations from elders, sheikhs and politicians, Tuur agreed to hand over the office of the president to Egal.

As is clear from Wilson's account, the Boroma process was anything but tranquil. There was intimidation, bribery and trickery. But from the hard bargaining, a set of rules emerged and decisions were made. What made it work? Credit has often been given to the common clan-family identity of most of the participants, to the respect enjoyed by the elders and to Islam. These certainly helped with a code of behaviour. However, the key factor, I suggest, was that the entire political elite was in the room, and that political calculations could be made solely on the basis of those who were present and the known quantities of their constituencies, finance, military capacity and personal reputation. Arteh's attempt at buying loyalty with money was heavily discounted because of his poor reputation and the clumsiness with which he implemented his plan. Symbolized by the sealed doors of the meeting room, the Boroma Conference was a complete and delimited political system, and, within that system, the key elements were known to all. It was therefore possible to bargain in such a way that all present had confidence in the result.

Political Finance

A sound process was not, in itself, sufficient: the *substance* of the bargain also needed to be workable. Drawing on the *Communist Manifesto*, 'the executive of the modern state is but a committee for managing the common affairs of the whole bourgeoisie',[10] I caricatured the origins of the Somaliland Republic as 'a profit-sharing agreement among the dominant livestock traders, with a constitution appended'.[11]

The budgetary skeleton of Somaliland politics was as transparent as the bargaining. The Berbera livestock merchants had money at a time when few others did, and were ready to use those funds for particular political purposes. As noted by Bradbury, the conferences and the resulting new government earned 'the backing of some of Somaliland's wealthiest merchants, who had interests in keeping Berbera free of conflict'.[12] The funds were small – just a few millions of dollars – but they were the only funds available, and were directed in a smart way.

The 1992 fighting in Berbera was known locally as the 'sheep war', because of its causes. It resembled the contemporaneous struggle for control of the port city of Kismayo. But several factors made it both necessary and possible for the traders to resolve the conflict. Traders must cooperate to use Berbera: water and fodder are scarce on the road to the port, and arrivals must be coordinated with the departure dates of ships. Health certification is essential and must be done collaboratively. The livestock traders' main competitors are Australia and New Zealand, not one another. In short, the trade is a positive sum game. This business community provided the fledgling national government with a loan of $7 million.[13] Berbera business district and port were Somaliland's first weapons-free zone: in 1993, it was striking to see money-changers sitting openly in the streets with their boxes of currencies fully on display.

The costs of organizing and hosting the conferences in Berbera, Sheekh and Boroma were covered by cash contributions from businessmen, along with funds collected among the Somali diaspora and contributions of food and housing from the local community. No single source of money dominated, and the delegates felt a sense of financial obligation to the Somaliland community – a fact which helps explain their readiness to reject Arteh's bribes.

At that time, livestock exports dominated the economy and the tax base of the government. In 1995, port revenues contributed over $10 million to government income, by far the largest share.[14] Telecoms companies began operations in 1996, leading to a threefold increase in remittances in a single year.[15] As the economy expanded, the tax base grew to include small business and, especially, the telecoms sector, and a 1999 report by the Ministry of Finance reports that of Somaliland's budget of $20 million, 'some 95% of the resources that finance the activities of the government are locally mobilised, mostly through taxation'.[16] In 2007, the budget was $40 million, still almost entirely from domestic sources.[17] At just $11 per capita per year, government spending was tiny: by comparison, excluding foreign aid, Ethiopia spends $60 per capita, Kenya $100 and Sudan $200.

The government repeatedly tried to capture the key sectors of the economy. In the early 2000s, it tried to increase taxes on the private sector with a proposed VAT rate of 30 per cent. The business sector organized against this, and won. The government tried instead to make backroom deals, including with the Total Red Sea Oil Company. It also tried to impose a monopoly on livestock exports – something that not even Siyad had succeeded in doing. The government's biggest effort was in trying to compel the telecoms companies to work through a single international carrier.[18] These efforts failed: businessmen resisted and the administration yielded. The government also persistently campaigned for international recognition that would allow it to take out sovereign loans. This also has not yet succeeded, leaving the government still dependent on bargaining with its domestic financiers. This situation may change as the country finally develops a minerals sector, including coal and oil.[19]

How Was Somaliland Secured?

In 1991, weapons were more plentiful in Somaliland than in Mogadishu. There were more armed men, more armed technicals, and more and bigger weapons systems, including arsenals of landmines, heavy artillery, tanks and even three-stage rockets. Fighters from different militia caused havoc in 1991–2 and fought another round of war in 1994. The SNM, once a cohesive liberation movement, had disintegrated. The men who had founded it and been prepared to sacrifice for its ideals were dead or demoralized.

This had the important, little-acknowledged benefit that there was no party vanguard determined to wield power indefinitely. Rather, there was a chance to renegotiate political authority. Following on from Matt Bryden[20] and Mark Bradbury,[21] Dominik Balthasar argues that the war that occurred in 1994–5 following the Boroma Conference, while apparently a disaster for the government, in reality served the critical purpose of consolidating its authority.[22] Barely a year after the conference, a group of political leaders from the Habr Yonis and Eidegalle clans held a meeting at Liiban and declared the government illegitimate. The Eidegalle militia took control of Hargaisa Airport, which was both a huge snub to the authority of the government and a major source of revenue, now controlled by the militia leaders themselves. After failed negotiations, Egal unleashed his forces – the emergent national army – to attack the militia and capture the airport. He won. Some months later he also attacked the Habr Yonis militia in Burao. The latter had modest external support: the business consensus in support of the government did not crack, and – with the exception of some ineffective support from Mogadishu – there was no external interference in Somaliland's political marketplace. Balthasar describes the 1994–5 war as a shrewd move by Egal, in which he used the military capabilities of his key backers, the SNM hardliners known as Calan Cas, before subsequently marginalizing them one by one.

It is interesting to note that the political dispute between Egal and his rivals, and the subsequent armed conflict, occurred at the same time as serious efforts at disarmament and demobilization. The disarmament programme began in August 1993, with a National Disarmament Commission (NDC), assisted by a Zimbabwean expert team consisting of former guerrillas. At times it was chaotic. For example, the demobilization camp at Mandheera was quickly overwhelmed without enough food rations. Most of the funds were from the government, with modest international support.

Somaliland's disarmament experience was unusual in that there was a lot of enthusiasm for it among the SNM fighters, especially the veterans. Within a few weeks of the campaign starting, Mandheera camp was filled to its limit of 5,000 men. The first disarmament rally was held in the Hargaisa stadium in February 1994, when men of the Fourth Brigade formally disarmed and handed over weapons to the president. On the second, in April, 350 men of the Fifth Brigade handed over fifteen tanks, thirty-six recoilless anti-tank guns, fifteen 120 mm mortars, twenty-six artillery pieces, five BM21 multiple rocket launchers, sixteen 37 mm anti-aircraft cannons (mostly mounted on vehicles) and two armoured personnel carriers. This list of weaponry indicates the size of the arsenal available in Somaliland, and the ceremony shows how the exercise was linked to building the authority of the government. Even more strikingly, when war broke out in Hargaisa in November 1994, the NDC did not abandon its work in other locations. Disarmament continued in Berbera, Awdal, Sool and Sanaag. On 13–14 January 1995, heavy weapons were handed over in Boroma. In February, disarmament continued in Tughdeer.

The 1994–5 war did not therefore cause a general rush to arms, but rather a consolidation of arms and armed men under the government. Egal had more guns than money, and his war-fighting strategy was based on organized forces rather than patronage.

The demobilization was undertaken before there were many civilian jobs available for the former fighters. The veterans' association SOOYAAL complained that its members were abandoned without recognition of their sacrifices, let alone pensions. However, many former fighters were recruited into the new national army with pay of $100 per month, a considerable incentive. The government spent an estimated $4.5 million re-equipping the army during this period.[23] But, more importantly, dissatisfied militia commanders had few places to turn for alternative sponsorship: the entire Somaliland business class was supporting the government, and none had succumbed to the blackmail of the Eidegalle militia at the airport. Finally, the readiness of the government not only to build a national army, but to use it to kill rebels, increased the risks faced by rebels: they might really forfeit their lives.

Implications

The people of Somaliland were lucky, but their leaders worked hard to take the slender opportunities that they had. Those opportunities may well have been specific to a particular historical moment, when the interregnum between old and new rentierism had just begun, and the technology of convening and communication was sufficient to bring the political elite together but insufficient to allow political entrepreneurs to renegotiate the bargain in real time.

Balthasar proposes that Somaliland conforms to Charles Tilly's dictum that 'war makes the state and the state makes war'.[24] However, clearly not *all* wars make states, as the wars in Sudan, South Sudan and southern Somalia have amply shown. We need to ask what was special about Somaliland in the 1990s that enabled war-fighting to help build a government rather than, as in most of the cases described in this book, do the reverse.

The Somaliland authority, acting de facto at the behest of the business community, successfully regulated violence. It did so despite the exceptionally high level of armaments and its very limited resources, indicating that the challenge is the relationship among the political budget, the price of loyalty and the regulation of the marketplace – not the power and money of the ruler. Drained of political finance, rebels' ability to mobilize was constrained and, with an impecunious non-rentier state, the prize was small. The government, for its part, suppressed rebellions by force of arms not monetary inducement. Fortunately for the Somalilanders, the regulation of political finance occurred at a time when they could also regulate political convening and communication, and political entrepreneurs had few other financing options.

Somaliland's developmental democracy is precarious. Its political finance could face the competition of rentierism in the executive, for example, with a flood of sovereign rents following international recognition or mineral exports. An able and strategic political-business manager would avoid the mistakes of Siyad and his successors, and maintain the domestic business finance contract, but there would be temptations to relapse into an oligarchic crony system. Somalilanders cannot rely on political leaders who are ready to follow Silanyo's example of selflessly conceding electoral defeat in the greater national interest. The regional environment will also be crucial: it is unclear whether the current benevolent protection afforded by Ethiopia and the neglect by other regional powers will prevail, or whether Somaliland will become the cockpit for regional rivalries. But, at the very least, Somaliland has demonstrated that it is possible to snatch stability and relative prosperity from violent turmoil.

9

Eritrea
A Museum of Modernism

Fascism and Maoism

Once heralded as 'the future that works', Eritrea today is a museum of modernism.[1] In the 1930s, Asmara was Africa's most modern city, and today the physical fabric of Eritrea's capital city is still the most modernist. When the Dergue was overthrown in 1991 and the city was opened up to foreign visitors, architectural historians were astonished and delighted to find one of the world's finest concentrations of modernist buildings in the world.[2] Many of Italy's greatest exponents of Nuova Architettura experimented in Asmara, and sixty years on, their creations remained, preserved by the fine, dry atmosphere, by neglect – virtually no new buildings had been erected in the city centre for thirty years – and because no battle was fought in Asmara.

Urban Eritreans are hugely proud of their city. Among those who treasured its fine boulevards and architectural delights was President Isaias Afewerki. After a particularly large, ugly and intrusive apartment complex was built that blocked the vista along Sematat Avenue, overshadowing a futurist Fiat Tagliero garage in the shape of an aeroplane,[3] he insisted that strict planning rules be enforced.

An irony of Eritreans' adoration of Asmara is that the city was built by Mussolini's Fascists for Italian settlers, and Eritreans were not part of it. Eritrean towns were racially segregated, although many Italians appear to have blithely ignored official prohibitions on inter-racial socializing. Eritreans were labourers, servants and soldiers, onlookers in the accelerated modernization that made their colony into the second most industrialized centre in Africa, after South

Africa. In the 1930s, the Italians built a spectacular railway up the escarpment from Massawa (later rehabilitated with the assistance of octogenarian Eritrean railwaymen in the 1990s), a ropeway, a superb road infrastructure and a beautiful modern city. The Italians put on an impressive demonstration of what a strong state could do. The Fascist emblem still adorns the building that later became the Eritrean Ministry of Education, another irony insofar as the Italians built no schools for Eritreans. Colonial-era education was provided by missionaries, notably the Swedish Evangelical Mission, which promoted an austere, disciplined Protestantism.

The Eritrean independence war did not begin in Asmara, with its industrial workers and educated bourgeoisie. It began in the lowlands, when the discontented leaders of Muslim communities and a handful of radical students made common cause. The Eritrean Liberation Front (ELF) was their vehicle, founded in Cairo in 1960, and organizationally modelled on the Algerian Front de Libération Nationale. The Eritrean People's Liberation Front (EPLF) was set up in 1970 by more radical elements in the ELF, among them Ramadan Nur and Isaias Afewerki. The EPLF was a rigorously vanguardist organization, drawing upon the Marxist-Leninism so prominent in those years, and especially Isaias's Chinese training. Following an intermittent internecine war with the ELF, the EPLF became the sole effective military opposition a decade later.

Forced by the massive military onslaught of the Ethiopian army into a strategic withdrawal to the mountains of the Sahel in northeastern Eritrea, the EPLF staunchly defended a small, arid but almost impregnable base under extraordinarily harsh conditions. For more than a decade, all activities were conducted underground or at night. The EPLF established a total society, communal and cashless, in which the necessities of life were allocated according to need. The Front set up schools for its own members and for the local pastoralist communities, clinics and hospitals. Its surgeons conducted plastic surgery in underground operating theatres. Its mechanics established workshops in which they rehabilitated captured trucks and tanks (fitting Soviet T55 tanks with Mercedes truck gearboxes that allowed them to travel up and down inclines far steeper than those for which they had been designed), plus factories for plastic sandals and sanitary pads for women fighters. The EPLF encouraged marriages between Christians and Muslims, aiming to create a unified Eritrean identity.

At the outset, the EPLF was Marxist-Leninist with a distinct Maoist flavour, but was compelled to adjust when the Soviet Union embraced its Ethiopian enemy. Writers on Eritrea have debated whether it was ideological, nationalist or pragmatic.[4] It was all of the above. Most important, however, was its political *culture*, which centered upon sacrifice, nationalism, modernism and military values, a combination which enabled the Front to survive during the years in which 'even the stones were burning'.[5] This culture had populist rhetoric and many of the EPLF's programmes – educating women, redistributing land, campaigning against female circumcision – were genuinely egalitarian and emancipatory. Nonetheless it was an exclusive and elite culture, drawn from the shared values of the Asmara bourgeoisie and the EPLF leaders.

For the majority of Eritreans, the experience of the liberation war and the liberation meant something different. Michael Mahrt has described how, for highland villagers, the protracted war was a general situation, or 'the happening things', with particular events such as battles or mass killings which 'were not seen as part of the same ongoing struggle for the nation's liberation, but as part of the current living conditions of their area...reminiscent of similar problems that, according to the villagers, had always affected their area'.[6] Mahrt's account chimes with historical accounts of banditry, rebellion and conflict in Ethiopia and Eritrea.[7]

Militarized Developmental State- and Nation-Building

The Eritrea that the EPLF leaders aspired to build after their military victory was a completely modern nation. The list of countries that they most wanted to emulate was headed by Sweden and Singapore. The means they intended to use were mass mobilization and vanguard state capitalism, with self-reliance added. Their project resembled a stylized version of nineteenth-century European state-building. One pillar was forging the nation in the image of the EPLF. Just three years after military liberation in 1991, Eritrea initiated compulsory national service in the army. This was explicitly intended to inculcate the values of sacrifice and national pride into the wider population, emulating the spirit of solidarity under fire of the fighters of the Sahel, who had achieved victory against all odds and by their own effort. It was also a means of mobilizing labour for infrastructural projects. Young Eritreans were ready to accept this as part of their contribution to building their new nation.

The second pillar was capitalism, but with party and state in a dominant position. At the time of liberation, the Eritrean economy was almost non-existent. There was no domestic business class to speak of and peasant farmers were chronically dependent on food aid. Government finances relied on aid, remittances from the large and dynamic diaspora, and the Red Sea Trading Corporation, which had been set up as '09' during the armed struggle as a mechanism for financing the EPLF and securing ammunition and parts for its weaponry. After 1991 it broadened its operations, and was brought under the centralized control of the party – renamed the Popular Front for Democracy and Justice (PFDJ) – and the presidency. In 1994, the PFDJ established the Hidri Trust as a corporate umbrella for the Red Sea Trading Corporation – which maintained secret off-shore accounts – plus banks, construction companies and manufacturing plants.[8] The Red Sea Corporation and other party enterprises were purged shortly afterwards on the pretext of weeding out corruption. It was in this nexus between party, commerce and finance that the first shadows were cast over the nature of the Eritrean state. Not once since its creation has the Government of the State of Eritrea (GSE) published a budget: in its first few years this may have been understandable in light of the need to build all institutions from scratch, but its opacity thickened rather than lightened over the following years.[9]

In 1997, when the Constitutional Commission presented its elaborate draft constitution to the president, following twenty-seven months of consultations throughout the country, Isaias received it and then made no mention of it. Eritreans have speculated over the reason, and one likely factor is that formalizing the institutions of government would have demanded some transparency in financial affairs. Eritreans have seen neither budget nor constitution since then – though in 2014 Isaias announced plans for a new constitution.

The shadowy economy also contributed to the first tensions with Ethiopia. For six and half years from 1991, the two countries shared the same currency, but Eritrea set an exchange rate that allowed it to attract a disproportionate amount of the foreign currency flowing to the two, and also bought coffee in Ethiopia using the Ethiopian birr and exported it for dollars.[10] The fact that Eritrean business-people had a prominent role in the Ethiopian economy, especially in Addis Ababa, generated both economic imbalances and political suspicions. The Ethiopian leadership suspected that Eritrea's 'Singapore' strategy entailed maintaining Ethiopia as a hinterland agricultural producer, with industry and finance dominated by Asmara. Eritreans argued that it was a wasteful duplication for Ethiopia – and especially Tigray – to subsidize infant industries that were already established in Eritrean cities. When Eritrea introduced its own currency, the nakfa, in 1997, Ethiopia simultaneously carried out a surprise and short-notice change in its banknotes, leaving the Eritrean central bank with millions of Ethiopian birr that were suddenly worthless.

Eritrea's regional policy was militaristic. Isaias confronted Sudan in 1994 and Djibouti and Yemen in 1996. In October that year, Eritrean generals joined in the planning of the Rwanda-led operation to remove Mobutu Sese Seko, and dispatched commandos and political advisors to the Congolese rebels. Following that rapid victory, Isaias is reputed to have said that his army could march all the way to South Africa. He considered himself the natural leader of the region. The Eritrean leadership also thought that the EPRDF leadership was not strong enough to hold Ethiopia together. Speaking to me in 1997, Sebhat Ephrem, then Minister of Defence, predicted that Ethiopia would disintegrate into its constituent nationalities in the same way as Yugoslavia had done. In the wake of the overthrow of Mobutu, Yemane Gebreab, head of Political Affairs at the PFDJ, is reported to have described Ethiopia as 'an overdressed Zaire', so rotten that it would fall apart if given a sharp military shock.

Isaias miscalculated. Whatever errors he made in the first seven years after liberation were as nothing compared to the blunder of the war with Ethiopia and its aftermath. Isaias dispatched an armoured brigade to punish Tigrayan militiamen for their encroachments in Badme in May 1998, part of what appeared to be an annexation of land that, on the common published maps, lay in Eritrea.[11] For Isaias, it began as just another exercise in brinkmanship, but he led his country over the precipice. For two years, the Ethiopian and Eritrean armies fed their young people into the Badme meat-grinder, until the Ethiopians used their underestimated battlefield skills to best effect, penetrating the under-defended mountains north of the disputed plain on humble donkeys and overrunning the Eritrean trenches from the rear.[12] The Ethiopian army went on to overrun the EDF on several fronts. It was a personal humiliation for Isaias, who was on the point of abandoning Asmara and repeating the EPLF's 1978 'strategic withdrawal' to the mountains of Sahel.[13] For reasons that have never been fully clear, Meles ordered his commanders to halt, and Isaias survived.

Funding a Garrison State, 2001–2011

Starting a war and then losing it brings poisonous rancour into national politics, but not necessarily regime change. Isaias Afewerki adopted a political-business strategy that successfully met his two goals of maintaining his defences against Ethiopia and keeping himself in power. In doing so he adopted a model of a tightly controlled political business, extracting political finance from illicit activities (mostly transnational) and using that money for the army. There was virtually no money for anything else at all, including patronage.

Isaias's first challenge was maintaining his army: the Algiers peace agreement of 2000 was a truce, not a full settlement, and Ethiopia remained in possession of Eritrean territory, most notably the part of Badme awarded to Eritrea by the Ethiopia-Eritrea Boundary Commission. Isaias feared the Ethiopians and he turned Eritrea into a garrison state.[14] This entailed maintaining a vast conscript army of over 200,000 soldiers. National service became an indefinite requirement, and the national education system was reformed to serve as a mechanism for surveillance of all young people and securing their universal entry into the army.[15]

But Isaias also needed a lot of money. His problem is encapsulated in two graphs that show the military spending of Ethiopia and Eritrea, both in US dollars and as a percentage of GDP.[16] Figure 9.1 shows that even after the war Eritrea's military spending was matching Ethiopia's, at about $600 million per year.

Figure 9.2 shows that Ethiopia, with its much larger economy, was able to bring military spending down towards the 2 per cent considered standard for Africa, but Eritrea was spending more than

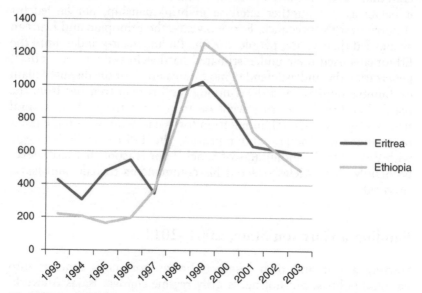

Figure 9.1   Ethiopian and Eritrean military expenditure (millions of dollar)
Source: SIPRI. Amounts in US dollars.

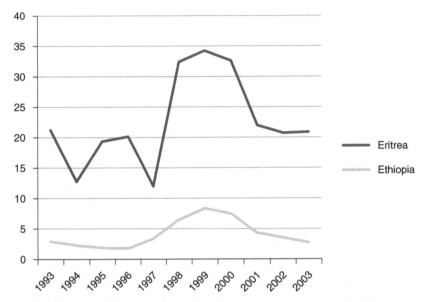

Figure 9.2 Ethiopian and Eritrean military expenditure (% of GDP)
Source: SIPRI.

20 per cent of its GDP on the army. More seriously still, while a militia army such as South Sudan's is mostly payroll costs, the EDF requires tanks, artillery and aircraft, plus fuel and maintenance, all of which need hard currency. In the decade 2001–11, Eritrea's exports were just $11–13 million per year.[17] The American ambassador, observing that Eritrea purchased Ukrainian Sukhoi aircraft and Russian MiGs, and hired aviation personnel to maintain and fly them, commented:

> if the GSE [Government of the State of Eritrea] bought materiel from Russia worth USD 50 million, it would have to spend the equivalent of all its diaspora tax revenue plus the value of nearly all of Eritrea's pitifully small exports. Clearly something else is at work here.[18]

Funding the army and buying enough fuel to keep the economy minimally functional demanded that Isaias devote huge attention to an extremely efficient operation of obtaining money, particularly hard currency, and ensuring that he had total centralized control over how it was spent. The business model he adopted was radically different to that of Sudan a decade earlier, when faced with a comparable financial predicament.

The UN Monitoring Group on Somalia and Eritrea has described how the country's formal economy was overshadowed by an opaque, offshore and largely illicit financial system controlled by leading members of the PFDJ.[19] This involves domination of all economic sectors, illicit activities such as money-laundering and arms trafficking, and obtaining payouts from foreign patrons. It was worth hundreds of millions of dollars.

The Red Sea Corporation or '09' was used to procure arms and ammunition during the armed struggle. Its illicit activities did not stop. It was folded into the party-run Hidri Trust conglomerate, which expanded to more than twenty companies. It has a virtual monopoly on government contracts and has forced other investors out of business. Hence diaspora investment – which briefly boomed in the 1990s – has entirely shut down.

Without remittances, estimated at $450 million per year, Eritrea could not survive economically. Through a monopoly on financial transfers operated by Himbol Financial Services, the PFDJ controls the exchange of hard currency remittances into nakfa. The party also extracted a 2 per cent income tax from Eritreans abroad (including those who have acquired other citizenship), which is paid in hard currency at Eritrean embassies and consulates, and is a strict precondition for obtaining official documents (such as birth certificates) or obtaining visas for either visiting Eritrea or allowing relatives to leave. This tax was condemned by the UN Security Council in 2011,[20] as a result of which a number of developed countries pressured Eritrean embassies not to collect the tax, leading to a decline in this source of income, and also in remittances.

The UN Monitoring Group for Somalia and Eritrea was tasked with investigating Eritrea's destabilization of Ethiopia, its sponsorship of insurgents in Somalia and its involvement in other trouble spots in the Horn and how those activities were financed.[21] It described many illicit economic activities and also mentioned sponsorship by other countries. The US Embassy in Asmara identified the 'regional sugar daddies' as Libya, Saudi Arabia, the United Arab Emirates, Qatar and 'various wealthy individuals', adding that 'the GSE has purportedly been offered financial pledges from the above-listed donors tied to anti-Ethiopian activity in Somalia and within Ethiopia proper'.[22] As well as cash, these donors provided food and fuel that kept Eritrea afloat. These investigations show money coming in and insurgents coming out, but reveal little about how they are connected internally within Eritrea, and do not explain the rationale for this political-business management strategy. Because of Eritreans' obsession with Ethiopia,[23] it is easy to assume that Isaias sought funds for the political objective of damaging Ethiopia, even if those means also damaged Eritrea as a whole. However, a political market analysis would require us to ask whether this is the right way round: it is equally plausible that serving as a regional insurgent generated illicit rents that kept Isaias's political and security budgets solvent.

The regional insurgency strategy was high risk because it involved Eritrea branding itself as the agent of Islamist destabilization of secular-Christian Ethiopia. This gave Ethiopia the opportunity to enlist the US on its side. When Ethiopia invaded Somalia in 2006, its main aim was to destroy Eritrean influence there. This objective could not be achieved by military action alone, and the political-diplomatic mechanism for this was international sanctions on Eritrea for its support of groups identified as terrorists, such as al Shabaab. In 2007, the US government threatened to declare Eritrea a state sponsor of terrorism and, in 2009, the UN Security Council mandated the UN Monitoring Group for Somalia to investigate Eritrean activities, putting Eritrea's entire system of political finance under scrutiny.

Eritrea's role in Sudan was different. Asmara had been a hub for Sudanese opposition since 1994. Eritrea supported the armed opposition in eastern Sudan, the Beja Congress and Rashaida Free Lions (collectively the Eastern Front), keeping tight control over their military activities. The Eastern Sudan Peace Agreement of October 2006 was first and foremost a deal between Khartoum and Asmara, in which the Sudanese paid off the Eritreans for ending the insurgency. Both Khartoum and Asmara wanted a deal for eastern Sudan that was discreet and efficient, and wanted to demonstrate to the international community that this was the way to do business, in comparison to the complex and expensive deal that had just failed in Darfur.[24] Eritrea withdrew its threat of violence in eastern Sudan and Khartoum provided a mixture of direct payoff in the form of cheap fuel and commercial opportunities. In fact, Eritrea was acting much like any other rent-seeking rebel on the periphery of the Sudanese political marketplace.

Isaias's second challenge was how to stay in power. After the disastrous war, Isaias's finances were so tight that he could not afford to pay off challengers – and in any case the immediate threat came from EPLF veterans who had profoundly internalized the values of sacrifice in a national struggle. In 2001, there was a brief Asmara spring of public debate and criticism of the president, culminating in a letter signed by fifteen prominent party members, insisting on reform. These men could not be bought off and only one was intimidated into recanting. Isaias clamped down decisively: he arrested his critics on 18 September 2001. Eleven members of the G-15 group have not been seen since, and most are feared dead after extended imprisonment in solitary and inhuman conditions.[25] Many others have since disappeared into the country's prisons. Eritrea has the worst internet connectivity of any country in Africa and the most controlled press. The University of Asmara was dismantled. The National Assembly has not met since February 2001.

The credible threat of elimination kept the price of loyalty down: Isaias could rule by fear. His threats were all the more effective because he could play on another real fear, which was the fear of Ethiopian designs on Eritrea, marked by Ethiopia's refusal to withdraw from Badme in fulfilment of the Border Commission ruling, and its sponsorship of a host of opposition groups.

Isaias coup-proofed his personal rule by using means well-adapted to his circumstances. His key innovation was to keep party and army separate, so that challengers within the party (who might have funds) could not organize violence, and army generals could not control political budgets. So Eritrea does not have a military establishment deeply vested in business or a multiplicity of parallel security forces, each with its own commercial structure. Neither does the PFDJ have its own armed security. Other techniques used by Isaias are familiar from the dictator's rulebook: sowing dissension and rivalry among the military elite, so that senior officers distrust and fear one another more than him, and using each commander's deputy as his spy, as well as shifting officers without warning or explanation.[26] Similarly, while senior party fund managers, especially Hagos 'Kisha' Gebrehiwot, were kept in place, their subordinates were frequently rotated and kept insecure.

Eritrea's finances were so tight that the country risked coming to a literal standstill when it suffered an economic shock. This happened when the price of oil rose, and Eritrea had no hard currency to pay even the discounted rate offered by Sudan. In June 2008, when the countries' vehicles were almost all immobile, Sudan stepped in with an emergency delivery of diesel.[27] What did Isaias exchange for this timely bailout? It is not clear if there was a specific bargain made. But Isaias might not have needed to make a threat: he had earned sufficient reputation as a troublemaker that his neighbours were well-advised to appease him before he opened the bargaining. Dan Connell has described Isaias's strategy as beginning with the premise: 'drawn from long experience of manipulation and betrayal, that if you trust no one, you can ally with anyone. There are no bad allies, only ineffective ones,' and concluding with his intent: 'to be a player in regional politics that local and global powers ignore at their peril'.[28]

The Seeds of a Rentier Political Marketplace

For the student of real political-business management, Isaias's model is an extreme and fascinating experiment in the separation of money from political business. However, this experiment began to break down and strategy had to change. The erosion of the plan came from within, with corruption in the army, and was accelerated when international pressures curtailed the criminal and insurgent rents. Then came a sudden change in economic fortunes with the arrival of mining companies and mineral rents, and new openings for strategic rents. Eritrea was moving towards a more conventional rentier political marketplace system.

The marketization of Isaias's strategy began when he started allowing generals to exploit illicit commercial opportunities in return for their loyalty. He licensed them to exploit the servile labour of military conscripts, in parastatals and agricultural projects,[29] as well as more conventional forms of corruption. The US Embassy described it in these terms:

> While some Eritreans manipulate the system in order to survive, the high-ranking officers are making fortunes on the backs of the conscripted army. Unraveling the depth of the military corruption is an ongoing effort, as anecdotes trickle out. The schemes and scams of individual military officers clearly occur with the full knowledge and support of the Office of the President in order to buy the military's loyalty. For example, military officers ranked colonel or higher as well as other high-ranking government officials are provided with free homes in Asmara and the surrounding areas. They are encouraged to choose the house they want and then the GSE expropriates the property...With the strangulation of the private sector by the GSE, the EDF generals have stepped in to fill the void. While the PFDJ controls many of the industries, the EDF generals have managed to get their individual fingers in the pie as well, especially in trade, smuggling and foreign exchange.[30]

Corruption intensified in a peculiarly unpleasant way as officers began profiteering from the haemorrhage of their own people. Eritrea has lost 300,000 of its citizens to flight in recent years, as young people try to escape indefinite military service and the general hopelessness of life. They and their families will pay thousands of dollars for the chance to leave, and this opened up opportunities for extortion.[31]

As the rate of escape accelerated in 2007, Eritrea's security chiefs found themselves unable to use the army to intercept escapees, because young conscripts might refuse to shoot at their peers and gain political courage from such elementary acts of defiance. Consequently, the generals hired militiamen from the Rashaida nomads, who live on the Eritrea–Sudan border, to do the job. The ICG describes how 'The apparent shoot-to-kill policy evolved into a chaotic "pay-to-leave" trade in which the threat from the Rashaida ex-paramilitaries "was crucial to generate revenues".'[32] Once the connections with these criminal elements were established, the Eritrean generals became part of the international human-trafficking network. The UN identified Brigadier General Teklai Kifle Manjus, commander of the EDF western region, and one of Eritrea's main arms smugglers, as the coordinator of this business, using the same networks and mechanisms for people as for arms.[33]

The horrors of the human-trafficking gangs, including torturing captives in the Sinai peninsula while phoning relatives in the diaspora to listen to their screams, and organ harvesting, gained sufficient publicity that, by 2013, Eritrea was under serious pressure to curtail this line of business, and indeed began to do so.

Isaias's regional insurgency brought him to the brink of being declared a state sponsor of terrorism by the US, and brought him to the attention of the UN Security Council. Because the actual mechanisms for supporting Somali and Ethiopian insurgents were so opaque, the UN Monitoring Group investigated all aspects of Eritrea's shadow economy that it could find, including the 'diaspora tax' and party-owned companies. The threats were effective in reducing Eritrea's support for Al Shabaab and other jihadis, although Security Council members took no steps to lift the sanctions when their ostensible goals had been achieved. Meanwhile, western countries with large Eritrean diaspora populations, such as Canada and the UK, took steps to ban the 'diaspora tax'.[34]

When the Eritrean economy and Isaias's finances were reaching the point of collapse, mining revenues pulled them back from the brink. The Canadian company Nevsun began exporting gold from the Bisha mine in 2011, and subsequently opened two more mines, which export copper and gold. Overnight, minerals became Eritrea's biggest source of revenue and transformed the country's balance sheet: its exports shot up from $13 million in 2010 to $388 million in 2011 and $457 million in 2012, of which fully 95 per cent were mineral exports to Canada.[35] The GSE owns a 40 per cent stake in the mine and there is little doubt that those revenues are personally controlled by the president.[36] The UN Security Council expressed its concern that funds from mining should not be used for destabilization and called for transparency in budgeting.[37] The mining sector is expected to expand as other companies arrive.[38]

The new geostrategic context has also given Isaias new opportunities. Eritrea's strategic location on the Red Sea was previously the basis for Ethiopia's alignment with the US, and then an inducement for Soviet backing. Saudi Arabia's decision to develop a Red Sea fleet, Egypt's dispute with Ethiopia over the Nile waters, and Russia's new assertiveness, have led all three of those countries to take an interest in Eritrea. Above all, the civil war in Yemen and the Saudi-led intervention have suddenly boosted the rental value of Eritrea's location. In the first months of 2015, Isaias restored diplomatic relations with Yemen – suspended since the two countries fought a brief war over the Hanish Islands in 1995 – and also received a delegation from the Houthis. Isaias certainly relished the prospects of new leverage and funds.

These elements change Isaias's business model. Instead of a near cashless political system and parallel illicit financing of the army, Eritrea is becoming something closer to a conventional rentier system. Army commanders are not only amassing personal fortunes but are also developing business interests. The country's big new source of revenue is conspicuously visible. Mines themselves could become the focus for extortion rackets, and claims on mineral rents could stimulate rent-seeking rebellions. Whether Eritrea becomes a tightly regulated marketplace with a dominant political-business manager, an oligarchic system run by a cartel of generals and party fund managers, or a deregulated and violent political marketplace, depends on the decisions of Isaias and the emergent political entrepreneurs.

Implications

The political career of Isaias Afewerki is a story of ideological commitment mutating into political-business management. Important elements of his system are criminal but, during the 2000s, it was run not for illicit enrichment but to maintain an army. This system had insuperable contradictions: it eviscerated the country and gave it a deserved reputation as a troublemaker, but it also opened the door for criminality and corruption to penetrate its leadership. Eritrea's political-business model is changing, but Isaias remains at the centre: it is run by him and for him. As the veteran EPLF leader Petros Solomon remarked to Connell just weeks before he vanished into the Eritrean gulag, 'Our dear president. Now, he says that Eritrea is less than the president. The president is more than Eritrea.'[39]

Eritrea still has the trappings of a modern state- and nation-building project, though they are wearing very thin. Isaias's use of a national myth and narrative, his pervasive militarization and his use of the education system to control the population all indicate a persistent 'state of exception',[40] redolent of the heyday of nineteenth-century European nationalism. The vocal diasporic opposition, expressing uninhibited views on numerous websites, point to a vigorous Eritrean imagined community in a way that has obvious historic echoes.[41] Eritrean nationalism has been sustained by a curious assembly of factors: a militarized political culture that has more echoes of Italian Fascism than its adherents care to admit, diasporic and online political imaginaries, and indeed Eritreans' common obsession with their leader-turned-tormentor. Isaias remains the pivot of Eritrea and people express grave fears for the future of Eritrea when he departs.[42] The president has no succession plan: Eritrea is a personally owned political-business corporation which risks disintegrating when its founder-owner dies or is removed. Eritrea's future is likely to be a political marketplace.

Younger Eritreans want to run away. Few are engaged in political debates: most just want a life. The values, norms, memories, dreams and debates that sustain a sense of Eritrean identity may be drowned in the turbulent waters of the political market. That may come in a flash flood, in the form of a political implosion, or could be the creeping flood of the pervasive corruption and marketization of political life, under the same ruler who has adopted a political-business model suitable to new circumstances.

10

Ethiopia
Is State-Building Still Possible?

The Ethiopian Configuration

If there is a governmental system that should qualify as a state (under any definition) in sub-Saharan Africa, it is Ethiopia. It has both the history and ambition to rank as a state. The Ethiopian state, however, tends to diminish on close approach. For every assertion about the continuity, legitimacy and order of Ethiopian governance, there is a counter-claim. Living in Ethiopia and conducting any kind of political or commercial business in the country is, for the most part, wholly different from Somalia, South Sudan or Sudan. The country is highly regulated and government bureaucrats are obsessed with procedural minutiae. Ethiopia does not feel like a place in which authority can be bargained. The Ethiopian government 'sees like a state'[1] and many Ethiopians experience the presence of the state and the ruling party in their everyday lives. Yet the forces of the political marketplace are present: they are most visible in the peripheries and in Ethiopian policy towards its neighbours, but also immanent within elite politics too.

The *idea* of a strong, legitimate political authority is deeply inter-nalized in the central and northern highlands. René Lefort in his study of the 2005 elections, describes the concept of power (*mengist*) in northern Shewa, the heartland of the Amhara.

> According to the great majority of interviewees, power cannot be contested, because it is divine by essence. According to the imperial myth, the late emperor was officially referred to as 'Elect of God',

'Power of the Trinity'. His successors...no longer claim this divine authority, but their mandate is still perceived as coming from heaven.[2]

He continues, 'Mengist cannot be shared. It is gained or lost only by arms.'[3] Insofar as power is God-given and indivisible, some of the key concepts of democratic government, such as division of powers between branches of government and choice of ruler by election, do not fit well. A ruler is to be respected and feared, not popularly chosen. Lefort quotes a proverb: 'The sun that comes up tomorrow will be our sun, the government that rules tomorrow will be our government.'[4]

Lefort is no cultural determinist, but earlier generations of scholars were. Writing from more of an Orientalist than an Africanist tradition, such writers treated Ethiopia as an anomaly, akin to an Asian state transplanted into Africa.[5] Commensurately, Africanists too often neglected Ethiopia. For example, Jean-François Bayart did not write about Ethiopia, on the grounds that its 'great tradition' of power and statecraft did not fit his account of the 'politics of the belly'.[6] This is a shame because closer study of Ethiopian imperial governance, including its regional and international diplomacy, in reality demonstrates that the politics of the court and interstate relations are 'ordinary' in precisely the sense that Bayart uses for politics elsewhere.

In ruling Ethiopia in the modern era, Haile Selassie showed what Bayart calls a 'Janus face': the progressive advocate of non-racial multilateralism abroad, and the traditional autocrat at home. In the capital, his government had some modernist bureaucratic trappings but was also a 'rhizome state' that sprouted everywhere – landlords, armed settlers, even priests, were representatives of the Crown. Combining temporal and spiritual authority, using the symbolic resources of rule, involving the Crown in both political and economic activities, the Emperor tried to be everywhere. He sat at the hub of a patronage system, in which he circulated members of the elite in and out of favour, and dispensed rewards (material and symbolic) and licensed the use of force through the feudal and armed settler systems and plunder of the lowland peripheries. All of this can also be seen as an apparatus for renting loyalties, keeping the system as inexpensive as possible.

Dame Margery Perham described Ethiopia as having institutions of government only in the capital, citing 'an official British report of 1906 [which] states that [Emperor] Menelik is an absolute despot and a few paragraphs later remarks that his power does not extend twenty miles beyond his palace'.[7] A century on, Meles Zenawi also argued that the actual presence of the imperial state scarcely reached beyond towns and army garrisons: 'for the majority of Ethiopians, the state was non-existent'.[8] This elaborate edifice was swept away, he said, by a taxi drivers' strike and less than half a dozen tanks. Meles continued his critique of the Dergue, which had built a vast military and administrative apparatus, but on very shaky foundations, as it lacked popular consent. People took every opportunity to escape, not least military conscripts who threw down their guns and surrendered at every opportunity.

Meles concluded that while custom and fear were two useful instruments of rule, they would only be effective if the main instrument were to be the delivery of real benefits to the people, with sufficient consistency and impact that thought patterns and expectations were to change. In short, governing Ethiopia demanded a project of making a different mode of governance hegemonic, in the sense (following Antonio Gramsci) of being thoroughly internalized. Hence one of the challenges of his government was for people to experience real state institutions, rather than merely the idea of being governed.

Historically, Ethiopia was governed as a military aristocracy that could be penetrated by men who built up wealth and military power on the borderlands. The social bandit is a recurrent figure in Ethiopian history. The Emperor Teodros II (who ruled from 1855 to 1868) was born Kassa Haile, a minor notable who acquired power and riches on the ungoverned frontiers of the realm, using these to seize power. Another theme is the wily courtier who outwits his rivals. The ascent of Ras Teferra Mekonnen to become Emperor Haile Selassie I was never preordained, and relied on his political skills to win first place in the Solomonic lineage.

The revolution is another crux of the paradox of Ethiopian statehood. Revolution is meaningful only when there is a state apparatus to overturn. By the early 1970s, the entire young intelligentsia of Ethiopia had embraced Marxism, as the scripture of modernity,[9] and the country then went through a revolution that, in rhetoric, symbolism, theatre and trajectory, resembled its sanguinary forerunners in France and Russia. Sometimes, indeed, Ethiopian revolutionaries seemed to be 'fighting over revolutions other than their own'.[10] Without doubt, many radical students and some army officers were absolutely sincere in their intent to create a transformed, modern socialist Ethiopia. They subjected themselves to extraordinary party discipline, up to death, and made huge personal sacrifices in pursuit of these ideals.

The imperial system disintegrated in 1974–5: the violence that followed was to destroy challengers to the Provisional Military

Administrative Committee (known as the Dergue) under Major (later Colonel) Mengistu Haile Mariam. The Red Terror in the cities killed tens of thousands and destroyed organized urban opposition. In the provinces, a plethora of nationalist and separatist movements had emerged as the old order fell apart, and these also threatened the new military rulers. In 1977, in response to the Somali invasion, the Dergue was able to call on nationalist sentiment and energy, and Soviet and Cuban military support. The counter-offensives not only drove out the Somali army but positioned the Ethiopian army to destroy multiple insurgencies in the south of the country.[11] The war against the Eritrean movements scored tactical successes but was unable to dislodge the EPLF. Meanwhile the Dergue created the largest army in sub-Saharan Africa.[12] The old hierarchy was decapitated and in its place was a massive military-party apparatus, a 'rage of numbers' of men and Soviet armaments.[13] A single party – the Workers Party of Ethiopia – became the mechanism for state patronage and the only ladder for individuals to gain career advancement. By 1980, a 'garrison socialist' government was consolidated.[14]

Throughout these titanic disruptions, important components of government remained, commandeered to the service of the new political masters.[15] For example, despite losing many members to political exile, the Ministry of Finance and Central Bank of Ethiopia maintained fiscal discipline, the Ministry of Foreign Affairs remained professional, and new institutions such as the Relief and Rehabilitation Commission and the Agricultural Marketing Corporation diligently pursued their tasks. The idea of a state was more important than who was ruling it.

Effective opposition was violently winnowed down to the EPLF and the Tigrayan People's Liberation Front (TPLF), both of which were centralized revolutionary military vanguards based in the highlands, each of which practised (at that time) their own version of garrison socialism, on a smaller and more intense scale. The forces of the southern and eastern peripheries, the Oromo, Somali, Sidama and Afar resistance fronts, were reduced to protracted but low-level insurgencies, unable to challenge the territorial control or political domination of the centre. And smaller insurgencies on the western borderlands, among the people of Gambella and Beni Shangul, and the western Oromo, sputtered on with the support of Sudan and the EPLF, also without significant military effect. However, the political import of these persistent rebellions should not be underestimated. They posed an ideological challenge to a unitary state, and that agenda returned with a vengeance in 1991, when they re-emerged to fill the political vacuum in large parts of the country following the defeat of the Dergue. The principle of national self-determination, widely if imprecisely known as ethnic federalism, was the logical outcome of this.

In Eritrea and Tigray, internecine fighting among resistance groups and the onslaughts of the army, in a brutal process of survival of the best organized, most ruthless and luckiest, were led by the EPLF and TPLF as the sole military-political contenders. The TPLF went on to create, from the remnants of other regional/national fronts, the Ethiopian People's Revolutionary Democratic Front (EPRDF). With more meagre resources than its Eritrean counterpart, the TPLF/EPRDF waged an extraordinarily effective political-military struggle. Rather than an adaptation of the EPLF's exercise in building a total society in the liberated zone, the TPLF/EPRDF approach was a perfection of a Maoist people's war, in which the front line was not a series of tenaciously defended trenches, but the allegiance of the people, among whom the front members lived. One TPLF slogan was: 'the people, politicized, mobilized and armed, can never be ruled against their will'. The ideological differences between the EPLF and TPLF led to a split at the height of the war.[16] While tactically disadvantageous to both, this split makes sense as a symptom of how seriously the leadership of the TPLF took its exercises in theorizing its struggle. Its ruling committees gave enormous attention to organizing combat forces, in such a way that a small attacking force could repeatedly destroy a larger defending force, which it did principally by means of targeting the front-line command and control capabilities of the enemy, leaving the majority of the defenders unable to fight intelligently. Even greater thought was devoted to the politics of the armed struggle, and ensuring that the political capabilities of the front did not fall behind its military prowess. Indeed, in 1989, the EPRDF leadership made its assessment that the military defeat of the government was now certain, but that the Front was not yet in a position to take *political* control of Ethiopia. Hence the military advance was deliberately slowed while political preparations were made, principally trying to develop political parties based in other Ethiopian nationalities such as the Oromo, waiting for the right moment to strike the final blow, which was delivered in February 1991 and took three months to unfold.

The key moment in the struggle had occurred some years before. In 1983–5, the TPLF leadership assessed that the greatest threat they faced was the destruction of the Tigrayan people in a famine that was generated in large part by the government's military strategy. Feeding and protecting the people rather than winning battles became the strategic priority. This included operations such as the organized evacuation of villagers to refugee camps in Sudan, building a road for relief supplies and targeting government grain stores to redistribute the food. This was the point of potential collapse for northern Ethiopia, when the fundamental societal variables were at a point at which survival was in doubt. The TPLF leadership not only survived this collective near-death experience, but from it forged what might be called a social contract for survival with its peasant support base.[17] Within the collective leadership of the TPLF, Meles was elected to the political bureau in 1983, with responsibility for training and propaganda. This gave him a strong base to influence the middle ranks of the Front and set a political agenda, and rise to become secretary general of the Front and its vanguard party, the Marxist-Leninist League of Tigray. What distinguished Meles was his formidable intellect. The arguments were lengthy and thorough: the TPLF out-thought its enemies.

Consequently, on taking power in 1991, the EPRDF was already 'seeing like a state' – or, to be precise, like a government. In the final months of its campaign, it had taken care to show that it would govern responsibly, for example, by allowing school students in the areas it controlled to sit for their exams, and allowing the examiners across the front lines to collect and grade the scripts. EPRDF forces entered Addis Ababa on 28 May, just three days before salaries and pensions were due – which were paid on time.[18] Government officials were instructed to return to work, which they did, and the institutional life of the state continued with modest disruption. The defeated army was disarmed, most of its members demobilized, and others absorbed into the EPRDF army, which in due course became the national armed forces. One of the most remarkable developments of modern Ethiopia is how the dispersal of control over the means of violence was ended after 1991. The national armed forces and security services, while constitutionally independent of the ruling party, emerged from the Front itself.

On a day-to-day level, Ethiopian governmental institutions are rule-bound to a fault. Officials are concerned, even obsessed, with regulations. Throughout revolutionary changes, bureaucracies have continued to function. They frequently frustrate their political masters as well as the ordinary people because of their resistance to reform. Ethiopian civil servants may choose to be studiously indifferent to political directives with which they disagree, but they invariably shelter their obstruction behind procedural detail. After taking power, the EPRDF leadership considered the civil service 'the next enemy we have to fight now we have overcome the Dergue'.[19] The strategy for re-orienting the bureaucracy was massive expansion, by creating a civil service college and training a new cadre of officials, many of them former EPRDF fighters. Later, the EPRDF sought to politicize the civil service in its own image.

Meles Zenawi in Government: Theory and Practice

Meles Zenawi developed a well-elaborated theory for how Ethiopia should escape from its predicament. He never had the chance fully to articulate this during his lifetime, but he published one book chapter and was working on a doctoral thesis, parts of which are available online.[20] In addition, Meles authored the Ethiopian Foreign Affairs and National Security Policy and Strategy,[21] which shows how his doctrine of national security was fully integrated with his theory of political economy. In a series of seminars held between 2008 and 2012, he explained his theory and its application at some length to a small group of political scientists and economists, who met in his office. I was one of them.

Meles argued that the rentier-predatory nature of the early post-colonial African state, compounded by external shocks, led in the 1980s to life-threatening crisis. The international response to this was neo-liberal economic reform. According to Meles, these reforms may have slowed the pace of economic deterioration but they did not address the fundamental issue, which was not the bloated size of the African state but its rentierist nature: 'you can not change a rent-seeking political economy by reducing the size and role of the state'.[22] In escaping one dead end, neo-liberal reform led African economies into a different dead end.

Meles's conclusion was that an activist state is needed to clamp down on rent-seeking activity and promote growth: 'Development is a political process first and economic and social process later. It is the creation of a political set-up that is conducive to accelerated development that sets the ball of development rolling.'[23] In Mushtaq Khan's terminology, his strategy was 'growth-enhancing' rather than 'market-enhancing'.[24] Speaking in 2010, Meles summarized how the EPRDF thinking had evolved:

For the first ten years after we took over, we were bewildered by the changes. The New World Order was very visible and especially in this part of the world. The prospect of an independent line appeared very bleak. So we froze the party. We fought a rearguard war to not priva-tize too much. We sent delegations across Africa to ask, how to handle the IMF? They said, 'say what they want you to say and do what you can get away with.' We said, 'we are a mass movement and cannot mislead the masses, we cannot do that.' But we began to change to a rent-seeking party. From the peasant to the very top, we were degenerating.

The stupidest event, the war with Eritrea, accelerated it. The war was started by idiots in Eritrea, but the response was equally stupid. We were more interested in protecting the interests of some groups than in the strategic national interest.

Meles said, 'The party decided the issue of war and peace with Eritrea, not the state. The war was prosecuted from party HQ.' He went on to describe how in the middle of the war, the party debated Ethiopia's war aims. Meles's view was that the country's central task remained the conquest of poverty, without which it would forever be vulnerable to internal collapse and external threat. After the war he expounded the same arguments in writing. He decried 'jingoism with an empty stomach'[25] and the obsessive preoccupation with the paraphernalia of physical security, which only undermined national development and therefore exposed Ethiopia to greater risk: 'our defense capability should not be built in a way that would have a detrimental influence on our economy'.[26] He observed that the vast military capability of the Dergue had not stopped it from being utterly defeated. Meles wrote, 'national pride is not a policy objective'.[27]

But while Meles sharpened his arguments, he lost the vote. During long sessions in 1999, 'The leadership formally decided, we would fight until our economy grinds to a halt. The vote was eighteen to two in the EPRDF Secretariat.[28] That showed that the elite had lost touch and had become a self-serving elite.' In line with democratic centralist rules, Meles implemented the agreed-upon decision, though he caused further controversy when, during the victorious military offensive of June 2000, he halted the advance of Ethiopian troops deep into Eritrea. Immediately after the war, the debate within the EPRDF resumed, with the issues broadened to include the fate of the revolutionary vanguard (the Marxist-Leninist League of Tigray, which had been silently forgotten in 1991), and the political-economic direction of the regime.

Meles's critics argued that he had been soft on Eritrea, running down Ethiopia's defences and leaving the country vulnerable to attack, and then, at the point of victory, preventing the army from destroying the EPLF completely. They argued that he had become a 'capitalist roader' – an agent of the bourgeoisie within the socialist movement – supporting a 'kulak line' in favour of richer peasant farmers and urban bourgeoisie, thereby submitting to imperialism. These references to historic debates within Marxism are instructive in showing the seriousness with which the EPRDF leadership takes doctrine and argument. Meles proved better versed in Marxist-Leninism than his adversaries, and also a master of procedural tactics. The core of his argument was that only accelerated economic growth could assure the security, even the survival, of the country, and that the question was not Communism versus capitalism, but rent-seeking versus revolutionary democracy. For Meles, Marxist-Leninism was not about building a socialist society now, but a question of developing the country's political economy to establish the class basis for development and democracy. He argued, 'let's be public about building a capitalist society'.

Each of the four parties constituting the EPRDF met and deliberated in parallel, but the key debate was within the TPLF. For a whole month, the TPLF Central Committee debated, day in and day out. Meles's group won by two votes, at which point his adversaries walked out, thereby surrendering the ruling apparatus to Meles, who said:

> Then the debate became smooth in all four groups, the revolutionary democracy line dominant. This started the renewal of the movement, beginning with the peasants. We said, you have to be rich, you have to be at the forefront of development. We gave them three tasks: get rich, teach others to get rich, and recruit others to the party. We targeted progressive farmers and had a similar process in the cities. It took two to three years. They were dark years, with the economy going down. Now it is more healthy.

In shifting the debate to theory, Meles's adversaries made a mistake, as this was the prime minister's favoured terrain for argument. They would have been better served by focusing on the organizational and political health of the EPRDF and governing institutions, because this was where Meles was weak. His political praxis became detached from the collective leadership and party apparatus, and he was increasingly running party and government as a one-man show. His 'renewal' inverted the former collective debate and decision-making: it was driven by Meles himself.

Meles's theory of the democratic developmental state drew from the experiences of Asian countries (most particularly South Korea and Taiwan), and applied the lessons to the very different circumstances of Ethiopia – landlocked, ethnically diverse, lacking the US security umbrella and the preferential market access that was associated with being an American ally at the height of the Cold War. His definition of the developmental state had the following components.

One, autonomy from the private sector. The developmental state should use and guide the private sector, but also be interdependent with the private sector. The class base of such a state should be an atomized and satisfied peasantry (as with the Bonapartist regime from the 1840s to the 1860s which is the grandfather of the developmental state). With the socially transformed peasantry as its bedrock, the developmental coalition will have the means to stamp out rent-seeking. The state should control the commanding heights of the economy so as to be able to lead the private sector (banks, utilities, some key production sectors).

Two, obsession with development. Development should be a matter of national survival. The ideology should be that growth is survival.

Three, hegemony (in the Gramscian sense) of developmental discourse. This requires a change in outlook and attitudes by state personnel and the productive sectors. Development is not a process of capital accumulation but should be defined as technological capacity development. Hence there needs to be a focus on education, especially secondary and tertiary, research and development. The day-to-day practice of producing goods contributes to this, in a dialectical approach to capacity building.

Meles argued that if Ethiopia were able to sustain fast growth for fifteen or twenty years, and thereby to become a middle-income country, that growth would, in itself, change social attitudes and political-economic behaviour. In order to achieve the necessary growth of 10 per cent or so per annum, all government activities would need to be focused on incentivizing growth and prohibiting or penalizing rent-seeking. Meles liked to give the example of corrupt customs officials in Taiwan, who exacted bribes worth 12 per cent of the value of imports of consumer goods, while not demanding bribes on imported capital goods, illustrating how value creation had been internalized in this way – so that even the thieves followed the norm.

Key to this strategy was the capture and allocation of rent by an activist state. Meles did not believe that rent could or should be eliminated, but rather that a developmental state should monopolize rents and allocate them strategically for value creation over the long term. Another way of framing this strategy is that the funds available for the ruler's political budget should be invested in development and state-building, not in maintaining or building a political base. Meles's investment policy, institution-building and political authoritarianism were all cut from the same theoretical cloth. In the categorization of the African Power and Politics Programme,[29] Ethiopia is an exemplar of long-horizon, centralized rent utilization, a 'developmental patrimonialism' that has the potential of securing sustainable growth.[30]

Ethiopia's investment policy has focused on industrialization including agricultural industries. The main vehicle for implementing this has been state-owned enterprises and endowment funds. The largest of these, the Endowment Fund for the Rehabilitation of Tigray (EFFORT), and several other party-owned enterprises were planned in the last days of the armed struggle and set up shortly after 1991. The initial aims were for the EPRDF to build its own economic and business base, and to invest in places that had been neglected because of poverty and war, so that the peasants would benefit from the post-war recovery.

In their study of the endowment funds, Sarah Vaughan and Mesfin Gebremeskel[31] document their role in the government's development strategy. While EFFORT and other endowment funds operate in profitable conventional sectors (for example, transport and leather processing) they also target investment to riskier and more innovative fields. They benefit from close association with the ruling party, with access to credit and land leases. Some of their business practices, for example, tax exemptions and preferential bidding for government procurement, may shade into crony capitalism, but they are scrutinized and regulated. Vaugan and Gebremeskel note:

> Our analysis suggests that it is unlikely that the endowment-owned companies in Ethiopia will be short-lived, however little they accord with international funder preference. The role that EFFORT-owned companies play in Ethiopia shows some important differences with similar commercial ventures in other countries. They do not seem to provide direct financial subsidies to the ruling party and political elite as is the case in Rwanda. Nevertheless they provide indirect resources and public goods that feed wider social, political and developmental processes.[32]

They continue, observing some of the threats to this strategy of state-directed development:

> For developmental patrimonialism to be successful, it needs not only to grow the pot [sic], but also to ensure reasonably equitable and sustainable access to it. In a transition economy of low productivity, poorly co-ordinated markets and opportunistic rents, unregulated entrepreneurialism has frequently led to non-developmental kleptocracy. It is not surprising that in just such a transitional context, the Ethiopian government is reluctant to rely on a private sector, some elements of which it sees as rent-seeking, law-breaking and uncooperative. Working instead with immediate political colleagues who are not only trusted, but who are 'on the inside' as far as the inner workings

of the state are concerned, undoubtedly carries an alternative set of risks, not least the political capture of resources which are not then used to serve economically productive or sustainable developmental ends.[33]

For Meles, the risk of internal inefficiency and corruption was less than the danger of pervasive and politically influential rent-seeking that would follow the privatization of land ownership and liberalization of the telecoms, power and financial sectors. He readily conceded that mistakes were made in economic management, but argued that the imperative of fast growth meant that it was better to make errors of commission and learn on the job than to be overly cautious and slow the economy. And, indeed, Ethiopia visibly developed under EPRDF rule, with new roads, bridges, dams, electrification, schools and health centres. This was the beginning of a transformation that, if sustained for another two decades, would truly change the face of the country.

Meles's critique of neo-liberalism was political as well as economic. He argued that political liberalization in a small open economy would simply deregulate political rent-seeking: 'Initially therefore the risk of democratic politics becoming riddled with patronage and rent-seeking will be there.'[34] He condemned liberal formulae in poor countries as 'trickle-up democracy' and feared a 'no-choice democracy' in which factions contested for which one could best loot the state. As a sitting head of government, Meles was careful never to criticize another African state. But he gave an interesting reaction to a paper in which I analysed the post-electoral violence in Kenya in 2007/08 as the culmination of a twenty-year process, during which the Kenyan party leaders' demand for ever-larger political budgets to pay for electoral competition served as the engine of plundering public money, stripping state assets and the resort to thuggery by party 'youth wings'.[35] Meles commented that even a well-established centralized government could quickly be pulled down by rampant rent-seeking in the political sphere.

The question follows: what kind of democracy is necessary – and possible – under these circumstances? Or, as Meles put it, 'how can the developmental state clean up the mess of patronage and rent-seeking in the initial stages of its establishment by anything other than undemocratic means?'[36] After 2005, Ethiopia's democratic trappings looked increasingly threadbare, and Meles's style of governance appeared more securitized and vanguardist.

The 2005 election campaign was the most open in Ethiopia's history, with vigorous public debate on a wide range of issues. The aftermath of the election was a disaster for democracy. The EPRDF went into the election weak and complacent. Meles said, 'we lost millions of votes. We were wiped out in the cities. The rent-seeking coalition was powerful enough to shake us. It was a difficult period.'[37] The opposition did not win, but it 'tried to force a decision', in Meles's words. It claimed overall victory based on early results. Opposition leaders refused to take their seats in parliament and challenge the government through constitutional means, and instead took to the streets. Meles publicly dismissed and derided the opposition, but he was deeply concerned at his party's failure to achieve hegemony – in both senses, of dominating the political landscape and internalizing its philosophy among the people.

In line with the best EPRDF tradition, Meles took the time to analyse the party's failure, and draw lessons. He explained that the EPRDF had been slow in establishing a social base in the cities, and (especially) had not drawn up policies that brought tangible benefits to urban areas.[38] The opposition was led by an elite that remained 'irritated by rhetoric, not transformed by our policies, and preoccupied with lingering issues about definition of Ethiopia. Some were ultra-patriotic, seeing us as a sin against the idea of Ethiopia'. In the rural areas, 'many still voted for us, others were sending a message'.

Internationally, Meles faced what he called a 'counter-revolution'. The head of the European Union election observer group, Ana Gomes, who declared the 2005 election result for the opposition, may have misspoken, but she represented international intolerance for illiberal politics. After the government crackdown on opposition protestors, human rights organizations and western governments vigorously condemned Ethiopia. Meles was confident that his government would ride out the storm: the US would continue to support Ethiopia because of counter-terrorism, and the Europeans would speak harsh words but continue their aid because Ethiopia was a shining example of poverty reduction and progress towards the Millennium Development Goals. He was right.

Having analysed his predicament, Meles decided that it was necessary to set the agenda, not react to it. Part of his task was international: he needed to explain the theory of the 'democratic developmental state' to the international academic and policy communities. Meles had many admirers among development economists, most notably Joseph Stiglitz, chief economist at the World Bank. Stiglitz writes that Meles 'showed deeper understanding of economic principles – and certainly a greater knowledge of the circumstances of his country – than many of the international economic bureaucrats I have known',[39] and credits him with having convinced the IMF to change its position on key policy issues.

Meles succeeded in winning supporters for his concept of a growth-led developmental state.[40] More challenging was the task of explaining that his project was a *democratic* developmental state. Democracy was not just a choice, Meles said, but a necessity: while historic Asian developmental states had been authoritarian, such authoritarianism was no longer feasible in an interconnected world and, in Africa's ethnically diverse societies, democratic legitimacy was a *sine qua non*. Inclusivity and decentralization were vital components of democracy, Meles argued, and Ethiopia's federal Constitution reflected this. He said his preference was to have two competing parties, each of which stood for developmental values, but in their absence the option would be a stable dominant party or dominant coalition, such as Japan or Sweden enjoyed in post-war decades. But Meles's theory of democracy was, in the end, postponing it until Ethiopia had achieved middle-income status.

Within Ethiopia, Meles's appraisal of 2005 led him to prioritize the second and third pillars of the developmental state: obsession with growth and the hegemony of developmentalism. He drew three concentric circles, representing: leadership; government and party cadres; and the mass organizations and local officialdom.

The innermost circle was the engine room of leadership. This was Meles's office, where Meles's own theoretical papers were debated with a close circle, including foreign intellectuals, seeking frank critique. Members of the EPRDF leadership attended, but largely as listeners. Once a conclusion had been reached, it was promulgated as doctrine for the rest.

The second circle was the government bureaucracy and institutions. Meles wrote policy documents for civil servants, which did not go into the political and ideological debates, or explain the political-economy framework. The need for these policy documents – and the fact that they dealt lightly with the EPRDF ideology – shows that the party still faced problems in bending the civil service to its philosophy. Governmental institutions are hidebound and bureaucrats are skilled at subverting political decisions through procrastination, sabotage or – that most effective of bureaucratic measures – strict working to rule.

The third circle was the mass organizations of the party. Meles again was the author of three long pamphlets, which formed the material for training party leaders across the country, as well as students. These were written to introduce and popularize the doctrine and vocabulary that was intended to reorient people's thinking. The party held hundreds of workshops in which tens of thousands of local party leaders reflected on the relevance of the democratic developmental theory to their own experience. The new vocabulary was also promulgated in every public pronouncement and across the media. Thus, the label 'rent seeker' became the favoured term of condemnation, used against any individual or group that was identified as obstructing national development plans. By contrast, 'developmental capitalists' are those who are patriotically pursuing value-creation and sustainable growth. Mega schemes such as the hydropower dams – notably the Great Ethiopian Renaissance Dam on the Nile – became a public rallying cry, an opportunity for citizens to contribute and to identify proudly with their nation's development.

Ultimately, Meles's democratic developmentalism was more a personal than a collective exercise, and the outcome was intellectually rigorous but organizationally dysfunctional. Everyday governmental issues were neglected. Meles's challenge was the practice. The TPLF had won its war on the basis of an organic connection between theory and practice, with the painstaking process of collective deliberation and decision-making serving as the gearbox that connected the controls to the engine. In place of these collective and consultative processes, Meles turned to pervasive public education and material incentives. After 2005, the EPRDF began a huge recruitment drive, expanding from 760,000 members to over 4 million in three years.[41] Party members had preferential access to state-allocated benefits, ranging from enrolment in higher education to subsidized fertilizer and small-scale credit. Sometimes they were the only ones who could get these benefits. Local administrative councils were expanded from about 600,000 members to 3.5 million.[42] Public-sector employees also obtained state-directed benefits. Speaking in 2008, Meles was confident that the EPRDF had consolidated the domestic political arena sufficiently, with one important proviso: 'Except in pastoral areas where there is no EPRDF presence and no basis for a democratic developmental state.'[43] In those peripheries, security was the priority, which was pursued using coercion and co-option.[44]

This policy rewarded unthinking compliance. While the numbers grew, the party infrastructure withered, and the EPRDF came to resemble the mass party of the former regime. Meles tried to justify this: he was sufficiently alarmed by the political challenges he faced to err on the side of emphasizing loyalty per se over informed and willing support. As noted by Kjetil Tronvoll:

> During the massive re-ideologization campaign undertaken after the
> 2005 elections, the EPRDF and the Prime Minister deliberately

employed an alarmist language, aiming to polarize the political landscape and to convince the people that, without EPRDF in power,
Ethiopia would turn into chaos.[45]

Tronvoll is unsympathetic to Meles's stridency and his readiness to
evoke alarm and fear. In reality, Meles himself was more worried than
he publicly admitted. He had a deep sense of the fragility of the
governing order, which he had expressed in the national security
white paper: 'failure to realize development and democracy has
resulted in our security being threatened.... The prospect of disintegration cannot be totally ruled out.'[46]

Co-equal as a threat was instability in the region. Meles was deeply
concerned with the potential of Eritrea, Somalia, Sudan and South
Sudan to imperil Ethiopia's developmental project. His rush to build
road and power infrastructure that linked Ethiopia with its neighbours was intended to advance both development and national security. Since 1994, I had discussed the challenge of Somalia with Meles,
providing him with a paper, 'Class and Power in a Stateless Somalia'.[47]
Meles liked to describe Somalia as the region's most perfect political
marketplace, in which no political rental contract could last longer
than a few months. In a 2006 update,[48] I identified the Islamic Courts
and their financiers as the potential basis for stabilizing the country,
in parallel to the way in which the mercantile class had laid the
foundations for working government in Somaliland. His response
was that my prescriptions would be workable if we were dealing with
Somalis only, but Eritrea had its agents in Mogadishu, and Ethiopia
could take no chances.

In 2011, Meles foresaw a 'perfect storm' of threats, in which a
post-Mubarak Egypt would externalize the blame for its internal
failings, turning against Ethiopia on the issue of the Nile, while also
combining forces with Saudi Arabia to support hostile forces in the
Horn of Africa.[49] He feared that Sudan would divide into an unstable
South, which would generate refugees and draw Ethiopia into its own
insoluble internal problems, and an embittered rump northern state,
which would become more Islamist and more oriented towards Egypt
and the Arab world. Should regional political strife and threats coin-
cide with domestic crisis, caused by routine buffeting from the liberalized global economic order, Ethiopia's national survival would, he
feared, be deeply jeopardized.

This sense of peril was the logic behind erecting barriers to entry
to Ethiopian political life, including laws that restricted foreign
financing for national NGOs, circumscribed the media and maintained government monopoly over internet and telecoms. Power in

all its forms – political, administrative, military and economic – became more concentrated, especially in the prime minister's office.

Was the strategy working? Ethiopia's economy performed well. But while Meles and his closest associates were obsessed with developmentalism, other Ethiopians were not. In 2008, he observed, 'The terms "rent-seeking" and "developmentalism" are common currency now, they are firmly entrenched in party discourse – but not social discourse.'[50] The project for a developmental state was not becoming hegemonic and Meles knew it. Just three months before his death, he made a candid assessment in a memorandum for the EPRDF Politbureau.[51] It reads like Meles's deathbed confession: 'Unless there is a strategic leadership capacity for implementation, having the policies right does not lead anywhere. We already have the right policies but we are still a long way from having the required strategic leadership capacity in place.'[52] He frankly identified the party leadership as the strategic weakness of the project, and discussed two problems it faced. The first was intellectual rigidity.

Our organization has never had its own policy 'think tank'. Policy research, design and implementation together have been the mission of the top political leadership of the party. This contributed to an effective policy process. There is no time wasted to lobby for a decision to be taken on a policy as the roles of policy researcher, decision-maker and implementer are given to the political leadership of the party. This is not usual in developed countries, in which policy study and research is done by universities, independent think tanks, and party-affiliated think tanks. Government ministries even have their own research and study wings. Policy research and study is a full-time job and also requires special knowledge. For this reason, it cannot be given to the political leadership of the party as its full-time job is different and it does not have the expertise required. Because we had elaborate policies, and elites outside the party were indifferent to these policy ideas, policy-making up to now remained the task of the political leadership of the party. We cannot continue this way.[53]

It is striking that Meles made no effort to distinguish between party and government. The second crucial problem was that of 'party membership and the recruitment process':

Party membership is voluntary. In principle, any Ethiopian who believes in the political programme of the party and is ready to meet required obligations to the party is eligible to be a member. Our party is a ruling party in power. Being a member of such a party can definitely provide a better job opportunity and access to power that can wrongly be used for self-enrichment. This gives the chance for rent collectors and opportunists to get into the party. The problem with the massive entry of rent-seeking individuals is not limited to their rent-seeking behaviour; but, their presence also repels genuine members from entering into the party as they don't want to be associated with such a crowd.[54]

Meles's proposed solution involved regular and relentless purging of the ranks – further military-style political command. He wanted to institutionalize his project, by bringing a new generation into leadership and stepping back from his own executive position in due course. But the gap between his own intellectual leadership and his followers was not narrowing at the time of his death on 20 August 2012.

Is State Building (Still) Possible?

For Meles's successors, continuing with the democratic developmental project requires exceptional political management skills.

Prime Minister Haile Mariam Dessalegn took over a prime minister's office that had become an apparatus for feeding information to Meles, for him to make the assessment and decision. None among the next layer of political leaders and security officers possessed the overall information or command required for the control of the ruling machinery, the single-minded pursuit of development and the resolute allocation of rent for such purposes.[55] The apparatus had two major faults. One was that the military command and security and intelligence services were subservient to Meles, not because of his position as prime minister, but because he served as the supreme intelligence, security and military analyst, and because he was a member of the political-military inner circle that had defeated the Dergue and run the country thereafter. None of his potential successors possessed those attributes in combination. The second was that the very effectiveness of centralization of rent allocation meant that the funds potentially available for use at the leadership's discretion were high indeed. The potential for political budgeting or corruption is commensurately high.

Members of the EPRDF leadership in general have a modest lifestyle and have devoted their efforts to the interests of the party and the nation. State rents and political budgets have become synonymous, allocated for public goods. This is possible because competitive politics has been almost entirely squeezed out of Ethiopian national life, to be replaced by a doctrinal commitment to developmentalism, by party and government alike. Ethiopia's government institutions have always been politicized, but never before have these institutions been so large and pervasive, and so explicitly dedicated to the political programme of a dominant party. Centralization has made procedures subject to political fiat. The continuing institutionalization of Ethiopian political life is less a case of rule *of* law and procedure than rule *by* law and procedure.

The immediate challenge for Ethiopia is the nature of competition within the political leadership of the EPRDF and the security services and army. Control over state rents is distributed among this elite, whose members have the power to appropriate those rents for personal enrichment (an 'elite cartel' model of systemic corruption[56]), for factional political budgets, or for both. Domestically, this system is sufficiently entrenched that it can deter new entrants. But Ethiopia is located in a troublesome neighbourhood, and navigating the turbulence of the region demands clear analysis and cohesive action, which the post-Meles leadership has yet to demonstrate. The army's rush into military deployment in South Sudan is an example of narrow interests overriding strategic wisdom.

Meles posed the question of how to achieve development and democracy in a country with a small open economy and a government with limited latitude for policy. It is the correct question and thus far it has no answer. Despite Ethiopia's troubles, it is still the leading candidate for establishing a developmental, institutionalized state in the Horn of Africa. The difficulties it is encountering and the uncertainty of its prospects are testament to the strength of the countervailing forces of the political marketplace.

11

Transnational Patronage
and Dollarization

The 'Non-Integrated Gap'

Strategists for the George W. Bush administration identified an 'arc of instability' stretching from West Africa to Afghanistan, with the Horn of Africa in the middle. Thomas Barnett, in *The Pentagon's New Map*,[1] calls this the 'non-integrated gap', arguing that this part of the world is not integrated into the global system. In this chapter, I argue the converse: that this region is actually well integrated, and is part of a global patronage system, in which political loyalties are instrumentalized and dollarized in a regional political marketplace.

Despite my best efforts, I have followed almost every writer in political science or current history, and used the internationally recognized country as my main unit of analysis. It is harder to do this in north-east Africa than elsewhere, because each of the three larger countries has been divided, and studying this region makes a mockery of the distinction between internal wars and international wars. The integration of conflicts is not captured by metaphors such as 'spill-over' or 'contagion'. It is better analysed through the lens of a transnationally integrated political marketplace.

The chapter begins with key elements of the 'new rentierism', introduced in chapter 3, which has emerged since the turn of the millennium. I then turn to the role of regional organizations, particularly the AU, and their role in political management and the 'new peacekeeping': militarized models for peace enforcement and atrocity prevention.

The Commodities Boom

Africa's twenty-first-century commodities boom was kick-started by US interest in the African oil sector, but its main engine has been Asia. Chinese and other Asian demands for oil and other minerals, and land for food, biofuels and land banking, have driven a surge of investment into Africa. In turn, this has generated investment in transport, power and communications infrastructure, and new prosperity. Asian investors, especially China, deal with governments and have little interest in domestic political issues in their target countries. As well as offering a state-led model of development, the Asian dethroning of the neo-liberal model as the sole alternative has allowed African leaders to innovate, though the only one to have taken the opportunity in a deliberate and strategic manner was Meles Zenawi.

Africa's oil production has boomed in the last fifteen years, and other industrial minerals – such as Eritrea's gold and copper – are following. Sudan started exporting oil in 1999, Chad followed in 2003, and Uganda and Kenya are set on the same path. In each of these countries, oil income is set to last between ten and thirty years, and will be much less than dreamed if oil prices stay low: it is a brief and precarious windfall. It is, however, enough to centralize the political budget and patronage system. These funds provide an opportunity for investment in public goods, but nowhere has this opportunity been seized. Rather, as illustrated by Chad, South Sudan and Sudan, rulers consistently prioritize political funding over state-building. The secondary investments in construction, real estate, energy and transport also tend to generate crony capitalism riven by corruption.

Oil states share a number of characteristics: their income is from enclaves with few connections to the wider economy; oil is a strategic commodity so it attracts security and foreign-policy interests; the price is volatile and the resource is depletable, so that proper management requires long-term planning; and almost no oil states husband their resource in a careful manner.[2] It is almost as though oil is an addictive narcotic drug: however much a country has, it craves more. This is the infamous 'resource curse': the propensity of oil-producing countries to suffer armed conflict and pervasive rent-seeking at all levels of society.

So far, no country in the Horn has gone through the entire cycle to the point of exhaustion of mineral rents, though post-secession Sudan is heading in that direction, and the 2015 oil price slump may dampen the twenty-first-century scramble for Africa's fossil fuels. If we include Yemen in our wider region – which is defensible on the basis of proximity and similarities of political economy – we can see how this may play out as oil rents diminish. Sarah Phillips has described the impact of the oil boom on Yemen:[3] 'In a very short period of time, the balance of power switched from a remittance-rich, relatively autonomous citizenry and a poor state, to a poor and relatively dependent citizenry and an oil-rich state.' We could add that competitive patrimonialism also increased. Saudi Arabia intensified its practice of direct payments to Yemeni tribal leaders, making the domestic political marketplace more competitive, and compelling the Yemeni government to spend more of its own loyalty payments. As the oil has dried up, the Yemenis are left with a highly deregulated political marketplace, and the government lacks the political finance for centralized management.

Artisanal minerals commonly determine a different distribution of power in a political marketplace, in favour of local political entrepreneurs. Minerals such as alluvial gold and diamonds, or near-surface coltan, can be extracted using simple technologies and exported by truck or light aircraft. The modest investments needed can be provided by small-scale businessmen who deal directly with provincial elites, such as army officers, rebel commanders or local chiefs. In a political market, these resources will directly accrue to those local elites, strengthening their bargaining vis-à-vis one another and central authorities. Therefore, unlike oil, or other minerals that require large-scale industrial investments, artisanal minerals tend to promote the decentralization of political authority. One example of this is gold in Sudan, which has empowered Darfurian potentates and military entrepreneurs. A better-known example is the mineral riches of the eastern DRC, which have provided a ready source of income for diverse groups, including the armies of neighbouring countries. This pattern of distributed political finance is not a good advertisement for the wider dispersal of mineral rents across society. But it does point to a potential policy agenda of dividing or atomizing rents, as a means of mitigating the political and economic impacts of the resource curse.

The 'great African land grab'[4] is a once-only opportunity for asset-seizing by politicians, especially those who can use their sovereign privileges to make land law or their connections to circumvent laws. Leasing large tracts of land to domestic and foreign corporations often amounts to mortgaging the future for immediate cash. The land grab is unfolding in two waves. The first wave involves the formal transactions themselves, in which documents are signed and money changes hands. The second is the physical acquisition of the land, in which bulldozers and armed guards arrive to dispossess those who live on and use the land. In the time lag between the first and second waves, the hapless residents of these lands continue as before, unaware that what they had considered their birthright, their livelihood and the anchor of their culture has been sold from under their feet. While oil rents feed inequality, corruption and resentment, and artisanal minerals become the focus for political entrepreneurs' conflictual rent-seeking, land-grabbing is an insult to the moral fabric of community and a provocation to populist rebellion.

Illicit Finance

The scale of Africa's losses due to illicit financial flows has become so vast, overshadowing official aid and debt relief, that several anti-poverty campaigning organizations have made it their priority.[5] These organizations estimate that $50 billion each year is spirited out of the continent. Raymond Baker disaggregates these flows into three elements: commercial tax evasion (estimated at up to two thirds of the total), the laundering of the proceeds of crime (up to a third), and corrupt payments and the theft of state assets (3–5 per cent of the total).[6] By far the largest way that Africa is deprived of funds is through multinational companies mispricing the value of internal transactions between different subsidiaries, so that it pays taxes where it chooses – typically where those taxes are lowest.

My concern here is not the illicit financial flows themselves but the political-business rationale for domestic elites to allow this to happen. African politicians are not innocent in these transactions: they gain a share. This is smaller than what would be a fair payment to a national exchequer under (for instance) a unitary global taxation system, but a payoff that is clandestine and under their direct control, which they can use to enrich themselves or fund political budgets. It is a collusive exercise in defrauding the citizenry.

Thus, an oil company may calculate the price it pays itself for oil as it leaves (for example) Chad or South Sudan, in such a way that it maximizes its own profit, minimizes taxes paid and also pays a sum into the offshore accounts of the ruler and his coterie. These funds, now secretly and privately held, can be 'round-tripped' and returned home. These are the perfect political funds: only the account holder knows where they are and how much they are, and so can be used for all manner of political favours. They can be leveraged for further political services. For example, cash-strapped European politicians have been known to call on African leaders' beneficence, as members of the transnational ruling elite recognize one another's most pressing financial needs and find collusive ways of meeting them.[7]

The arms trade is a particularly notorious source of illicit finance. It has been informally estimated that 40 per cent of all bribery in international trade is associated with arms deals.[8] On the supply side, the business of manufacturing weapons has a curious economic logic: European countries want to maintain their production capacity but their domestic requirements are too small to make their products competitive, so they must export. Their products are the immediate successors of weapons built for the Cold War.

Tanks and jet fighters are rarely tested in action against their ostensible peer threats. For controlling a road junction against the threat of a militia, there is no difference between a T55 and a T72 tank except the higher cost and maintenance complexities of the latter. Similarly, the Sudanese airforce's preference is bombing civilian targets, which means that rolling bombs out of the cargo doors of Antonov transport planes is no less fearsome than an airstrike that uses an expensive fighter-bomber such as a MiG29. The Ethio–Eritrean war was a very unusual conflict in which both sides used third-generation fighter planes – but many of these on both sides were flown by Russian and Ukrainian mercenaries, who made sure not to shoot one another down.

High-end conventional weapons systems are vanity products. Consequently, arms manufacturers do not compete on the product specifications themselves, except in the same way that Porsche and Jaguar compete on their interior trim and hypothetical top speeds. The competition is on the side benefits: an elaborate apparatus of offsets, kickbacks and commodity barter (especially oil) for arms, and – in the case of the US and (to a lesser degree) France – the security pact that comes with being a major arms purchaser. At a time when the world's major weapons purchasers (particularly the US) have stagnant procurement budgets, the pressure on manufacturers to export is growing. Africa's defence budgets grew by 8.3 per cent in 2013, far above the world average.[9]

When generals are serious about war-fighting, they buy Landcruisers and small arms and rent militia. There is no shortage of bribery and corruption in these transactions and in the budgets of combat units – for example, payroll fraud and selling fuel – but the levels of finance involved are far lower. Fraud in supplying frontline units will show up in poor performance on the battlefield – and indeed it does, which is why armed conflict in a deregulated political marketplace is more often a matter of rough bargaining among political-military businessmen than testing armed forces in combat.

Uganda illustrates the nexus between political budgets and defence budgets, facilitated by arms procurement. President Yoweri Museveni maintains a high defence budget, which enables him to divert, without domestic challenge or international scrutiny, significant funds to his political budget at the same time as licensing army officers to accumulate private fortunes through commercial activities. The Ugandan journalist Andrew Mwenda analysed the counter-insurgency against the Lord's Resistance Army (LRA) in northern Uganda, during the 1990s up to 2006, as 'an integral part of Uganda's foreign-aid-driven reconstruction process... The threat from the north was turned into an opportunity.'[10] Mwenda does not subscribe to the conspiracy theory that Museveni deliberately prolonged the conflict, but argues rather that the war continuously presented opportunities which the president and military turned to their advantage. Most important of these opportunities was the chance to expand military spending beyond 2 per cent of GDP. Ugandan defence spending increased from $42 million in 1992 to $110 million in 2001 and $260 million in 2010. This had a particular advantage for Museveni, because Uganda's regular budget was subject to close donor scrutiny, so the opportunities for graft or politicization were diminished. The defence budget, by contrast, was off-limits for both foreign donors and national parliamentarians. Mwenda continues:

> As defence spending grew, so did procurement of military supplies become ever more riddled with inflated purchases of junk equipment – tanks, jet fighters, helicopter gunships and anti-tank guns, expired food rations and undersize uniforms. Ghost soldiers became so endemic in the military that by 2003 between one-third and two-thirds of the army were actually dead or missing. In 1998, Uganda had invaded Congo, and soldiers there began to plunder the resources of their mineral rich neighbor. From this point, military corruption and plunder became a key strategy through which Museveni rewarded army officers...In spite of huge increases in the size of the defence budget, the money was not going into the army.[11]

Since 2009, this campaign has been extended well beyond Uganda's borders. Ugandan troops have been deployed in South Sudan and CAR. With the enthusiastic backing of the Kony 2012 campaign in America, it is legitimized, financed and supported by the US and AU. This provides a perfect pretext for maintaining an inflated defence budget, which keeps army officers content and greases the wheels of the patronage machine. Meanwhile, Uganda is able to support clients in South Sudan (notably JEM) and in CAR, and its officers can pursue business interests such as commercial logging.

Aid Rents and Global Governance

During the darkest years of the late 1980s and into the violent confusion of the 1990s, international aid was an important source of basic sustenance, a resource transfer and a source of political rent. Practitioners and critics of official development aid and humanitarian relief engaged in some fierce debates on, among other things, the ethics of assistance in war zones and political conditionalities attached to governmental aid. These questions were not resolved: members of the 'humanitarian international'[12] learned some painful lessons from its efforts in the war zones of the Horn and Central Africa. The debates themselves were refashioned a decade later when those involved in practical relief efforts found themselves at loggerheads with (among others) the Save Darfur movement.[13] The Darfur rebels were uninterested in the political administration of a liberated area and had little direct access to relief aid – which was, by this time, much more tightly monitored than before – and instead focused their efforts on what we might call 'human rights rent', which is the assistance and political leverage that local political entrepreneurs can obtain from international actors, by dint of solidarity for their cause.[14] Another opening is 'negotiation rent': political entrepreneurs try to secure a seat at an internationally sponsored mediation, which brings the immediate benefits of per diems and the bigger potentials of international networks and leverage, which may translate into a formal role in a rent-allocation peace deal.

But the most significant change over the fifteen years from Operation Restore Hope to Save Darfur was, however, that humanitarian relief simply became relatively less important as a source of money. In the early 1990s, southern Sudanese commanders contrived starvation camps in order to attract food aid that they could then loot to supply their troops. By the time of the 2013 civil war, bags of maize and sorghum were small change for South Sudan's petro-kleptocrats.

Official aid is more significant. In a rough parallel to the dual structure of the minerals business, official development aid (ODA) functions differently from the artisanal humanitarian NGO relief. In 1999, following a decade of decline, ODA to Africa began a sharp increase. Unlike the earlier peak in the late 1980s, which was disproportionately emergency relief, this expansion was driven by debt relief, direct budgetary support, technical assistance and (in the case of the US after 2003) aid to the health sector, in particular for HIV and AIDS. The Cold War format of aid-as-loyalty payment was thus diluted and disguised. Countries such as Uganda and Ethiopia were major beneficiaries, while Sudan and Eritrea missed out because of international ostracism.

The Ethiopian government resolutely centralized control of aid rents. As a large and very poor country with, after 1991, a reputation of a government committed to poverty reduction, it naturally attracted very large amounts of development aid. The Ethiopian strategy was to study carefully the merits and demerits of each potential development partner, and prioritize accordingly. It is instructive that this was articulated most clearly in the White Paper on Foreign Affairs and National Security:

> It is important to know in detail the development cooperation policy of each country.... We have to differentiate between assistance that contributes significantly to our development and the building of a democratic order and aid that has a more modest impact. This requires detailed study. Who provides what must be known, and the priorities worked out, in order for our work to yield results? Spontaneous and haphazard activity can only negatively impact the effective and efficient utilization of foreign assistance. That is why the need to have proper studies cannot be over emphasized.[15]

The British were preferred for direct budgetary support, the Germans for technical assistance, the Chinese and Italians for infrastructural projects. Insofar as the Ethiopian project of the developmental state merged the political budget into the national development strategy, this was a strategic means of enlisting donor support for national political aims. In parallel, Ethiopia's NGO law confined international NGOs to working on government-approved development projects, and imposed such tight restrictions on foreign funding and areas of operation for domestic NGOs that most of those involved in public-policy debate were forced out of business. Meles defended this restriction – and the associated press law – on the basis that civil society should not be a Trojan Horse for rent-seeking political interests.

At a lower level of the hierarchy, relief aid remains an important resource, and all the old tricks of diversion and manipulation are relearned by a new generation of local political entrepreneurs. This was the case in Somalia, especially during the famine of 2011. Stealing humanitarian aid is likely to re-emerge in South Sudan as the war drags on and the government finds itself unable to pay its commanders.

In the 1990s, the aid business took a governance turn. Though this was ostensibly an exercise in undoing some of the excesses of neo-liberal dogma and 'bringing the state back in', its impact has rather been to integrate recipient countries into a new apparatus of glo-balized governance. This issue will be discussed further in chapter 12. Here, the key point is that resources provided for good govern-ance are more likely to be co-opted into a patronage marketplace, than to challenge it.

External support to governmental institutions, such as a depart-ment of education or a ministry of finance, may generate a bubble of technocratic integrity. But the survival of that bubble depends wholly on the character, power and political longevity of the individual patron. A dedicated, professional and powerful governor of the central bank may be able, if he is adept and lucky, to carve out a niche. But should those political conditions change, or should he be replaced, that bubble is likely to be pricked. Absent such a patron, no amount of goodwill, effort, money, expertise or patience will have a result other than generating at best a Potemkin institution, and more probably a pile of documentation that optimistically speaks about sincere commitments to build capacity, reform systems and comply with best practices. Efforts at security-sector reform and disarmament, demobilization and reintegration have commonly met the same fate. These are more likely to be used to promote the fac-tional and financial advantage of individuals than to reform and institutionalize. The demands of a payroll peace – providing armed men with army salaries – will normally trump those of professional-izing the military.

Counter-Terrorism Rent

After a post-Cold War hiatus, strategic and international security rent returned after 2001. America's counter-terror strategy, entangled within the regional strategic rivalries of the Greater Middle East and the 'new peacekeeping', has created an exceptionally well-financed rentier political-security market with the added bonus that counter-terror patronage also comes with intelligence technologies and a legal vocabulary that is perfectly suited for justifying secrecy and repres-sion. For the Horn's leaders, counter-terror rentierism was a return to a familiar business model. Just as an earlier generation of leaders had used geostrategic rents to pursue domestic political agendas, so too counter-terrorism rent was manipulated for diverse other pur-poses, all of them to do with consolidating power, and often uncon-nected with defeating terrorist groups. Cold War era rentier rulers had a real, if rarely used, option of defecting to the other side. Contemporary political CEOs cannot credibly threaten to do this, but they can play the vulnerability card, presenting themselves as sufficiently reliable to deserve support, and sufficiently fragile to need it.[16]

The most time-honoured and straightforward form of security rentierism is, literally, to rent out a plot of land as a foreign military base. There is no better example of this than Djibouti, a Franco-American garrison with a small hinterland. French Somaliland was created as a naval post on the sea route east of Suez in the 1890s. After granting it independence as Djibouti in 1977, France kept its military facilities and paid the government accordingly. Djibouti was also Ethiopia's railhead and an important port and, when the 1998 war shut Ethiopia off from Eritrean ports, it gained a lot more trade. After 2001, the US military set up a military base for, among other things, armed drones overflying Yemen and Somalia. The president of Djibouti finds himself in the comfortable position of being valued by three powerful governments, receiving payments accordingly, and also being able to play the three patrons against one another in minor but locally significant ways, as needed.

Ethiopia has bent its counter-terror alliance with the US to serve its own ends. Meles brushed off America's public criticism of his electoral and human rights record because he knew that the US cared more for his readiness to host US special forces and send his own troops into battle against Somali Islamists. The entire Somalia operation, from the earliest commando operations, through the 2006 invasion to AMISOM and the UN Monitoring Group, has served Ethiopia's goal of rolling back Eritrean influence. Ethiopians knew that the invasion would strengthen jihadism in the region – which indeed it did[17] – but were willing to take that risk. More recently, Ethiopia has used counter-terror legislation for domestic repression.

Without counter-terror rents, the Somali Federal Government would not exist. Its National Intelligence and Security Agency is largely controlled by the US, and its army is subordinate to AMISOM, which in turn is a product of African and international counter-terror strategy.

In the second Clinton administration, the SPLA benefited from being Khartoum's biggest military adversary. Although the US intelligence assessment was that the SPLA was not an effective operational partner, Washington did not want it to fail. Since 9/11, when Khartoum began a discreet intelligence partnership with the CIA, the SPLA has not obtained counter-terror rent as such, but has continued to obtain strategic rent because of the extent to which American domestic constituencies have been invested in the southern Sudanese cause. Meanwhile, Ethiopia, Uganda and Israel have all supported the SPLA in pursuit of their own political interests.

The Sudanese switch from hosting bin Laden to providing the CIA some of the best intelligence on al-Qaeda illustrates Khartoum's opportunistic security policy. Bashir's hope that this would translate into normalizing relations with Washington – with associated funds – was not fulfilled, but as soon as NISS began sharing some of its files with the CIA, it generated animosity from al-Qaeda, including threats, so there was no going back. Sudan's policy was delicately balanced: it kept close links with Hamas and allowed Iran to transit arms supplies along the Red Sea coast, actively supported the Libyan opposition in 2011, and kept lines open to former proxies, just in case they could ever prove useful again.[18]

Just outside the Horn we can see other variants of counter-terror rentierism. Chad is a fine example. Fort Lamy (now N'djaména) has an important place in French military history: it was here that General Jacques-Philippe Leclerc assembled his Free French forces in 1942, and led them across the desert in a march that ended in Paris two years later. French interest in Chad was mostly sentimental until the 1980s contra war against Gaddafi, when Hissène Habré became a strategic client. In 1991, during President François Mitterand's uncharacteristic departure from established Francafrique policy, France threw Habré to the wolves and permitted Idriss Déby to take power. Since then, the French military has kept a base, made more strategic by the growth of Saharan jihadism. Déby contributed 2,000 soldiers to fight in the Malian desert in 2013, in support of the French-led Operation Sérval. The immediate quid pro quo was that France was publicly silent on Chad's role in supporting the CAR rebels and Déby's domestic repression.[19] A bigger prize is that N'djaména will be the headquarters of the French army's Operation Barkhane, a Sahel-wide counter-terror programme.

For a decade, Yemen's President Ali Abdullah Saleh ably used the threat of al-Qaeda-linked insurgents to maintain generous American security assistance. Saleh compared ruling Yemen to 'dancing on the heads of snakes' and, on the eve of the Arab Spring, Sarah Phillips described how 'crisis has kept the system running, and has been, to a significant degree, a deliberate choice of Yemen's power elite'.[20] Solving the security crisis by defeating al-Qaeda was not in Saleh's interest, as he discovered in late 2005 when his near-complete defeat of the jihadists resulted, not in American accolades and rewards, but in cutbacks in security aid and criticism over corruption. Saleh was more threatened by a diminished political budget than by Islamist militants, and it is probably no coincidence that three months later, twenty-three militants escaped from a maximum-security prison, some of whom 'went on to establish al-Qaeda in the Arabian Peninsula, putting Yemen's problem with militant jihadis back on the international agenda'.[21]

Saleh's logic is familiar to American counter-terror specialists. The Harmony Project at West Point has observed the perverse incentive for a government, with a low level of internal terrorism threat but a high level of counter-terror assistance, 'to prefer a non-zero level of terrorism', and (prior to al Shabaab) it put Kenya in this category.[22] The Harmony Project's proposed solution to this problem is to link counter-terror assistance to the recipient government's level of effort, not to the level of terrorist threat. But, even if this could be implemented, it would not address the deeper structural problem: an American global counter-terror strategy, designed on the premise that war needs to be taken to terrorists' supposed foreign sanctuaries. Implementing this, either with US combat troops or paying and equipping front-line governments to do the task, creates the biggest-ever rentier opportunity for security business managers. Small by the metric of American defence spending, the funds provided are enough to fatten political budgets nicely, feeding militarized kleptocracies.

A particular twist on counter-terror rentierism is its converse: the denial of essential services and supplies to those whom the US fears might support, deliberately or inadvertently, an organization designated as terrorist. For example, in 2011, US counter-terror legislation impeded relief agencies' operations in al Shabaab-controlled areas, at the cost of seriously delaying an international response to a disaster that cost as many as 250,000 lives. American restrictions on banks transferring money to Somalia are also threatening the flows of remittances.

Criminal and Law-Enforcement Rents

The Horn of Africa does not produce illegal drugs in large quantities,[23] and neither is it a transit point for drugs destined for developed markets, so it is not a significant client of international counter-narcotics policies. The Horn is not part of the outer perimeter of fortress Europe. Criminal and law-enforcement rents are niche opportunities rather than a central component of political finance. The niches, however, are revealing. Khartoum was long a well-known if discreet hub for illicit transnational activities, and is likely to remain so, especially while US financial sanctions compel businesses to operate on a cash basis. Maritime piracy briefly brought in huge funds to coastal Somalia, and in due course counter-piracy provided bigger and steadier revenues. Arms and human trafficking provided opportunities for senior generals and party members in Eritrea. Organ harvesting in eastern Sudan, targeting refugees from Eritrea and Ethiopia, is another profitable niche.

The marginal role of criminal rents in the Horn is a matter of circumstance rather than policy: the opportunities have been too few for the region's political entrepreneurs to develop them at scale. Should a suitable conjuncture occur, the political-commercial structures and skills exist for the openings to be taken. The handful of instances that have thus far transpired also illustrate the ability of entrepreneurs to exploit both criminal rents and law-enforcement rents, including switching between the two and even obtaining both at the same time.

The 'New Peacekeeping'

The African Union was set up at the turn of the millennium with diverse objectives. Paramount among them, after a decade in which American and European interest in, and aid to, the continent had reached an all-time low, was finding 'African solutions to African problems'. With the near-simultaneous triumph of the African National Congress in South Africa, signalling victory over white racist rule, and the Rwanda genocide, signalling that national sovereignty could not be a shield for mass atrocity, the continental organization, the OAU, needed to be reinvented. The AU was conceived in Libya in 1999 and born in Durban in 2002.

Given the political and economic realities of the first fifteen years of the new millennium, it is no surprise that the AU's actual functioning reflects political market principles. This is evident in the AU's most active department, Peace and Security, and in the way in which mechanisms for the resolution of African conflicts according to principles of negotiation are being replaced by security-sector rent-seeking. I will call the latter phenomenon 'the new peacekeeping', with the word 'new' serving as a placeholder for a better descriptor of a phenomenon that has little to do with peace.

Let us begin with the now-banal observation that African states broker international resources for internal power.[24] The associated 'resource curse' has been measured by Bruce Bueno de Mesquita and Alastair Smith[25] who find that UN Security Council membership has a malign impact on a country's economic growth, presumably because council membership attracts international patronage and permits rulers to pursue less-than-optimal economic policies.

Setting up the AU and in particular its peace and security architecture similarly brought rentier opportunities, for both African member states and the AU Commission itself. Initially they took the opportunity because of international disinterest in Africa, and later the AU could safeguard a measure of political space because of the stand-off at the UN Security Council between the 'P3' (the US, Britain and France)[26] and, at different times, China and Russia. When, for example, tensions between the US and Russia were paralysing business at the Security Council in 2012, the AU Peace and Security Council (PSC) position on the border war between South Sudan and Sudan was adopted almost verbatim by the UN Security Council.[27] For the US, the AU was emerging as a useful intermediary in the 'new peacekeeping', circumventing the UN, while for China and Russia, it was useful to gain African votes and promote the principle of regional solutions for regional problems. This approach spectacularly broke down over Libya in 2011.

The AU is an ideal place in which to observe the value of legitimacy in political bargaining. The organization holds its Ordinary Assemblies of Heads of State and Government (summits) twice yearly, and most African leaders attend. There are also frequent extraordinary summits, occasional meetings of the PSC at the level of heads of state, and subregional summits, notably of the Economic Community of West African States (ECOWAS), the East African Community and, for the Horn, IGAD. All are remarkably well attended. Despite the pressures on their time, African leaders make it a priority to attend these meetings. They provide the opportunity for conducting the bargaining that keeps regional political markets functional.

Bargaining between the men who run Africa's political business needs to done face to face in private. More important than the formal business of the summit is the chance for personal meetings in hotel suites. Former heads of state play an important role in making the system run: first, they are exceptionally well-connected and, second, there are few people in whom a sitting ruler can confide, and a retired president is one of them. The gathering as a whole is an excellent illustration of the fractal nature of political markets. The interactions between national leaders are banally similar to those between village chiefs or provincial governors.

A forum of this nature is too useful to escape the attention of the superpower. This is illuminated by the exception: the instance when the AU was brusquely spurned. This happened, of course, over Libya in 2011, when the P3 peremptorily blocked the visit by African leaders to meet with Colonel Gaddafi, and then denigrated and blocked their attempt to negotiate a handover.[28] UN Security Council resolution 1973 garnered the support of the three African members of the Council, on the promise that military action was to be conducted in accordance with the 'responsibility to protect' and the AU's peace effort would be supported. It was a cynical stratagem that deceived and angered the Africans and also Russia, and violated the emergent principle of listening to regional organizations, if not necessarily deferring to them.[29] However, although African leaders' wisdom on Libya has subsequently been vindicated, NATO's Operation Unified Protector was brute demonstration of where global power really lay.

This came shortly after France had called the shots in Côte d'Ivoire, removing Laurent Gbagbo (and taking him off to the ICC for good measure), also thereby completing the rehabilitation of the Burkinabe putschist Blaise Compaoré, whom many West Africans had considered the premier candidate for international justice because his fingerprints were all over unusually sanguinary insurrections in Liberia and Sierra Leone.[30] When the fallout from Libya ignited the dry tinder of northern Mali, France also took the lead in military action, enlisting Déby as its favoured gendarme this time.

In the early 2000s, the AU adopted a five pillar 'African Peace and Security Architecture', including the AU Peace and Security Council, a mediation capacity, an analytical and early warning system, an African Standby Force (ASF) that could intervene in emergencies, and a funding mechanism. By the time of the Mali crisis, the ASF existed notionally as five regional brigades. However, first in Mali and then in the creation of the 'Force Intervention Brigade' within the UN Stabilization Mission in the DRC (MONUSCO), consisting of South African and Tanzanian troops to combat the M23 rebels, the ASF was bypassed. This was formalized with the creation of the Africa Immediate Crisis Response Capacity (AICRC) which serves as an instrument for ad hoc action by militarily capable African governments to dispatch troops, with AU authorization, on enforcement operations.

At the fiftieth anniversary summit of the AU in May 2013, heralded as a celebration of the continent having cast off the colonial yoke, French President François Hollande surprised his hosts with an invitation to all African heads of state to Paris for a special summit, with predetermined date (December) and agenda (peace and security, including combating organized crime). After some countries, led by Algeria, expressed their dismay at what appeared to be a French hijacking of Africa's institutions, the Elysée Summit for Peace and

Security in Africa went ahead, with economic issues added to the agenda.[31] The peace and security declaration focused on financing and operationalizing the AICRC and measures for African countries to serve as a forward line of law enforcement and immigration control, against drugs traders and human traffickers.[32]

In August 2014, President Barack Obama did the same, though he was careful to emphasize good economic news from Africa and to encourage commercial investment – indeed the tenor of the economic business was that the US was lagging behind China. The hard business was, however, security. Just ten weeks earlier, on 28 May, in his commencement address at West Point, Obama announced a $5 billion Counterterrorism Partnerships Fund, which 'will allow us to train, build capacity, and facilitate partner countries on the front lines'.[33] At the US-African Leaders Summit, he announced the African Peacekeeping Rapid Response Partnership ('A-Prep') to build the capacity of six selected African militaries to rapidly deploy peacekeepers, at a cost of $110 million a year, in addition to ongoing American support for peacekeeping missions.[34]

These two summits advertised the fact that the AU and Africa's subregional organizations have become brokers in the global flows of security rents. This was a remarkable turnaround for African-led peacekeeping. In 2006, the Bush administration had made the transition from AU to UN peacekeepers the centrepiece of its Darfur policy and, in 2008, when the UN-African Union hybrid operation in Darfur (UNAMID) was deployed, the UN Department of Peacekeeping Operations (DPKO) had made it clear that it did not want to be seen as a precedent or a model. Similarly the UN initially did not want to become involved in AMISOM in any guise. Part of the reason was simple institutional rivalry and protectiveness of DPKO jobs and contracts.[35] But the UN also has a set of principles that determine peacekeeping operations that can only be worked around with difficulty, including reluctance to deploy troops from one country in a neighbouring country, restrictions on rules of engagement, and onerous political and human rights reporting requirements. These constraints became a problem as the US sought to merge peacekeeping and counter-terrorism, notably in Mali and Somalia.

By comparison, African countries contributing troops through the AU, ECOWAS and IGAD are more flexible on the political purpose and mandate of the military operations they are prepared to authorize, more ready to take casualties and to stay the course. The AU's readiness to intervene is founded more in the practices of political bargaining and peer pressure than the legalities of the responsibility to protect or Article 4(h) of the Constitutive Act of the African Union, which specifies 'the right of the Union to intervene in a Member State pursuant to a decision of the Assembly in respect of grave circumstances, namely: war crimes, genocide and crimes against humanity'. Adopted in the shadow of Rwanda, Article 4(h) has never been invoked, and was only hinted at regarding Darfur in 2004.

If we examine the negotiations that lead to the dispatch of a military mission, and its subsequent expansion (in numbers and mandate), we can see how the 'new peacekeeping' is an extension of political bargaining over position in a globalized hierarchy. It is a game of rent-seeking in which sovereignty is instrumentalized, and the main function of the AU is to regulate the sovereignty, including legitimizing its abrogation.

Consequently, mediators are selected from the countries of the region, and blessed by the AU (or a subregional organization). In turn they use their position to advance their political-business interests, including deploying their own soldiers as peacekeepers. Western countries subsidize their military budgets in hard currency, while they also have the opportunity to deploy in the neighbourhood where they can pursue political and commercial interests. For the government of Burundi, whose own civil war was settled through a 'payroll peace' deal that hugely expanded the army, contributing troops to Somalia and CAR helps meet the costs of this bloated military and develop an *esprit de corps*. For other troop contributors in the region (Chad, Ethiopia, Kenya, Rwanda and Uganda), the domestic function is to subsidize military budgets and expand political budgets.

The African Union Mission in Somalia began as a mechanism for Ethiopia to obtain international backing for its political goals, in the wake of its invasion of 2006. Subsequently, AMISOM has become all of the following: a multinational African army to support the Somali government in its war against al Shabaab; a counter-terrorist force; a peacekeeping force; an anti-piracy force (using private military companies); a mechanism for putting African troops on the international payroll; and a means of resourcing the AU Commission as a nodal point in the global patronage system. Though under AU auspices, the troops were at first funded directly by international donors, including the US, UK and European Union, and later also supported by a UN-administered trust fund. It initially consisted of troops from Uganda and Burundi. Kenyan troops were formally integrated in 2012, just four months after they crossed the border in Operation Linda Nchi ('Protect the Nation') to attack al Shabaab. Having been operationally coordinated with AMISOM from the outset, Ethiopia followed the Kenyan lead and formally integrated 4,000 troops into the mission in 2014. For Kenya and Ethiopia, this not only covers their costs but also facilitates their political grip on the country. The two neighbours are competing to control Somalia: this rivalry has already generated tensions in the Gedo region that adjoins both countries and will need to be managed if it is not itself to generate future conflict.

Other configurations are seen across the wider region. In Mali, Chad provided combat troops through a separate, AU-facilitated channel, in support of the French and UN mission. The Force Intervention Brigade in DRC was formally part of MONUSCO but retained its own command and control. In CAR, parallel and loosely coordinated French and AU interventions were replaced by a UN mission. The AU Regional Task Force to combat the LRA consists of Ugandan and South Sudanese troops with US advisors and air assets. In Darfur, UNAMID's troops are almost entirely African, but managed through DPKO. The UN Interim Security Force for Abyei (UNISFA) consists of an Ethiopian brigade – a unique case of a single country providing all the troops for a mission. The Protection and Deterrent Force (PDF) in South Sudan is deployed within the UN Mission in South Sudan (UNMISS) and includes troops from Ethiopia, Kenya and Rwanda. It is supposed to enable Ugandan troops, deployed in a combat role in South Sudan in support of the government, to withdraw, but it is likely that (on the AMISOM model), those Ugandan troops will eventually become incorporated into the PDF. Uganda will not want to withdraw from a large part of its extended security perimeter and zone of influence, handing it over to its regional rivals, especially Ethiopia. Part of the logic of deploying troops from neighbouring countries in South Sudan is that, should the South Sudanese belligerents attack the PDF, then they would not simply be taking on the contingent on the ground, but the army of that neighbour too. South Sudan risks becoming the cockpit for regional rivalries.

A counter-example is Chad. Déby was keen to preserve his freedom of manoeuvre within his country, and an essential part of this was keeping the UN out of his internal affairs. He could see how international concern for Darfur was limiting the Sudanese government's ability to act, and did not want anything comparable – such as a peacekeeping mission with a broad mandate – in Chad. His vision of a peacekeeping mission was an expansion of his defence pact with France, and he accepted a compromise with the European Force for Chad/CAR (EUFOR) in 2007, mandated alongside the UN Mission to CAR and Chad (MINURCAT). Neither mission had a political or human rights component, and at the first opportunity Déby wound them up – and became a troop contributor himself, notably in Mali and in the Multinational Joint Task Force for combating Boko Haram along the north-eastern borders of Nigeria.

On the principle that the budget is the skeleton of the system, we can trace the finances of the new peacekeeping and infer the political incentives that arise. Overall, since 2008, while troop contributions from the countries that traditionally provide the backbone of UN peacekeeping missions (in Africa: Ghana, Kenya, Nigeria and Senegal; in Asia: Bangladesh, India and Pakistan) have remained stable, the numbers of troops from the 'new peacekeeping' countries of east and west Africa have shot up.[36] Rwanda has increased its UN peacekeepers from zero in 2004 to 5,660 in 2015; Ethiopia from 1,000 in 2003 to 7,858 in 2015 (plus 4,400 serving with AMISOM). The three UN missions in Sudan and South Sudan were budgeted at \$2.69 billion for 2013/14, fully a third of the global UN peacekeeping budget.[37]

The DPKO prefers that AU peacekeepers are 're-hatted' under the UN as soon as a mission is consolidated. For the most militarily active missions this may not happen quickly, and African-mandated peacekeepers are increasing in numbers and costs. AMISOM troop numbers are over 22,000 and its budget is expanding.[38] The AU Regional Task Force against the LRA consists of 2,500 troops (mostly Ugandan), half of its projected total. However, African troop contributors prefer the UN because its pays in a more timely and reliable way, and the P3 also prefer the more direct control they can exercise through DPKO. Thus, Ethiopia insisted that UNISFA should fall under the UN and not the AU, and the African forces in Mali and CAR were 're-hatted' as UN missions. The AU is left with the more dangerous and experimental missions: Africans' comparative advantage is their readiness to die.

Between a half and a third of the expenditure of a peacekeeping mission is on uniformed personnel costs. These are small outlays compared to the costs of deploying US or European combat troops, but they are a substantial subsidy to African defence budgets, especially as they are hard currency.

As has been the fate of many attempts to build modern institutions and realize political ideals, the AU has succumbed to the relentless political-commercial logic of the rentier marketplace, and is becoming a subcontractor in the market of providing international security. That security agenda is not set in Africa. The AU's particular niche is regulating sovereignty on behalf of the deals brokered between Africa's military powers and their financier-patrons in Washington, DC, and Paris. The regional military powerbrokers, especially (at this time) Chad and Ethiopia, are exploiting the opportunities to their tactical advantage, but at the cost of repurposing the African peace and security architecture as a platform for rentier militarism.

Peacemaking in the Political Marketplace

If warring politicians are sincere in their intent to make a deal, they will not need a third-party facilitator. The contenders are perfectly well aware of the resources at stake, know one another sufficiently well, and have all the negotiating skills needed. They will not trust one another, but will have enough confidence in the system itself – the rules of the marketplace and the sound judgement of their counterparts – that they can come to a workable arrangement.

If the contenders call in a third party, it is not because they need a forum, skills or confidence-building, but because the mediator provides a missing ingredient. This may be a discreet channel between two senior politicians, or (more likely) the common benefits of external resources. In recent years, however, what is most common is that mediation is imposed by foreign powers, especially the US, making use of a regional intermediary. The mediators therefore find themselves operating in a marketplace in which their formal 'square table' with recognized belligerents, a tripartite agenda (power-sharing, wealth-sharing and security arrangements, with a civil society/democracy add-on), and a focus on constitutional-type documents, is poorly suited to real politics. The proceedings within the conference hall will be a sideshow to bargaining conducted elsewhere, including parallel tracks between the parties and the Americans. In these circumstances it is likely that the people who believe most in the peace process and are most heavily invested in its outcomes are the mediators themselves, and insofar as their own status and interests are vested in the process, in desperation they will try to force the parties into accepting it.

International mediators are obliged, by the norms of their institutions, to include provisions for accountability for human rights violations. This so goes against the grain of the political markets that in 2013 the AU withdrew its cooperation from the ICC. Mediators are also expected to engage with civil society. This also makes political entrepreneurs uncomfortable, but it is a provision they can more readily work around, by the expedient of setting up their own loyal NGOs. Meanwhile, local civil society leaders want a seat at the table (and associated access to resources), while for the mediators and their backers they are useful as 'proxy publics'[39] which substitute for broader consultation.

A peace agreement in the political marketplace is as good as the political conditions under which it was signed: as soon as those conditions change, it will be renegotiated. The foundation of any workable agreement is that contending politicians come out of the negotiations with more resources than they entered. Such deals require expanding budgets, and will fail when that budgetary expansion stalls. A variant formula for a peace deal is a security pact in which signatories join forces to eliminate their rivals, thereby reallocating existing rents in their favour. Either way, it is likely to be an 'interwar' rather than a peace.[40]

Third-party mediators become trapped in a carousel of talks. They are understandably reluctant to walk away because the 'give war a chance' logic, even if it were an ethical option, does not operate in a political marketplace where there is rarely decisive victory. Instead, mediators have developed stratagems for staying involved and negotiate layers to a deal. There is no longer a single agreement, but rather talks first aim at framework agreements and declarations of principles, or creatively worded variants of these, and then, after a purportedly final agreement, the parties may add an 'implementation matrix' or similar in order to maintain the pretence that they are not reopening issues that have already been agreed. A persistent mediator will find that pursuing the deal entails becoming more closely involved in the internal bargaining among the members of the cartel who constitute each party, and in turn in the bargaining between cartel members and their clients. This process can result in a mediator becoming engaged, literally, in village politics. If the peacemaker becomes a peace enforcer, the outcome is the same, except on a grander scale. The current fashion for deploying peace enforcement troops from neighbouring countries entangles international peacekeeping with regional power politics.

It is tempting to conclude that the political marketplace of the Horn will be the graveyard of international efforts for conflict resolution. However, those efforts also serve purposes other than creating peace and stability, and their protagonists can always find reasons for their failure on each particular occasion, and refinements to sustain the mechanisms. The most powerful international actors are deeply entangled in the market of loyalties, in pursuit of their interests, so that peace talks are only one component of their overall political-business activities. The US government, for example, has far more vested in its counter-terrorism and defence strategies (of which the new peacekeeping is a small component) than in peace in South Sudan or development and democracy in Ethiopia.

Globalizing Patronage

Bringing together the strands, we can draw several preliminary conclusions about the trajectory of the Horn of Africa. First, there is a regional patronage hierarchy in the Horn and much of what seems chaotic is an interstate contest over who occupies which place in the hierarchy. Some are rising: Chad. Some are attempting to rise: Uganda. Some are declining: Sudan. Some tried to rise but fell far and hard: Eritrea and South Sudan. Ethiopia is joining the militarized rent-seeking scramble.

Second, the countries of the Horn are integrated into a global power hierarchy in a subordinate position, but they are able to exploit sufficient niches to sustain political budgets. One can see similarities with Central America and the Caribbean and parts of South-East Asia, where economic and political structures are strongly influenced by proximity to powerful countries with major domestic markets and the capacity to extend their policy frontiers well beyond their own borders. For all these countries, American, European and East Asian policies on counter-terrorism and extra-territorial policing, along with demand for oil and other primary commodities, have generated new sources of rent, and opportunities for their political leadership. For the Horn, proximity to Saudi Arabia and Qatar, both persistent practitioners of monetized patronage, is a key factor.

Third, globalization has wrought several important changes on how patronage functions. The political marketplace is integrated vertically, with the same features occurring at different levels, and horizontally, with the patronage systems of different countries that were previously separated now merged. Rulers in one country can more easily sponsor clients in another. The bargaining power of provincial clients is therefore increased, while rulers' capacities for illicit financial dealings has also increased.

Fourth, the AU and IGAD are succumbing to the temptation of specializing in brokering 'new peacekeeping' deals and earning their keep on the commissions thereby earned. 'African solutions' risk becoming a simple rebranding of a Euro-American franchise, with payoff.

And last, on current trends, a regional political marketplace is thriving within the globalized political economy. Patronage-based political orders should not be treated as a phenomenon that is passing into history, then contrasted with globalization as the way of the future. Patronage and globalization are not in fact opposites: the two evolve together like a double helix.

12

Towards a More Perfect Marketplace?

Political Circuitry and the Public Sphere

The political marketplace is a materialist, instrumental framework that provides little space for ideals and norms. Its values are monetary. It is hierarchical and elitist: politics is the business of a relatively small number of individuals, almost all men, who have money and guns. The logic of political markets reduces people to commodities and interpersonal relations to bargaining over material reward, and it evens out local societal and cultural factors in favour of the common currencies of the dollar and the Kalashnikov. It relegates public debate to background noise: what matters is the business transacted among political elites, usually in secret. The information that counts is the political-market data: 'who, whom and how much'.

In this chapter, I argue that transformations in information and communication have made the political marketplace more efficient and inclusive, but at the expense of the public sphere and public goods – including state-building. I distinguish between political circuitry, through which political business is transacted, and the public sphere, in which public debate is conducted. In the Horn, the two are diverging. For political CEOs and aspiring political entrepreneurs alike, the circuitry of political-market communications and information is what matters. Political entrepreneurs may have ideals and try to pursue political agendas; they may engage with public debate. But the demands of operating in a marketplace in which power is continually transacted for material reward mean that the determinant of success becomes political-business capabilities, nothing else. Political ideals will be instrumentalized or will be irrelevant.

A marketplace requires an arena to meet, rules (formal or informal) for bargaining and flows of information. One of the perverse qualities of a political market is that as it becomes more efficient – information flows more freely, and barriers to entry and transaction costs are lowered – the price of loyalty rises rather than falls. It follows that a more perfect market is more attractive for its junior or aspirant traders. Conversely, for a senior political-business manager, controlling elite connectivity – the arena, the rules and the information – is no less important than possessing a sufficient political budget. Political CEOs spend massively on intelligence, and their subalterns try to outwit them. This contest makes the public sphere less relevant: either the political marketplace is strengthened, or the power of the ruler is strengthened.

State-builders, however, have a tougher task. In seeking legitimacy through producing public goods, they face judgement in the court of public opinion. The work of establishing public institutions and promoting value-creating economic development is difficult enough. A hostile public sphere makes the job harder still. Censorship is the tribute that the state-builder pays to the power of the public sphere.

The Imperial Model: Hub and Spokes

In the colonial and imperial era, there was no distinction between political circuits and the public sphere because the general public was not important in politics. All that mattered were the relations between ruler and elite. Control of the political circuitry could be achieved through the physical design of infrastructure such as roads and telephone lines. In colonial geography, the capital city and port were the hubs to which roads, railways, telegraph and post were connected. Imperial Ethiopia followed precisely the same model, and post-colonial states inherited it. Members of provincial elites met in the capital or not at all. Telephones were few and calls went through operators; two-way radios in police stations were the only means of long-distance communication in areas without working telephones.[1] There was a central postal system and national newspapers and radio. Two-way radios, typewriters, stencil machines and copiers were registered. Every educated person was known. It was an elementary task for government to monitor potential dissidents and control communications.

Sudan and Ethiopia had a similar design of political circuitry to the Ottoman Empire, described by Karen Barkey as a 'hub and spokes with no rim'.[2] The Ottomans ran a patrimonial system that extended over a vast area, in which central power was maintained by devolving authority – most characteristically tax farming – to local potentates. With no empire-wide common public spaces, those at the hub controlled the bargaining with each spoke. They could set the times, participants and the agenda for each round of political talks, and controlled the information about each deal, so that the next supplicant would be ignorant of what had been agreed with others. This model provided for local particularities, which allowed the empire to persist for centuries and accommodate enormous diversity, but which also contained the germ of its own demise. Within each province, the particularities of the devolved convening mechanism – the vernacular used in informal gatherings, the shared terms of local debate – generated centrifugal nationalisms, which ultimately tore the empire apart.

Sudan was an Ottoman frontier province, and the Ethiopian empire survived just beyond those frontiers. Legacies and echoes remain: one need only look at the road and rail maps of the two countries. In Sudan today, diversity is managed through a combination of flexible federalism – in which new states are carved out from old ones in response to particularly intense local pressures – and a carousel of peace negotiations, which awards different forms of devolution to different provinces. Ethiopia has formalized political devolution on the basis of nationality with its federal Constitution.

The imperial era hub-and-spokes model created a public sphere at its hub but not elsewhere. Typically, the public sphere began with a parliament, a university and a radio station, which the government could scrutinize or control.

I discovered this in 1996 when I tried to bring a portable manual typewriter into Ethiopia. It was a gift for the SPLA commander of Blue Nile, Malik Agar Eyre – I knew that one of the scarcest items in the field was that basic item. To my surprise, at Addis Ababa Airport, the customs officer insisted that I surrender the machine, and produced a 1950s ordnance that determined that all typewriters had to be registered with the Ministry of Interior. The customs officer knew that it was an anachronistic edict, as there was no restriction on laptop computers, but he knew each regulation and his job was to enforce them all. After some discussion he was content with my explanation that I planned to export the typewriter (though I did not say it would be illegally handed to a rebel commander in a neighbouring country) and let me take it in.

It was not an absurd idea in the 1950s – or indeed for some decades afterwards – for a government to seek to control communications by registering typewriters and stencil machines (there were no photocopiers).[3] For the revolutionary students of the early 1970s, access to a stencil machine was a rare privilege that could only be enjoyed clandestinely, with the aid of a friendly faculty member.[4]

Provincial dissenters suffered huge communicative disadvantages. Any form of political transaction needed people to meet in person, and given the distances and poor infrastructure – time between small towns was measured by days of travel – this created a hierarchy of connectedness. Living, working or studying in the capital was, in itself, membership of an elite club. A provincial town within a day's travel of the capital was next best. Life in a more remote provincial town might be attractive for a social anthropologist, a missionary or a truly dedicated development worker, but for a schoolteacher or administrative official it was akin to being stranded as a distant observer of national life. Schoolteachers assigned to villages felt as though they had been sentenced to exile.

Rural rebels were even more disadvantaged. Some provincial insurrections rumbled on for years, hardly registering on the national political radar. Rebel commanders might be oblivious to the defection or death of their lieutenants for weeks or months. As late as the 1990s, frontline commanders in the SPLA carefully hoarded every notebook or even each stray piece of paper, in order to send written instructions or record decisions. My choice of typewriter as a gift to Malik was based on my experience in the Nuba Mountains a year earlier. There, SPLA Commander Yousif Kuwa Mekki had convened conferences in the hills, including a consultative assembly and a meeting on religious tolerance, but there exists no written record of the deliberations or even some of the resolutions, because the Nuba fighters lacked paper and pencils.

Three things changed the hub-and-spokes model, making a rim – connections within and between remote areas. These were: the expansion of higher education, especially the explosion of provincial universities and colleges; the internationalization of governance; and the communications revolution. All are recent. The creation of the rim has meant that political information flows more freely and political transactions among hitherto isolated members of the provincial elite have become far easier. With better information, lower-level political entrepreneurs get better deals. The political market is more efficient and the price is higher. But better political chances for individuals have strengthened the marketplace, at the expense of more transformative political agendas, including state-building.

The Politics of Intellectual Life

The modernization era, from the 1960s to the 1990s, introduced public politics to the Horn. During these decades, the region was the locus of some extraordinary experiments in political ideology: revolutions, nationalism, Islamism, and public protest for honest government. For most of this period, public politics was a metropolitan affair, focused on universities, parliaments and national media.

Political community was built around convening and communication. Capital cities – the hubs – were the arena for an emergent public sphere, marked by intense but spatially limited political interaction and the politics of modernity. Where representative assemblies did not exist, schools and colleges stood in: by these means emerged the Graduates Congress in Sudan, the Ethiopian student revolutionaries and the Somali Youth League. Newspapers and national radio brought together readers around a shared cultural, social and political agenda.[5]

In 1970, universities in the Horn were few, small, metropolitan and high status. Sudan possessed just four: the University of Khartoum (the largest and most prestigious), Omdurman Islamic University, Cairo University (Khartoum Branch) and Al Ahfad College for Women. Juba University was founded in 1975, an outcome of the 1972 peace agreement. Sudan enrolled just 5,000 students in its five public universities as recently as 1989.[6] Ethiopia had Haile Selassie I University (renamed Addis Ababa University in 1975) and a small university in Asmara, founded in 1958 as Catholic College of Santa Famiglia. The Somali National University was accredited in 1969. Elsewhere in east Africa, the University of Dar es Salaam, famed for its radical influence on the whole continent (its students included Yoweri Museveni and John Garang), had a student body of just 1,500 in 1970, of whom no more than 5 per cent were considered revolutionaries and a further 10 per cent were nationalists.[7]

When the entire cadre of a nation's undergraduates were concentrated in a single institution, their classes and debates were the fulcrum of the country's future, and the political and social bonds formed at university helped to shape a shared idea of the nation among its aspiring leaders. Such a concentrated and intense national intellectual life has never been repeated.

The 1960s and 1970s were an era of intellectual ferment and creativity in Africa's universities. Sudan's first military dictator, General

Ibrahim Abboud, was brought down by a popular uprising in October 1964 that was initiated, to a large degree, by faculty and students at the University of Khartoum. Twenty years later, the Staff Club at the University was again the focal point for opposition to a military ruler. Throughout this period, the University of Khartoum boasted one of the finest faculties of social and political sciences in Africa and the Middle East,[8] producing a cadre of remarkable and radical political theorists, social anthropologists and economists, as well as some of the most innovative thinkers and practitioners in the emergent field of refugee studies, the forerunner of humanitarian studies.[9] The university was the anteroom for national politics: in its halls, cafes and cloisters, political battles between Communists and Islamists were fought out, sometimes literally with iron bars, in a way that prefigured the country's national political drama over the following decades. The discontent of Darfur's Daud Bolad began when his position as president of the Khartoum University Students' Union did not translate into a national political position.[10]

Addis Ababa University was similarly an exceptional institution. Founded in 1950 to produce an elite for imperial administration, within twenty years it became the intellectual and political powerhouse of revolutionary thought and practice.[11] In contrast to Sudan, which had a well-established Communist Party, Marxism in Ethiopia was a student project, distant from lived realities, but all the more fervently pursued and rigorously debated for that abstraction. Although thousands of students were to be murdered in the Red Terror of 1976–8, graduates and dropouts from the classes of the late 1960s and early 1970s defined the political history of Ethiopia and Eritrea for the next four decades. Among them were Meles Zenawi and Isaias Afewerki.

In this era, social movements were an urban phenomenon, in symbiosis with the state, sharing the same communicative space, making demands on the state, and thereby serving to strengthen the state. The central demand of anti-colonial movements was the right to self-determination, which consolidated government, rather than individual human rights or an end to atrocities, which limited it. Ethiopia's revolutionaries similarly sought to take state power and use it.

The aspirations and expectations of the students of that era – all of them political modernists, whether revolutionaries, reformers or technocrats – were not realized. Some of them died or were exiled. Many were exhausted, abandoning politics for other pursuits, or abandoning principled politics for the political marketplace. But others continued to believe in the ideals that had animated their youth. The afterlife of these ideals, often mutated into new forms, influenced the politics of later decades.

But the younger generation is different, and the material conditions of higher education are a good starting point for explaining the change. Replicating the Arab world's 'universities of large numbers',[12] there has been a massive expansion in tertiary education. Today, there are scores of universities and other higher-education institutions, public and private, and many of them are far larger than the national universities of old. It is hard to find a definitive listing. Ethiopia has ninety-three universities, polytechnics and colleges of higher education.[13] A Wikipedia search[14] finds today that Sudan has twenty-seven public and seventeen private universities and higher-education institutes, which have over 9,000 faculty and 300,000 students;[15] South Sudan has fourteen universities; Somalia has ninety-two and Somaliland has fifteen. The University of Djibouti was established in 2006. Although campuses still cluster in capital cities, most large provincial towns now have public universities.

The only country to have moved backwards is Eritrea. Having dismantled the University of Asmara, Eritrea provides vocational training in seven colleges, allocating students to courses. It is a conspicuous anomaly, in which education is the anteroom to military service.

Thus, the Horn's universities are widely spread. Standards have declined: classes are larger and learning by rote is common. In Ethiopia, the huge numbers of graduates are trained to staff local government, schools and the development bureaucracy. The government wants loyal cadres with specific technical skills, not freethinkers.

Nonetheless, these new student bodies provide geographically dispersed fora for transmitting political information, convening provincial intellectuals and aspiring politicians, and organizing newsletters, petitions and protests – a nascent localized public sphere. Consider Darfur. Students in its three universities are almost all from Darfur itself, and through their social and family networks and research projects, they provide connections between villages, IDP camps and politicians. They have a stronger ethnic or regional consciousness than the previous generation of students who congregated in Khartoum. Darfurian graduates' expectations of ascending to posts in the civil service or the professions, let alone national leadership, are limited. Instead they seek personal advancement through finding a patron in the political or business class. Through numbers alone, each graduating class is making the retail sector of the political marketplace more competitive, inclusive and efficient.

Transnational Intellectual Careers

Students and faculty are becoming globalized, not only because they use the internet, but also in their employment opportunities and career paths. This phenomenon at scale began in the 1970s. At the same time as repression drove thousands of the most educated into exile, the oil boom in the Gulf generated a job-seeking exodus of Arabic speakers. The countries of the Horn lost many, possibly a majority, of their graduates.

The internationalization of career openings came home in the 1980s, with the expansion of international relief programmes. Western NGOs and specialized UN agencies set up (first) emergency relief and (then) rehabilitation programmes. International relief funds also spawned local NGOs, some drawing from the same donors, and others (such as Islamic agencies) tapping new sources. The particular significance of the NGO rush was that their operations focused on the remotest areas, and they provided transport, communications and employment for educated personnel in a completely new way. Their Landcruisers were often the commonest passenger vehicles on country roads, their aircraft the majority at provincial airfields. In some areas – for example, Somalia and southern Sudan – relief agencies were virtually the *only* providers of these services for the entire 1990s. United Nations peacekeeping missions arrived in the 2000s and ramped up transport, communications and employment even more. This international aid presence reduced the costs and obstacles that had formerly prevented members of rural elites from connecting with one another in their home provinces. International aid work built a rim that connected the spokes.

The NGO-UN penetration of the 1980s also changed the career options of political intellectuals, in ways that were just as significant as the physical networking of the peripheries. International aid agencies provided a form of internal asylum for political dissidents. They needed to employ English-speaking graduates, and those they attracted included liberals interested in the welfare of the poor or human rights for all. For former civil servants, this employment not only came with a better salary, but with international connections and intellectual stimulation. The advantages were comparatively greater for women, who were undervalued in national bureaucracies. The meeting rooms of UN agencies, NGOs and their donors became alternative sites for convening political debate. Perhaps most importantly, employment by foreign agencies provided political protection. Men and women whose public-service jobs were insecure because of their political sympathies, or who might have been threatened with harassment or detention, gained physical and career security because their names became known to foreign friends, and they had a chance of escape when threatened by state security officers. Once absorbed into this network, professionals could find work elsewhere in the world, or consultancy work back home, which made it unattractive to return to employment in the national civil service or academia.

During Africa's independence struggles and the first post-colonial decades, civil society was represented by trade unions, political parties and nationalist associations, universities and the press. The project was simultaneously building and reforming states, and was symbolized by the demand of independence-era African social movements and their metropolitan allies for self-determination – a concept with an ambiguous relationship to individual human rights.[16] Since then, not only has the focus of rights advocacy changed – to exposing governments' abuses of power and seeking to limit their authority – but the very meaning of 'civil society' has changed as well.[17] In the 1990s, a new instrumental definition of 'civil society' became evident: it is what western governments and foundations can fund.[18] Meanwhile, civil-society activism becomes a livelihood strategy for individuals.[19] In southern Sudan, the vernacular term is 'civil societies', with the plural indicating that what counts are registered local civil-society organizations (CSOs) that fit the donor template. These CSOs became ubiquitous in almost every sector.[20] With their independent channels for foreign finance and their capacity for convening and communication, they threaten rulers' business models. The Ethiopian civil-society law of 2009 places prohibitive restrictions on CSO work except in service delivery, and other governments are adopting similar legislation.

The absorption of African professionals into international bureaucracies can be seen as a co-option by external institutions and interests,[21] but co-option also occurred in the other direction, as Africans used foreign agencies for their own purposes too. African elites penetrated the international aid system up to a high level and co-opted the international organizations for their benefit. Some governments (Senegal and Rwanda are examples) have proactively placed members of their educated elites within international organizations and have benefited as a result. The mutual penetration of multilateral agencies by African elites means that African and multilateral governance have come to overlap, and occasionally fuse.

Wherever governments are fashioned under international tutelage, there is a revolving door between multilateral agencies and senior governmental posts. Liberia, Sierra Leone and Côte d'Ivoire provide a rich set of cases, including heads of state. In the Horn, the choice of a senior UN official, Tijani Sese, to head a 'rebel' coalition formed at the behest of international mediators in peace talks, and subsequently to head the Darfur Regional Authority, is one example. The logical outcome of the integration of the Somali government into its foreign sponsors would be to staff Villa Somalia with Somali members of this multilateral elite, and we might expect something comparable for South Sudan and Eritrea in due course.

The ostensible purposes of this apparatus are development and state-building. There are celebrated critiques of how these aid institutions have drawn the political sting from development work, and even depoliticized governance and human rights.[22] One element of this is that national staff members repurpose their jobs for different goals. Sometimes this is simple personal advantage, but it can also involve using a post in an aid organization as a platform for uplifting a community or advancing a political agenda. By these means, the complexity, competitiveness and global integration of the political marketplace are deepened, and the ability of national politicians to regulate that market is reduced.

Convening and Communication Transformed

The third transformation is the most spectacular: media, telecommunications and information technology, supplemented by better transport infrastructure. The history of the Horn during the modernization era is filled with examples of the inordinate power that came with control over centralized media and communication. In 1976, Nimeiri was saved in part because the Minister for Telecommunications, Bona Malwal, ensured that Radio Omdurman stayed on air and loyal during the attempted military takeover by the National Front. In the thirty months after the downfall of Siyad Barre, Somalia's sole radio station was the scene of three confrontations, each of which determined the country's political future. Garang's coup-proofing strategy for the SPLA after 1991 involved keeping SPLA Radio closed and directly controlling all two-way field radio-sets.

Such centralized media and communications now belong to history. In 1999, a mobile phone company in Uganda advertised with the slogan 'Uhuru has a new name'. Uhuru – Swahili for 'freedom' or 'liberation' – is a deeply symbolic word in east Africa. The company was making a point of greater significance than its advertisers may have realized. The promise of personal freedom to the owner of a mobile phone also heralded change in political circuitry. Tajudeen

Abdul-Raheem of the Pan-African Movement joked that the mobile phone companies had a point.[23] Since the advent of FM radio and mobile phone towers, he said, the military coup was in decline. No longer was it possible for an army officer to dispatch one unit to State House to arrest the president, another to surround the parliament, and a third to the national radio station to announce a coup, and thereby take power overnight. The decline of the coup is one of the few trends that reduces turbulence. It has added to the longevity of political CEOs and stabilized their patronage orders. It has made political marketplaces more predictable and therefore more efficient.

The combination of satellite phones, mobile phones and the internet – along with better roads, more vehicles and more domestic air traffic – has connected the provinces. The impacts have been different on the public sphere and on political circuitry. Density of mobile phone ownership or internet connectivity are indices of public access to information and opportunities for expression. But it is rare for those platforms to be organized in a manner that brings access to real politics. Kenya's Ushahidi and Huduma are exceptions that illustrate this general rule. In the Horn, the level of rancour on political websites seems inversely related to the level of political access or influence, and political-business managers simply ignore most of this, regarding it as background noise. Nonetheless, as with the potential for provincial universities to nurture localized identity politics or populist sentiment, niche websites have served to advance particular political agendas, such as support for militant groups.

The impact of these technologies on the reach and efficiency of political circuits is a distinct issue, restricted to the political elite. So the Thuraya satellite phone, although expensive and scarce, has become a *sine qua non* for a political-military entrepreneur who operates anywhere beyond the reach of mobile phone coverage, for example, in the desert. The politician or commander who possesses a handset and phone credit can call up anyone, anywhere, and be reached at almost any time. Costly though it is to own and use, the Thuraya has lowered the transaction costs of bargaining.

Twenty-five years ago, the 1989 Darfur intertribal peace talks required all the leaders to assemble in al Fashir, not only for the talks themselves, but for the preparatory stages of agreeing the participants and chair and setting the agenda. In 1991, Daud Bolad's rebellion in Darfur was organized through written messages smuggled by hand and he had just one solar-powered two-way radio.[24] By 2006, Darfur's rebels would be seen, in breaks between the negotiating sessions at the peace talks in Abuja, speaking on their Thuraya phones, pacing up and down in the hotel car park (where the signal was best) and sharing Khartoum's latest proposal with interlocutors in Tripoli or N'djaména to see what better offers might be forthcoming. This intense networking and sharing of political market intelligence put the rebels on nearly the same informational level as the government.

The new political-communication circuitry can occasionally allow opponents to catch a ruler by surprise. Satellite phones are a superb tool for tactically coordinating military attacks. They enable momentary alliances. But they do not help with building the collectivity of a political movement or settling complex issues. Thus, the Chadian rebels, backed by Sudan, outwitted and overran the Chadian army up to N'djaména in February 2008, but then halted at the gates of the palace to renegotiate their posts in the government to be formed the next day, which turned out to be a fatal hesitation. The rebels needed to meet and discuss in depth the entire package of governmental power, and their last-moment face-to-face encounter was their first opportunity to do so.

Another instructive comparison is between the public protests in Sudan in 1985 and 2013. The April 1985 Popular Uprising was clandestinely organized by the trade unions, drawing on the discipline of collective action and party organization. Bringing people on to the streets, keeping them off the streets on the 'dead city day', and ensuring that the demonstrations were non-violent and targeted on certain locations, was a formidable organizational achievement. The army command abandoned Nimeiri partly because they recognized that the protestors' resolve and discipline was such that they could outlast and out-think the government. By contrast, the September–October 2013 protests were loosely coordinated by social media and mobile phones: they were more rapid and spontaneous but lacked the qualities that had made the 1985 uprising so formidable.[25] The government wielded two effective countermeasures. One was the threat that if the demonstrators brought down the government, the likely outcome would be chaos, as in Libya or Syria. The looting and burning of shops and petrol garages – some of it surely carried out by agents provocateurs – reinforced this message. The second was singling out individual organizers and intimidating or co-opting them. Back in 1985, the national security services had found it much harder to penetrate the trade union alliance's underground cells, especially the shadow committees that sprang into action when the top layer of leadership was arrested.

The lesson is that better information and communication helps subordinate actors, but only in certain ways. Specifically, it helps them as individuals in the political marketplace. Transactions are easier and cheaper. The deals they get are better. It follows that participation in the marketplace is more attractive. These technologies have not assisted the kind of detailed lengthy planning that undergirds sustained political struggles. Information technologies may democratize the political marketplace, but they will not transform it.

Greater density and frequency of political communication pose huge problems for a national political CEO. It is a reality he cannot reverse. The ruler will still possess more and better information than other members of the political elite, but that gradient has become shallower. He can spend more on intelligence gathering, but that has the danger that it empowers the intelligence officers. While the transaction cost of each individual bargain is reduced, this is outweighed by the tremendous increase in the number of bargains that have to be transacted. Administering a patronage system of this nature is expensive and time-consuming.

The political CEO's adaptation to this new reality is seen in the changing nature of political agreements, which has emerged as a consequence of the deregulation of the time interval for renegotiating a deal. As outlined in the previous chapter, political agreement itself has become a slippery concept. When communication and convening were scarce, meetings held greater significance. The proceedings of a parliament or an intertribal peace conference were scrupulously recorded and were, by common consent, respected. Today's agreements may be up for renegotiation the day after they were signed. Conflict resolution has become less a matter of drafting a constitutional document as the embodiment of a political settlement, and more a matter of making a contingent bargain over rents. This is a sea change in the intensity of political turbulence.

The political CEO in a political marketplace has a simple response to the elusiveness of a robust bargain: become the master of turbulence. He will be uninterested in the public sphere and public opinion, and will concentrate on the immediacies of political bargaining: staying afloat in today's ever-more-turbulent political waters.

The political CEO may succeed, through technical prowess and vigorous policing, in controlling the political circuitry, and become an authoritarian, repressive ruler. His intelligence and security services will keep the price of loyalty down, but insofar as there is any state-building agenda, it is a police state. He will have shifted the locus of political contestation to bargaining among security and intelligence chiefs. If the subaltern political entrepreneurs escape his controls and bargain hard, the outcome is a more competitive political marketplace, and possibly one that includes representatives from across diverse societal groups. Either way, the politics of ideas, fiercely debated in a small but lively public sphere, which defined the previous generation, will not return.

The serious state-builder has a different challenge. He is concerned with a form of legitimacy built on providing public goods, and the verdict on his project will ultimately be found in the public sphere. It follows that the strictest controls over public media and political freedoms are found in aspiring developmental states, such as Ethiopia. Meles Zenawi became infamous for his fierce censorship. He saw repression not as an end in itself, but the counterpart of a determined attempt at inculcating a new developmentalist ethos into society. That was the weakest element in his project, both because it mocked the adjective 'democratic' that he appended to his developmental project, but also because his effort at mass indoctrination differed from any authoritarian predecessors chiefly in that it was accompanied by impressive economic growth. Meles's successors have repressed the public sphere even more vigorously, using counter-terrorist legislation as the pretext for imprisoning journalists and bloggers. It looks less like protecting a developmental project and more like entrenching an oligarchy in power.

Challenges to the Political Marketplace[26]

The political marketplace offers little solace or opportunity to those who are less self-seeking, who want to challenge the entire system because they are revolted by its corruption and inhumanity, or because they genuinely believe a different order is possible. But there is some solace nonetheless.

Overall, the current political marketplace era has been a period of economic growth during which human-development indicators have improved. In the Horn, there have been three motors for progress: Ethiopia's developmental project, Sudan's economic boom and Somali entrepreneurship. The latter two show that there can be prosperity within a political marketplace. If that economic growth is sustained, it is possible that it will generate productive sectors that in turn will create a new non-rentier political economy, perhaps regardless of how that growth was achieved in the first place.

As political markets advance, people see dearly held values and norms being trampled. Some grasp their own meagre pickings from the marketization of public life. Others are contemporary political Luddites, mounting raids on the symbols of the new order, putting some to the torch, but ultimately dispersing or submitting. The commonest strategies of the powerless are flight, invisibility and stealthy sabotage, in the tradition described in the literature on peasant economies.[27] Wendy James[28] has described how people on the Sudan–Ethiopia borderlands have tried to be as invisible as possible, drawing on a cultural archive of avoiding the encroachments of violently extractive powers from either direction. Janet Roitman[29] details comparable efforts to escape the depredations of authority in central Africa.

Men and women who organize public challenges to political-business managers typically draw on repertoires of moral populism.[30] They claim authority by asserting that they represent the will of the people. They elevate the virtues of custom and community – obscuring changes and internal differences – and pit the local group against 'dangerous' outsiders or elites. They attack political elites as corrupt and amoral, and intent on depriving the community of its rights and identity. But examination of a few examples will show how, rather than forming a sustained challenge to the political marketplace itself, moral populist projects usually become instruments for political-business managers.

Ethnic-particularist claims to self-government provide a rich set of cases, ranging from the insurgencies in the Nuba Mountains of Sudan, to contests for control over regional government in Gambella and Beni Shangul states in Ethiopia. Localized nationalisms tend to arise when a central government has managed a hub-and-spokes model on a case-by-case basis, but cannot manage – or pay for – the rising demands of better-connected and better-informed provincial political entrepreneurs. Other examples are local vigilante groups, organized to provide security where the police are absent, incompetent or corrupt, which are prime candidates for co-option by political-military entrepreneurs as militia, party youth wings or the enforcement arms of protection rackets. Radical Islamist rebellions such as al Shabaab draw upon popular sentiment, and their conspicuous suppression of corruption and other transgressions of their code wins them credence. They can call upon an Islamist moral and political register, and an international network of committed jihadist recruits and financiers. Islamists – of both civic and jihadi strains – are candid about their political-business strategies and their readiness to work with, rather than against, the grain of the political marketplace.

The realms of spiritual and material power and politics intersect. Spiritual power or status is subject to material bargaining, and vice versa, and religious authority is often marketized and sometimes militarized.[31] However, moral and spiritual authority can also challenge the marketplace, both through articulating humane norms and also because popular resistance can call upon customary, localized values and spirits. For example, local healers and rainmakers were strong supporters of the Nuba resistance against the Sudanese government, the Nuer Prophet Wutnyang mobilized the 'White Army' in the 1990s, and politicians and chiefs often invoke the memory or spirits of the dead, as a power with which there can be no negotiation.

Can resistance to the political marketplace call on civil, inclusive, cosmopolitan values? Corresponding values are deep-rooted in the societies of the Horn, including in Muslim[32] and Christian traditions, and within local institutions which promote norms of dialogue, reciprocity or social justice. Even the most proficient operators in the political marketplace defer to more humane norms in their social interactions and public statements. Hypocrites they may be, but voicing a principle is a first step towards acknowledging it, from which it is a smaller step to respecting it, at least sometimes.[33] Human rights activists, women's groups and spiritual leaders in the region, and some diaspora groups, regularly condemn violence, exploitation and corruption. A small but vocal regional civil society is emerging, whose members are vigorously promoting discourse on human rights and peace.

However, civil-society groups and spiritual or 'traditional' leaders are all readily absorbed into political markets. This diminishes their capacity to mobilize the kinds of non-violent social movements that brought momentous political changes in the past. The days have gone when a single protest in the capital city could give a credible impression that, as Mohamed Ahmed Mahgoub said of the 1964 uprising in Sudan, 'anyone who could walk appeared to be on the streets'.[34] Trade unions and student organizations filled public squares and called governments to account in the 1970s and 1980s. The uprisings of 2011 in Tunisia and Egypt resembled those earlier demonstrations of people's power in choreography and political demands, but were built upon different and less durable organizational models. They appear less as the harbinger of a new era of popular democracy, midwifed by social media, than a spectacular but transient display of communitas – a structureless society based on solidarity and equality[35] – that served as an ironic rite of passage from one form of disenfranchisement to another. The Arab Spring revolutions removed dictators who had centralized and securitized corruption, then replaced them not with liberal democracies but with an accelerated marketization of politics. Libya and Syria are the most dramatic manifestations of this.

In Kenya, civic opposition took a different route, recognizing that protest needed to maintain the state against which it was ranged, an insight that sparked Kenyan activists to create Huduma alongside Ushahidi.[36] The first web platform, Ushahidi, was set up to allow citizens to report in real time on the 2007 election, enabling people to expose violations and pre-empt cover-ups. This was a crowd-sourced version of classic adversarial rights reporting. The second platform, Huduma, allowed people to provide and find information about shortcomings in the provision of services such as health and education. Launched alongside the government's Kenya Open Data initiative,[37] this marked a shift to a collaborative exercise between government and people in building state capacity, through an online public sphere. Such an emancipatory public sphere is not an evident prospect elsewhere in north-east Africa: instead public debate is repressed and co-opted.

The call for justice resonates in all societies and challenges the arbitrariness of power. However, mechanisms for administering justice are subject to political market forces, including hiring lawyers, buying judges, and assessing, paying and collecting fees and fines. Shopping among courtrooms and legal systems, selection of advocates, judges and juries, and plea bargaining are all examples of political markets at work, and not only in north-east Africa.

Partly as an effort to overcome the problems of existing judicial systems, local justice activists and international donors have promoted tools of transitional justice. As the name implies, this is premised on a one-time transition from one political-constitutional order to another, such as occurred with the ending of military dictatorships in Latin America or the end of apartheid in South Africa. Selective prosecution, truth-telling, lustration and other measures are intended to serve as a process of social healing and reckoning with the past. Where the 'transition' is from one configuration of political uncertainty to another, the logic is different. For instance, selective prosecution may be seen (correctly) as driven by political decisions, in the same way that anti-corruption measures in systemically corrupt societies become a means of weeding out political opponents.[38] This is not an argument against prosecutions as such – indeed they may play a more significant deterrent role in a society in which the same structural conditions are going to recur – only that they must be seen for the political acts that they are. Just as efforts at institutional capacity-building that create bubbles of technocratic integrity depend on individuals and their positions in patronage marketplaces, so too do attempts to achieve acts of justice.

In post-war Burundi, Peter Uvin found international civil servants talking about better institutions, but '[w]hile Burundians were often talking about the same aims, they did so in terms of people: they spontaneously desire "better people" rather than "better structures" '.[39] Their model was 'wise men whose impartiality, knowledge, and sense of justice are so widely accepted that they are chosen to advise in [resolving] local conflicts'.[40]

This reflects a wider truth: important forms of resistance emerge from within the logic of personalized politics itself. Powerless members of communities want their leaders to act with civility and personal integrity, and commonly see political failings as the failures of individual leaders. People also want their leaders to be capable and effective – that is, to possess political-business skills. Meanwhile, members of the political class value a political entrepreneur – whether peer or client – on the basis of his reliability in fulfilling the terms of a bargain, knowing a large number of people and being able to assess them, and skill in translating material resources into a political following. All agree that a public figure requires personal reputation and societal management skills. This implies that honourable individuals may still generate and sustain civil moral values that allow them to resist the depredations of the system, and perhaps to humanize or even change it.

Towards a More Perfect Political Marketplace

The net impact of the changes traced over time in this book has been to advance the political marketplace and make it more efficient. Many of those changes have advantaged senior political-business managers. Prominent among these are new sources of rent, especially security cooperation. Another development favourable for national political CEOs is the eclipse of the coup d'état. An equal number of changes have disadvantaged them, such as faster and wider flows of information and cross-border integration. These factors have made the political marketplace more competitive and thereby increased the price of loyalty. There are more and better-informed claimants who can demand higher payments, and political CEOs need to spend more money, run a bigger and more elaborate intelligence system, and allow more time for bargaining, to stay on top.

It would be an error to characterize this contest as a tussle between authoritarianism and democracy. The marketization of politics operates on a different plane and rewards a different brand of politician, who is neither dictator nor democrat, but political entrepreneur. Still less should we celebrate the empowerment of subalterns as a triumph for inclusivity. The logic of political markets generates today's paradox of democratization: political competition and an open public sphere increase the marketization of politics. As David Booth observes, 'Under typical conditions, citizen pressure…will normally lead to more effective clientelism, not better public policies. So the normal form of "democratic deepening" is not a solution.'[41] There is no clear solution to this dilemma. A starting place for studying it is that we must be very cautious in drawing lessons from earlier historical periods and applying them to today's era of globalizing political markets.

What would a more perfect marketplace look like? Rather than constructing a model, let us examine the best examples we have: Somalia, Darfur in the late 2000s and South Sudan. These systems are dollarized. Loyalty is fully commoditized and regularly open for renegotiation. Flows of information and channels of bargaining are rapid and open. They are integrated across borders and with regional and global patrons. The means of violence are distributed among diverse men, some of them inside the governing apparatus, some of them outside, some with a foot in each camp.

Advanced political markets are turbulent and conditions fluctuate. At times, political finance is so readily available and competition among patrons so fierce that any hoodlum with a handful of sawn-off Landcruisers, a score of armed men and a Thuraya phone has a fair chance of advancement. Such moments of low entry barriers to the market tend to be transient, though they will surely recur – quite probably in South Sudan, possibly if central power collapses in Eritrea. At other times, loyalty markets become tighter, and the opportunities for upward mobility are limited by the need to climb up a less flexible clientship hierarchy.

A political market with near-perfect competition would be an arena of creative destruction, as political-business ventures prosper and crash, and new competitors outperform the old or innovate entirely new political products. The life cycle of national political CEOs also drives change. As the political fortunes of the men at the apex stall, decline or collapse, political entrepreneurs at the next level down will seize opportunities and establish new political enterprises or take over established ones. In extremis, international recognition will be won or lost by political businessmen's success vis-à-vis their peer-rivals and their ability to sell their wares to the international dispensers of sovereignty.[42] Intergovernmental clientelism channelled by American security funding and the new peacekeeping will reconstitute the sovereign order as a negotiated patronage hierarchy.

The biggest problem facing a political CEO is that as the political market becomes more perfect, the cost of loyalty rises. The political graveyard of the Horn is filled with politicians who failed to pay their way. One option – the cheap and old-fashioned one – is to repress and centralize control. The rulers of Eritrea and Ethiopia have been most successful in doing this, in their different ways, but each faces constraints that grow more formidable year by year. The expensive option is to beg, borrow or steal enough to pay the going rate – or, as Salva Kiir did, deliberately pay over the odds. As he enters yet another term in office, Omar al Bashir is trying to chart a middle course. When the current rentier boom – oil, aid and security cooperation – turns to bust, there will be more casualties.

Today's advanced political marketplaces are militarized, and violence plays the essential purpose of signalling a politician's intent and seriousness. But there is a paradox to violence in the political marketplace: while violence is embedded as an essential communicative and bargaining device, violence itself generates inefficiencies and risks. Once an act of violence goes beyond threat or symbolic harm, it generates emotions including the intoxication and sense of impunity of the immediate victor, bonds of solidarity among those who are fighting, and the impulse to revenge by those who have lost. Fighting follows its own escalatory logic and thereby multiplies uncertainty. Fear clouds judgement. Violence is a currency whose exact value is unknown until it is paid.

The history of the Horn shows that governments and revolutionaries inflicted the most extreme violence during the modernization era of attempted state formation. Under conditions of marketization, political businessmen inflict episodes of mass killing when information systems break down or they make miscalculations. The market rewards targeted, discriminate violence, and a political entrepreneur who is excessively bloodthirsty will rarely prosper. But when power hierarchies can be resolved by no other means, battle or massacre remains the ultimate decider. The convergence between war and commerce is even closer than suggested by Clausewitz's famous dictum, 'The decision by arms is, for all operations in war, great and small, what cash payment is in bill transactions.'[43]

Decision by arms occurs when one party submits to the will of the other. Defeat is a subjective decision and depends upon what is considered the boundary between acceptable and unacceptable losses, including loss of human life. Societal changes associated with the demographics of urbanization and mass higher education, combined with the information and communication revolution, have already altered those norms, and will continue to do so. Tolerance for violence is declining. Today's rent-seeking rebellion is usually played out in rural areas, with militarized tribalism as its gearbox. Its urban counterpart may emerge as the street protest and campus demonstration: less violent, with wider participation and more equitably gendered. So far, urban protest has lacked sufficient political financing, organization and strong allegiance among its protagonists to make it a favoured vehicle for political entrepreneurship. However, this will surely change as young political entrepreneurs develop business models that better leverage urban unrest for political advancement. Possibly, violence will become limited and even mostly symbolic, and entry-level political entrepreneurship will be widened to those with skill-sets that do not include coercion. It is possible, for example, to envisage regular contests between unarmed demonstrators and the police, in which unwritten rules determine which side concedes and for what price, or an electoral marketplace in which votes are auctioned.

I will not conclude this book neatly: it does not offer a thorough theorization but rather select histories of political agency in turbulent times. The Horn of Africa's political marketplace will – by its very nature – change in reaction to events. But let me end with an observation and a warning. This account of the encroachment of the political marketplace, and the general (though not unchallenged) triumph of its mercantile logic over other ways of organizing political and social life, can be seen as an example of Karl Polanyi's 'great transformation' to a commoditized global society.[44] The monetization of global politics will not easily be reversed, but its trajectory must surely be altered before it destroys the social order in the world's poorer and weaker countries.

Concluding Thoughts

I opened this book with a description of how the Sudanese negotiator at the Darfur peace talks, Dr Majzoub al Khalifa, practised retail politics alongside the formal negotiations. His bargaining was of course the centrepiece of the talks, and the labour of producing the eighty-seven-page document that was the Darfur Peace Agreement was the sideshow. In an article in the *London Review of Books*,[45] I described Majzoub as 'king crocodile' with the thick skin of a reptile, who was as vexatious to his colleagues as he was fearful to his adversaries. A few weeks after it was published I met Majzoub at his office in Khartoum. We had a long discussion about the situation in Darfur in which he, characteristically, did not concede a single point. He returned time and again to his principles: he would not give in on a certain claim because it would have wider repercussions, and that would be a violation of the legitimate demands of others. Majzoub took pride in managing a complicated and perilous system: for him, it was not only a career but a calling. Deeply aware of the uncertainties of politics, he was a master of *tajility* – the art of prevarication. Only when he walked me to the door, did he clap his huge hand on my shoulder and say, 'Fair article, fair article.'

Majzoub died in a car crash in 2007, and in his honour the Sudanese presidency published a compendium of tributes. Among them was included an excerpt from my article, translated into Arabic. The managers of the political marketplace in the Horn of Africa are sophisticated and studious, and appreciate the ironies of their circumstance. They know how to be civil when appropriate and may indeed prefer to practise a different kind of politics, but for the time being they, and their challengers, have no option but to sharpen their political-business skills.

An efficient and integrated advanced political marketplace of the kind that is in prospect is distasteful. To the extent that the fabric of a Weberian, rule-governed system existed, it is being corroded by the acid of real politics.

There are two types of measures that might halt the advance of the political marketplace and generate a more humane political order. One would involve taking the money out of international politics – or at least reducing it and making it more transparent. International policy reforms could make politics less conducive for rent-seekers and better structured to provide public goods. These reforms should begin at the top: regulating political finance. The two greatest dangers to the Horn are mineral rents and counter-terrorism funding, followed closely by any form of international security cooperation (including peacekeeping) that increases the size and opacity of military budgets. Illicit financial circuits are a complementary evil. Though we should try to reduce political financing, we cannot eliminate it. Rather, if we see political budgets as necessary for these (and any) political systems, then there should be ways of providing these funds in a more predictable and transparent way.

The other agenda is human morality: acknowledging civility and integrity amid the turbulence of the political marketplace, and recognizing and rewarding people who show those qualities. The final paradox of real politics in the Horn of Africa is that it is simultaneously an impersonal and dehumanizing system, and one that operates, visibly and inescapably, through the actions of men who use their power to get their way over others. Poor and powerless women and men understand this quite well, and respond as best they can to preserve humanity at the margins. The point of departure for challenging this cruel reality is to be honest to their experience and insight.

Notes

Chapter 1   Introduction: Observing the Business of Power

1 James 2007, p. 100.
2 Geuss 2008.
3 Compare how an ethical business in a developed economy may be run with the intention of promoting fair trade or environmental conservation, but will prosper only if it meets basic tenets of commercial viability.
4 Cf. Uvin 2009.
5 Firearms have been used as a currency in many parts of Africa over centuries. See Guyer 2004, pp. 43–4.
6 Mahmoud 1984.
7 'Explaining the Darfur Peace Agreement', an open letter to those members of the movements who are still reluctant to sign from the African Union moderators, May 2006, at: <http://fletcher.tufts.edu/World-Peace-Foundation/Activities/Sudan-Peace-Archive/~/media/Fletcher/Microsites/World%20Peace%20Foundation/Explaining%20the%20Darfur%20Peace%20Agreement.pdf>.
8 Andreski 1968, pp. 108–9.
9 See de Waal 1997, pp. 127–31.
10 FDRE 2002.
11 These encounters began when Paulos Tesfagiorgis, a veteran Eritrean freedom fighter, patriot and staunch advocate for human rights and peaceful cooperation, approached Meles discreetly in 2007 to explore possibilities for peace between Ethiopia and Eritrea. Meles asked Paulos to convene a small group to engage with him on a wider range of issues,

in a confidential but frank setting. Other members of the group were Abdalla Hamdok, Charles Abugre and Andre Zaaiman.
12 Author's notes, seminar, 16 October 2010.

Chapter 2   The Political Marketplace: Politics is Business and Business is Politics

1 Guyer 2004, p. 129.
2 Ibid., p. 130.
3 Scott 1976, p. 1.
4 Jackson and Rosberg 1982, p. 18.
5 World Bank 2011, pp. 108–11.
6 Ferguson 2006, p. 186.
7 Geuss 2008.
8 Tilly 1985, p. 169.
9 Williams 2014.
10 Porter 2008.
11 The 'sixth force' consists of complementers: firms that provide a necessary complementary product. Examples are arms dealers and bankers in tax havens.
12 Quoted in Schumpeter 1954, p. 100.
13 See Michael Johnston's 'syndromes of corruption', Johnston 2005, 2014.
14 See Konrad and Skaperdas 2006.
15 Cf. Olson 1993; Tilly 1990; North et al. 2009.
16 Anderson 1983; Tarrow 1994.
17 World Bank 2011.
18 See also Schatz 2009. Schatz notes that 'a general sympathy for interlocutors is…the hallmark of ethnographic research' and raises the practical and ethical difficulties of 'a hypothetical researcher who, although intending to conduct an ethnographic study, genuinely does not enjoy spending times with particular individuals (local strongmen, perpetrators of violence, corrupt police officers and extremist ideologues come to mind)', pp. 7–8. I can testify to those difficulties.
19 Bratton and Van de Walle 1997, p. 458.
20 Van de Walle 2001.
21 Duffield 2001; Keen 1994, 2005; Reno 1999, 2011.
22 Monga 1997, p. 56.
23 Bayart 2009.
24 Clapham 1996.
25 Chabal and Daloz 1999; Chabal 2009.
26 Mbembe 2001; Schatzberg 2001; Ellis and ter Haar 2004.
27 Putzel and Di John 2012.
28 Booth 2012; Kelsall 2013.
29 Booth 2012, p. 48.
30 Rawls 1971; MacIntyre 1981; Geuss 2008.

Chapter 3 The Horn of Africa: Subcontinental War in Three Acts

1 The electoral symbol for Sudan's ruling National Congress Party in 2010 was a tree, superimposed on a map of Sudan, with its roots following the course of the Nile and its tributaries in southern Sudan. I often expected to see one of these defaced with an axe cutting the tree trunk at the north–south boundary, depriving the tree of its roots, but never did.
2 With apologies to Jean-François Bayart, who prefers to see the African state as a rhizome. The incommensurability of the metaphors should not be taken too seriously.
3 There is a substantial literature on this: I have been very sparing in referencing.
4 Laitin 1999, p.156.
5 Woodroofe 2013.
6 Bates 2001, p.114.
7 Bates 2008, p. 20.
8 Ibid., p. 138.
9 Cf. Clapham 1996, pp. 25–6.
10 Cf. Quinlivan 1999.
11 Laitin 1999, p. 157.
12 de Waal 2004a.
13 Her meeting with Garang was described as 'a demonstration of support for a [future] regime that will not let Khartoum become a viper's nest for terrorist activities'. See 'Quote of the Day', *The Washington Post*, 11 December 1997, p. A30.

Chapter 4 Darfur: The Auction of Loyalties

1 From the Arabic *tajiil*, delay. See Daly 2010, p. 77.
2 Daly 1991, pp. 106–8, 123, 260–1, 347.
3 'Tribe' in Sudan and South Sudan refers to the administrative unit formalized in the 'native administration' system of government and is a translation of the Arabic *qabila*. Tribal chiefs are government appointees, but are almost always drawn from families that are historically powerful.
4 El-Tom 2011. See Bolton 2010 for a critique of El-Tom's translation.
5 Tubiana 2007.
6 Abdul-Jalil 1984.
7 El-Tom 2011, p. 211.
8 Mahmoud 1984.
9 His taste in costumes suggests this was a pervasive character trait.
10 Burr and Collins 1999, 2006.

11 Commission of Inquiry 1992, p. 80.
12 Harir 1994.
13 Roessler 2014; Flint and de Waal 2008, pp. 24–5.
14 Flint and de Waal 2008, pp. 62–3.
15 El-Tom 2011, pp. 2010–11.
16 Ibid., p. 213.
17 Ibid., p. 213.
18 El-Tom 2013, pp. 39–47.
19 de Waal et al. 2014.
20 Flint 2010.
21 Hobbes 1996, p. 62.
22 Flint 2008, p. 37.
23 Elbagir 2008.
24 Flint 2008, p. 38.
25 Nouwen and Werner 2011.
26 They were not asking for aid for the populations under their control, but direct support to them and their cause.
27 See Jumpert and Lanz 2013.
28 SIPRI military expenditure dataset.
29 Tubiana 2011.
30 Ibid., p. 28.
31 Qatari foreign policy is an exemplar of the political marketplace. See Dickinson 2014.
32 de Waal 2013b, p. 370.
33 de Waal 2004b, p. 27.
34 I will not here engage in debate as to whether this constituted genocide. See de Waal 2007d.
35 Fadul and Tanner 2007, p. 295.
36 Hansen 2013.
37 Debos 2011, p. 415.
38 Ibid., p. 416.

Chapter 5 Sudan: Managing the Unmanageable

1 It was also my first morning as Sudan researcher for Africa Watch.
2 Deng 1989, 1995.
3 Scott 1998.
4 Sudanese in different parts of the country were 'citizens' or 'subjects' accordingly, as described by Mamdani (1996).
5 Cf. Scott 2009.
6 Kameir and Kursany 1985.
7 Patey 2014, p. 30.
8 Stiansen 2004, p. 157.
9 El-Affendi 2013, p. 445.
10 Gallab 2008, p. 92.

11 African Rights 1997, pp. 102–3.
12 Brown 1992, p. 210.
13 World Bank 2003, p. 45.
14 Ibid., p. 2, para. 13.
15 Brown 1992, p. 228.
16 Stiansen 2004, p. 165; Gallab 2008, pp. 88–90.
17 See the US cable, reproduced by Wikileaks, on 413 'grey' parastatals (US Embassy Khartoum 2008).
18 Alsir 2014.
19 Alsir Sidahmed also points out, 'It is hard to imagine how Sudan under any regime could have survived oil prices of $100 a barrel if it was not producing oil itself' (Alsir 2014, conclusion (Kindle edition, no page)).
20 Patey 2014.
21 US Embassy Khartoum 2008.
22 World Bank 2007, pp. 23–4.
23 Ibid., p. 23.
24 Small Arms Survey 2009, p. 8.
25 Indeed, in the last days of the campaign, the NCP made two cash payments to Sadiq al Mahdi, amounting to $1.5 million, to encourage him to participate in the elections, so as to make them more credible. Sadiq took the cash but his party still boycotted.
26 Abdalla 2010.
27 World Bank 2007, pp. 7, 61–2.
28 de Waal 2010, p. 24.
29 I handled the 'Two Areas' file for the AUHIP from December 2010 to June 2011. I will write the full story elsewhere.
30 African Rights 1995.
31 Adam Mohamed Ahmed, 'We Cannot Win through War, Gosh Says,' *The Niles*, 25 July 2013, at: <http://www.theniles.org/articles/?id=1965>.
32 Komey 2012, p. 6.

Chapter 6   South Sudan: The Boom and Bust of a Kleptocracy

1 I chose not to attend the independence celebrations in Juba.
2 Cf. Pinaud 2014.
3 A note on terminology: southern Sudan refers to the southern region or southern states of the united Sudan, up to July 2011; South Sudan is the independent republic from July 2011; in 1983 the SPLA and SPLM were founded as SPLA/M; later the initials were reversed to SPLM/A, and in 2005 they were formally separated with the SPLM becoming a political party and the SPLA the armed forces of southern Sudan, and later South Sudan. The separation between SPLA, SPLM and government is a legal fiction.
4 Author's discussions with South Sudanese leaders.

5   Burr 1998.
6   'Tribe' refers to units as constituted and recognized through the native administrative system. Ethnographers of South Sudan also categorize each major ethnicity, such as Dinka and Nuer, as consisting of several tribal units. See Ahmed 2002 for tribal elite as a class.
7   Prendergast 2014.
8   Copnall 2014, p. 167.
9   See: <http://fletcher.tufts.edu/World-Peace-Foundation/Program/Research/Sudan-Peace-Archive/Timeline>.
10 See: <http://southernsudan2011.com/>.
11 Ten of the seventy-nine counties were overzealous and recorded more than 100 per cent turnout. Of the votes cast within southern Sudan, 99.57 per cent were for independence. When the numbers were published, the tally for Western Equatoria State was omitted, causing a ruckus.
12 Deng 2005, p. 6.
13 A political but not biological cousin to his near namesake.
14 Tvedt 1994, p. 80.
15 Kameir and Kursany 1985, p. 26.
16 Tvedt 1994.
17 Quoted in African Rights 1997, p. 63.
18 Garang 1987, 1992.
19 For the militarism and brutality of the early SPLA, see inter alia, Nyaba 1997, African Rights 1997, Hutchinson 1998, Madut-Arop 2006, Leonardi 2007 and Thomas 2015.
20 Karim, Duffield et al. 1996.
21 Wöndu and Lesch 2000.
22 Rolandsen 2005.
23 Johnson 2012, p. 169.
24 Natsios 2012, p. 177.
25 Deng 2013.
26 *Sudan Tribune*, 'TEXT: Minutes of Historical SPLM Meeting in Rumbek 2004', 12 March 2008, at: <http://www.sudantribune.com/spip.php?article26320>.
27 Alier 1992.
28 Small Arms Survey 2006–7.
29 Rands 2010, pp. 42–3.
30 Young 2012, pp. 121–2.
31 World Bank 2007, p. 72.
32 Snowden 2012, p. 19.
33 Due to the depreciation of the Sudanese pound, the dollar value was $220 a month.
34 Snowden 2012, p. 20.
35 Ibid., pp. 37–9.
36 Peter Martell, 'South Sudan to Arm Militias against Uganda Rebels', AFP, 27 September 2010, at: <http://m.reliefweb.int/report/369051>.
37 Lewis 2009, pp. 39–44. A ship carrying some of these tanks was hijacked by Somali pirates.

38   Lewis 2009, p. 66; World Bank and SIPRI data.
39   Speaking at a seminar on preparing a National Security and Defence White Paper, Juba, September 2007.
40   'Edward Lino: There was No Coup in Juba', 9 February 2014, at: <http://paanluelwel.com/2014/02/09/edward-lino-there-was-no-coup -in-juba/>.
41   Leonardi 2013, p. 185.
42   World Bank 2013.
43   Ibid., pp. 9–12.
44   Larson et al. 2013, p. 21.
45   French and Travis 2012.
46   Conversation with the author, 21 January 2012.
47   Guigale 2012.
48   An ethnic Nuer, Gatdet was in Juba at the time the killings started and escaped to begin the rebellion.
49   Radio Tamazuj, 'Oil Companies Reject Loan Request by Kiir Government', 6 August 2014, at: <https://radiotamazuj.org/en/article/ oil-companies-reject-loan-request-kiir-government>.
50   Small Arms Survey 2014.
51   Javier Blas and Katrina Mansion, 'War-torn South Sudan under Economic Attack from Fall in Oil Price', *Financial Times*, 21 December 2004.
52   For South Sudanese the initials 'PDF' of course conjure memories of the Arab militia and not their own protection.
53   Resolutions of the 28th Extraordinary Summit of the IGAD Heads of State and Government, Addis Ababa, 7 November 2014, paragraph 4.

Chapter 7   Somalia: A Post-Apocalypse Workshop

1   de Waal 1993, p. 10.
2   UNOSOM II, 'Background', at: <http://www.un.org/en/peacekeeping/ missions/past/unosom2backgr1.html>.
3   Mohamed Ibrahim and Jeffrey Gettleman, 'UN Chief Pays Surprise Visit to Somalia', *New York Times*, 9 December 2011.
4   Cf. International Crisis Group 2008.
5   Lewis 1998, p. 105.
6   Lewis 1961.
7   Compagnon 2013.
8   The US hesitated at first. The Soviet invasion of Afghanistan changed the calculation. Lefebvre 1992, pp. 208–9.
9   World Bank 1991, p. 5.
10   Maren 1997.
11   Askin 1987; Tucker 1982; US Senate 1980.

12   General Accounting Office 1989, pp. 9–10.
13   Besteman and Cassanelli 2000.
14   Cf. Coolidge and Rose-Ackerman 1997, p. 15.
15   Quoted in Keith Richburg, 'Orphan of the Cold War: Somalia Lost its Key Role', *Washington Post*, 15 October 1992.
16   Lefebvre 1992, p. 250.
17   Jamal 1988, p. 206.
18   Coolidge and Rose-Ackerman 1997.
19   World Bank 1991, p. 2.
20   World Bank 1983.
21   Isaias Afewerki has done the first and Jaafar Nimeiri did the second.
22   Jamal 1988, p. 208.
23   Cf. Olson 1993; Bates 2008.
24   Kapteijns 2013, p. 93.
25   Powell, Ford and Nowrasteh 2006; Leeson 2007.
26   Marc Lacey, 'Amid Somalia's Troubles, Coca Cola Hangs on', *New York Times*, 10 July 2006.
27   Kulaksiz and Purdekova 2006, p. 5.
28   Hassan and Chalmers 2008, p. 13.
29   Collins 2009a, 2009b.
30   Collins 2009b, pp. 163–4.
31   Ibid., pp. 65ff.
32   Ibid., pp. 93ff.
33   Ibid., pp. 110–34.
34   Kapteijns 2013.
35   Aidan Hartley, 'Somali Companies Go to War over Banana Exports', *Reuters*, 17 February 1995.
36   Ken Menkhaus (2003, pp. 419–20) frames this issue in slightly different language.
37   de Waal 1996, p. 28.
38   Johnson et al. 2009.
39   Menkhaus 2003, p. 419.
40   Johnson et al. 2009, pp. 54, 65.
41   The investigation was done by Abdirazak Fartaag, who was head of Somalia's Public Finance Unit during 2009–11. See Warah 2012.
42   Drysdale 1994, p. 181.
43   Simons 1995, p. 116.
44   de Waal 2004a, p. 207.
45   Watts, Shapiro and Brown 2007.
46   Ibid., p. 15.
47   Ibid., p. 21.
48   Ibid., pp. 21–2.
49   Marchal 2011, p. 15.
50   Marchal 2004, pp. 140–3.
51   Collins 2009a, pp. 143–4.
52   Marchal 2011, p. 16.
53   Watts et al. 2007, p. 65.

54 See Hoehne 2009.
55 Djibouti and Sierra Leone joined later.
56 Roggio 2012.
57 Marchal 2011, p. 23.
58 Ibid., p. 65.
59 Maxwell and Majid 2015.
60 Aynte 2012.
61 Marchal 2012.
62 United Nations Monitoring Group 2012a, p. 8.
63 Ibid., p. 18.
64 Ibid., p. 236.
65 Ibid., p. 8. The United Nations Monitoring Group exposure generated a vigorous response from SCS lawyers and public relations consultants.

Chapter 8   Somaliland: A Business-Social Contract

1 Omaar 1994; Flint 1994; Bryden 1995.
2 Gilkes 1993.
3 Bradbury 2008.
4 Spears 2003; Balthasar 2013.
5 Collins 2009b.
6 Balthasar 2013.
7 Africa Watch 1990.
8 de Waal 2002.
9 Wilson 1994.
10 Marx and Engels 2010 (1848), p. 15.
11 de Waal 1996, 2007b. Nicholas Eubank (2012) in his study of revenue bargaining makes similar points.
12 Bradbury, 2008, p. 110.
13 Ibid., p. 112.
14 Ibid., p. 111.
15 Collins 2009b, p. 170.
16 Eubank 2012, pp. 472–3.
17 Bradbury 2008, pp. 236–7.
18 Collins 2009b, pp. 189–91.
19 'Somaliland to Drill Oil by 2014', *Somaliland Press*, 31 October 2012, at: <http://somalilandpress.com/somaliland-to-drill-oil-by-2014-36905>.
20 Bryden 1999, p. 137.
21 Bradbury 2008, p. 123.
22 Balthasar 2013.
23 Bradbury 2008, p. 116.
24 Balthasar 2013; Tilly 1990, p. 67.

Chapter 9   Eritrea: A Museum of Modernism

1   See Abdulrahman Babu (2002) for a description of the EPLF in the field as 'the future that works'.
2   Denison, Ren and Gebremedhin 2007.
3   Arguaby the world's most beautiful petrol garage, it was designed by Giuseppe Pettazzi, completed in 1938 and restored in 2003.
4   Iyob 1995; Pool 2001.
5   Pateman 1990.
6   Mahrt 2009, p. 24.
7   Tareke 1991.
8   US Embassy Asmara 2006.
9   The African Development Bank politely states, 'Since the national budget is not publicly available, the task of assessing the quality of public finance management remains difficult.' African Development Bank 2009, p. 5.
10   Styan 2004.
11   Even the maps used in Ethiopian schools place Badme in Eritrea. During the hostilities and aftermath, Ethiopia has not used maps to demonstrate the location of Eritrean 'aggression', because it lies north of the line on those maps. The question of de facto administration and the use of force to determine international boundaries is a separate question, on which Ethiopia has strong arguments.
12   Ethiopia's national symbol is the lion, but its generals joked that they owed more to the hardworking and loyal donkey than they ever did to the lion.
13   See Connell 2005, pp. 10–11 and 133–4 for related details.
14   Tronvoll and Mekonnen 2014.
15   Riggan 2009.
16   The data source is SIPRI's military expenditure database. See: <http://milexdata.sipri.org/files/?file=SIPRI+milex+data+1988–2011.xls>. No figures for Eritrea's spending after 2003 are available.
17   IMF data also see Trading Economics, at: <http://www.tradingeconomics.com/eritrea/exports>.
18   US Embassy Asmara 2007b, para. 6.
19   United Nations Monitoring Group 2011, 2012b.
20   UN Security Council Resolution 2013, 5 December 2011, para. 10.
21   United Nations Monitoring Group 2011, p. 97.
22   US Embassy Asmara 2007b, para. 8. The cable also obliquely refers to officially organized prostitution, observing that influential Arabs 'enjoy short recreational breaks in Massawa'.
23   The obsession is reciprocated but asymmetrical. Asmara controls Ethiopian rebels based in Eritrea and uses them as pawns. Ethiopia has hosted and supported Eritrean opposition groups but without a strategy for making use of them.

24 I was alerted to this when a discussion I was having with Abdalla Jabir in Abuja in April 2006 was interrupted because he needed to fly home – with Sudanese intelligence chief Salah Gosh, in Gosh's plane.

25 Three went into exile and one recanted and joined the government, later going into exile.

26 International Crisis Group 2010.

27 This was also the date, according to World Bank statistics, when Eritrea's GDP per capita (going down) was surpassed by Ethiopia's (going up), the two crossing at about $190.

28 Connell 2009, p. 42 and p. 43.

29 Kibreab 2009.

30 US Embassy Asmara 2007a, paras 9–10.

31 International Crisis Group 2014, p. 8; Poole 2013; van Reisen, Estifanos and Rijken 2012; United Nations Monitoring Group 2012b, pp. 20–21.

32 International Crisis Group 2014, p. 8.

33 United Nations Monitoring Group 2012b, pp. 20–21.

34 However, in 2014, the Eritrean Embassy in London was still enforcing the 2 per cent tax. See Plaut 2014.

35 See: <http://www.tradingeconomics.com/eritrea/exports>.

36 Nevsun's website contains the following summary of Eritrea: 'Single party state. No corruption. UN arms embargo/sanctions have no impact on Bisha or Nevsun.' See: <http://www.nevsun.com/projects/eritrea/>.

37 UN Security Council Resolution 2023, 5 December 2011, paras 12–14.

38 On 20 March 2015, the Nevsun mine was attacked and damaged by an Ethiopian airstrike.

39 23 August 2001, Connell 2005, p. 135.

40 Woldemikael 2009, 2013.

41 Anderson 1983.

42 International Crisis Group 2013.

Chapter 10   Ethiopia: Is State-Building Still Possible?

1 Cf. Scott 1998.

2 Lefort 2007, p. 258.

3 Ibid., p. 259.

4 Ibid., p. 267.

5 Cf. Levine 1965. In the Oxford University Library system, the African literature is collected at Rhodes House, with the exception of Ethiopia, which is in the Oriental Reading Room, along with Somaliland (because the latter was initially governed from Bombay).

6 Bayart 2009.

7 Perham 1948, p. 72.

8 Author's notes from a seminar held at the prime minister's office, Addis Ababa, 16 October 2010.

9 Balsvik 1984.
10 Donham 1999, p. 131.
11 Africa Watch 1991, chapters 4–5.
12 Tareke 2009.
13 Africa Watch 1991, chapter 17.
14 Markakis 1990.
15 Clapham 1990.
16 Young 1996.
17 de Waal 1997, chapter 6.
18 Some civil servants were paid twice that month, as – fearing the worst – their managers paid salaries early before the capture of the city.
19 Vaughan and Tronvoll 2003, p. 94.
20 Zenawi 2012; n.d.
21 FDRE 2002.
22 Zenawi n.d., p. 32.
23 Ibid., p. 8.
24 Khan 2012.
25 FDRE 2002, p. 38.
26 Ibid., p. 30.
27 Ibid., p. 23.
28 The Standing Committee of the EPRDF Executive Committee.
29 Booth 2012; Kelsall 2013.
30 David Booth argues that Ethiopia and Rwanda were uniquely able to follow this strategy because of their particular histories of conflict and the governments, headed by former liberation movement leaders, which emerged. Meles did not agree with this but nonetheless was unsure about the preconditions under which an activist developmental state could be established. Meles would also have disputed the use of the word 'patrimonialism'.
31 Vaughan and Gebremeskel 2011.
32 Ibid., p. 59.
33 Ibid., p. 60. See also Chanie (2007) for a critique of Ethiopian decentralization policies as a mode of clientelism.
34 Zenawi n.d., p. 10.
35 'The Political Marketplace: A Political Economy of Rentierism and State Fragility', unpublished paper, 4 November 2009.
36 Zenawi n.d., p. 11.
37 Author's notes, seminar, October 2010.
38 Author's notes from a seminar held at the prime minister's office, Addis Ababa, 22 October 2008.
39 Stiglitz 2002, p. 26.
40 Khan 2012.
41 Aalen and Tronvoll 2008, p. 18.
42 Tronvoll 2010, p. 132.
43 Author's notes, seminar, October 2008.
44 Markakis 2011.

45 Tronvoll 2010, p. 124.
46 FDRE 2002, p. 23.
47 De Waal 1996.
48 De Waal 2007b.
49 Author's notes, personal discussion, prime minister's office, 20 February 2011.
50 Author's notes, seminar, 23 October 2008.
51 Meles Zenawi 'The renaissance movement and the question of building leadership capacity and institutions', internal memo prepared for EPRDF Politbureau, May 2012 (in Amharic).
52 See p. 2.
53 See pp. 32–4.
54 See pp. 5–6.
55 Cf. Altenburg 2010, p. 2.
56 Cf. Johnston 2005.

Chapter 11 Transnational Patronage and Dollarization

1   Barnett 2004.
2   Kaldor, Karl and Said 2007.
3   Phillips 2011, p. 68.
4   Cotula 2013.
5   See: Global Financial Integrity, at: <www.gfintegrity.org> (set up by Raymond Baker); the Tax Justice Network, at: <www.taxjusticeafrica.net>; and the ONE Campaign's 'Trillion Dollar Scandal', at: <http://www.one.org/scandal/en/>.
6   Baker 2005.
7   The allegations that Nicolas Sarkozy obtained funds from Muammar Gaddafi is the latest in a line of unconfirmed reports that leaders, including Felix Houphouët-Boigny and Omar Bongo, assisted with French candidates' electoral expenses.
8   Roeber 2005; Feinstein 2011.
9   SIPRI data.
10 Mwenda 2010, p. 45.
11 Ibid., p. 52.
12 I coined this term in 1992; see de Waal 1997.
13 See de Waal 2007c.
14 See Bob 2006.
15 FDRE 2002, p. 31.
16 See Lefebvre (1992) for Cold War era examples.
17 Hoehne 2009.
18 Military intelligence officers even kept connections with Joseph Kony.
19 Marchal 2013.

20 Phillips 2011, p. 11.
21 Ibid., p. 43.
22 Watts et al. 2007, p. 28; emphasis in the original.
23 The stimulant leaf khat or chat, grown in Ethiopia and Kenya and consumed within the region, Yemen and by the Somali diaspora, is a part exception. It is considered a social problem rather than a law-enforcement issue in the region.
24 Bayart 2009; see also Englebert 2009, p. 95.
25 Bueno de Mesquita and Smith 2010.
26 The 'P5' are the five permanent, veto-wielding members of the Security Council, and the 'P3' are the three western nations that generally act together.
27 African Union Peace and Security Council communiqué of 24 April 2012 and UN Security Council Resolution 2046 of 2 May 2012.
28 The first AU leaders' visit to Tripoli was scheduled for the day that the NATO air action began, and was stopped. The African leaders subsequently met with Gaddafi, but too late and with too little political momentum to have a positive impact.
29 de Waal 2013b.
30 See inter alia Soré 2011; also see Dörrie 2012 for an analysis of Compaoré as a political entrepreneur who specialized in 'solving' conflicts he has himself initiated – a more effective version of Isaias Afewerki's business plan. Compaoré finally overreached in 2014 and was deposed.
31 China initiated this trend with its Forum on China–Africa Cooperation which met at summit level in 2006. This focused on trade and investment.
32 See: <http://www.elysee.fr/declarations/article/elysee-summit-for-peace-and-security-in-africa-final-declaration/>.
33 See: <http://www.whitehouse.gov/blog/2014/05/28/america-must-always-lead-president-obama-addresses-west-point-graduates>.
34 See: <http://www.whitehouse.gov/the-press-office/2014/08/06/fact-sheet-us-support-peacekeeping-africa>. The US's assessed contribution to UN peacekeeping is 28.8 per cent and its total (multi-year) commitment to nine ongoing peacekeeping operations in Africa is over $9 billion.
35 Kofi Annan's first act as Secretary General in January 1997 was to make DPKO senior to the Department of Political Affairs within the UN. This can be seen as subordinating independent political advice to the implementation of peacekeeping operations, which, for obvious financial reasons, are determined principally by the P3.
36 Perry and Smith 2013.
37 United Nations General Assembly 2014.
38 AMISOM's budget is complex. Between 2007–12, the US provided $429m, the EU provided €444m and the UN trust fund $787m.
39 See Lang 2013, p. 8, for this in a European context.
40 Debos 2011.

Chapter 12   Towards a More Perfect Marketplace?

1   In Darfur between 1985 and 1987 for my fieldwork I did not use a
    telephone a single time.
2   Barkey 2008.
3   Nick Couldry makes this point with regard to Iraq in the 1990s (Couldry
    2012, p. 10).
4   Harry Mapolu, a radical student at the University of Dar es Salaam,
    has written an engrossing account of producing the magazine *Cheche*
    in 1969–70 (Mapolu 2010).
5   Cf. Anderson 1983.
6   Gassim 2010, p. 50.
7   Hirji 2010, p. 42.
8   In Egyptian universities, by contrast, the humanities and social sciences
    were considered 'garbage faculties', with predictable consequences for
    public intellectual life. See Kepel 1993, pp. 135–8.
9   I went to Khartoum in 1984 because at that time it was the world's
    intellectual centre for refugee studies: the university and the Commissioner
    of Refugees, just across the street, were producers of intellectual capital,
    not consumers of products generated elsewhere (see Karadawi 1999).
10 Flint and de Waal 2008, p. 20.
11 Balsvik 1984; Donham 1999.
12 Cf. Kepel 1993, pp. 135–6.
13 Wikipedia lists 157, many of which have uncertain status. In 2012, the
    Ministry of Higher Education listed thirty-four public universities, fifty-
    two polytechnic colleges and seven private universities.
14 Conducted on 28 August 2014.
15 Gassim 2010, p. 53.
16 Moyn 2010.
17 Mary Kaldor (2003) captures part of this with her distinction between
    'old' and 'new' social movements, but this does not fully address the
    specifics of anti-colonial movements.
18 de Waal 2003, p. 486.
19 See Englund (2006) for a case study of this in Malawi.
20 The exception is the security sector, though local vigilantism and private
    security contractors may yet generate security-sector NGOs.
21 Bayart 2009; Krause 2014.
22 Ferguson 1990; Abrahamsen 2001.
23 Discussion, February 1999.
24 El-Tom 2011, pp.169–70.
25 See de Waal 2013a.
26 This section draws heavily on the research team for the Justice and
    Security Research Programme, including Tim Allen, Vesna Bojicic-
    Dzelilovic, Tatiana Carayannis, Rachel Ibreck, Mary Kaldor, Anna
    MacDonald, Holly Porter, Mareike Schomerus and Koen Vlassenroot.
27 Scott 2009.

234

Notes to pages 210–216

28 James 2007.
29 Roitman 2005.
30 I owe this insight and term to Tim Allen. It is one of the three organizing logics of the Justice and Security Research Programme, along with public mutuality and the political marketplace.
31 Ellis and ter Haar 2004; Guyer 2004, pp. 76–9.
32 Muslim thinkers have long articulated the need for restraint in the use of violence and respect for persons, arguing that civilization should aim at making power more humane, not imposing norms on others. Civil space implies a forum for deliberative democracy and free use of public reason for expressing grievances and voicing criticism bound by agreed rules. Ezzat and Kaldor 2006.
33 Keck and Sikkink 1998.
34 Mahgoub 1974, p. 190.
35 Cf. Turner 1974.
36 Thigo 2013.
37 See: <https://opendata.go.ke/>.
38 Nouwen and Werner 2011.
39 Uvin 2009, p. 66.
40 Ibid., p. 189.
41 Booth 2012, p. 57.
42 See Pierre Englebert's 'rational policy fantasies', Englebert 2009, chapter 9.
43 Clausewitz 2003, p. 137.
44 Polanyi 1944.
45 See de Waal 2006.

Bibliography

Aalen, Lovise and Kjetil Tronvoll, 2008. 'The 2008 Ethiopian Local Elections: The Return of Electoral Authoritarianism,' *African Affairs*, 108/430: 111–20.

Abdalla, Abd-al Wahab, 2010. 'Sudan: The Ugly Election,' Making Sense of Sudan, 22 April, at: <http://africanarguments.org/2010/04/22/the-ugly -election/>.

Abdul-Jalil, Musa, 1984. 'The Dynamics of Ethnic Identification in Northern Darfur, Sudan: A Situational Approach', in Bayreuth African Studies Series, *The Sudan: Ethnicity and National Cohesion*, pp. 49–62.

Abrahamsen, Rita, 2001. *Disciplining Democracy: Development Discourse and Good Governance in Africa*, London: Zed Books.

Africa Watch, 1990. *Somalia: A Government at War with its Own People*, New York: Human Rights Watch.

Africa Watch, 1991. *Evil Days: Thirty Years of War and Famine in Ethiopia*, New York: Human Rights Watch.

African Development Bank, 2009. *Interim Country Strategy Paper for Eritrea, 2009–2011*, Tunis: African Development Bank Group.

African Rights, 1995. *Facing Genocide: The Nuba of Sudan*, London: African Rights.

African Rights, 1997. *Food and Power in Sudan: A Critique of Humanitarianism*, London: African Rights.

Ahmed, Abdel Ghaffar M., 2002. ' "Tribal Elite": A Base for Social Stratification in the Sudan', in Abdel Ghaffar M. Ahmed (ed.), *Anthropology in the Sudan: Reflections by a Sudanese Anthropologist*, Utrecht: International Books, pp. 65–80.

Alier, Abel, 1992. *Southern Sudan: Too Many Agreements Dishonoured*, London: Paul & Co.

Alsir, Sidahmed, 2014. *The Oil Years in Sudan: The Quest for Political Power and Economic Breakthrough*, Toronto: Key Publishing.

Altenburg, Tilmann, 2010. *Industrial Policy in Ethiopia*, Bonn: German Development Institute, Discussion Paper 2/2010.

Anderson, Benedict, 1983. *Imagined Communities: Reflections on the Origin and Spread of Nationalism*, London: Verso.

Andreski, Stanislav, 1968. *The African Predicament: A Study in the Pathology of Modernisation*, New York: Atherton Press.

Askin, Steve, 1987, 'Food Aid Diversion', *Middle East Report*, 145 (March–April): 38–40.

Aynte, Abdi, 2012. 'Understanding the al-Shabaab/al-Qaeda "merger"', March, unpublished paper.

Babu, Abdelrahman M., 2002. 'The Future that Works', in Salma Babu and Amrit Wilson (eds), *The Future that Works: Selected Writings of A. M. Babu*, Trenton, NY: Africa World Press (first published 1981), pp. 239–42.

Baker, Raymond, 2005. *Capitalism's Achilles Heel: Dirty Money and How to Renew the Free-Market System*, New York, Wiley.

Balsvik, Randi Ronning, 1984. *Haile Selassie's Students: The Intellectual and Social Background to Revolution, 1952–1977*, East Lansing: Michigan State University.

Balthasar, Dominik, 2013. 'The Wars in the North and the Creation of Somaliland', *Reinventing Peace*, 28 October, at: <http://sites.tufts.edu/reinventingpeace/2013/10/28/the-wars-in-the-north-and-the-creation-of-somaliland/>.

Barkey, Karen, 2008. *Empire of Difference: The Ottomans in Comparative Perspective*, Cambridge: Cambridge University Press.

Barnett, Thomas, 2004. *The Pentagon's New Map: War and Peace in the Twenty-first Century*, New York: Berkley Books.

Bates, Robert, 2001. *Prosperity and Violence: The Political Economy of Development*, New York: W.W. Norton.

Bates, Robert, 2008. *When Things Fell Apart: State Failure in Late-Century Africa*, Cambridge: Cambridge University Press.

Bayart, Jean-François, 2009. *The State in Africa: The Politics of the Belly*, London: Polity.

Besteman, Catherine and Lee Cassanelli, 2000. *The Struggle for Land in Southern Somalia: The War Behind the War*, Brighton: Haan Publishing.

Bob, Clifford, 2006. *The Marketing of Rebellion*, Cambridge: Cambridge University Press.

Bolton, Caity, 2010. 'JEM's Black Book and the Language of Resistance: Transcribing Tyranny', *Making Sense of Sudan*, 8 June, at: <http://africanarguments.org/2010/06/08/transcribing-tyranny/>.

Booth, David, 2012. *Development as a Collective Action Problem: Addressing the Real Challenges of African Governance*, London: Overseas Development Institute, African Power and Politics Programme.

Bradbury, Mark, 2008. *Becoming Somaliland*, Oxford: James Currey.

Bratton, Michael and Nicolas van de Walle, 1997. *Democratic Experiments in Africa: Regime Transitions in Comparative Perspective.* Cambridge: Cambridge University Press.

Brown, Richard, 1992. *Public Debt and Private Wealth: Debt, Capital Flight and the IMF in Sudan,* London: Macmillan.

Bryden, Matt, 1995. *Somaliland and Peace in the Horn of Africa: A Situation Report and Analysis,* Addis Ababa: United Nations Emergencies Unit for Ethiopia.

Bryden, Matt, 1999. 'New Hope for Somalia? The Building Block Approach', *Review of African Political Economy,* 26/79: 134–40.

Bueno de Mesquita, Bruce and Alastair Smith, 2010. 'The Pernicious Consequences of UN Security Council Membership,' *Journal of Conflict Resolution,* 54/5: 667–86.

Burr, J. Millard, 1998. *Quantifying Genocide in Southern Sudan and the Nuba Mountains, 1983–1998,* Washington, DC: US Committee for Refugees.

Burr, J. Millard and Robert O. Collins, 1999. *Africa's Thirty Years' War: Chad, Libya, the Sudan, 1963–1993.* Boulder, CO: Westview Press.

Burr, J. Millard and Robert O. Collins, 2006. *Darfur: The Long Road to Disaster,* Boulder, CO: Markus Wiener.

Chabal, Patrick, 2009. *Africa: The Politics of Suffering and Smiling,* London: Zed Books.

Chabal, Patrick and Jean Pascal Daloz, 1999. *Africa Works: Disorder as Political Instrument,* London: James Currey.

Chanie, Paulos, 2007. 'Clientelism and Ethiopia's Post-1992 Decentralisation', *Journal of Modern African Studies,* 45/3: 353–84.

Clapham, Christopher, 1990. *Transformation and Continuity in Revolutionary Ethiopia,* Cambridge: Cambridge University Press.

Clapham, Christopher, 1996. *Africa and the International System: The Politics of State Survival.* Cambridge: Cambridge University Press.

Clausewitz, Carl Von, 2003. *The Essential Clausewitz: Selections from 'On War',* London: Cassell.

Collins, Gregory, 2009a. 'Connected: Exploring the Extraordinary Demand for Telecoms Services in Post-collapse Somalia', *Mobilities,* 4/2: 203–23.

Collins, Gregory, 2009b. 'Connected: Developing Somalia's Telecoms Industry in the Wake of State Collapse', PhD thesis, University of California Davis.

Commission of Inquiry, 1992. *Chad: Report of the Commission of Inquiry into the Crimes and Misappropriations Committed by Ex-President Habré, His Accomplices and/or Accessories,* N'djaména: Commission of Inquiry, 7 May.

Compagnon, Daniel, 2013. 'State-sponsored Violence and Conflict under Mahamed Siyad Barre: The Emergence of Path Dependent Patterns of Violence,' *Reinventing Peace,* 22 October, at: <http://sites.tufts.edu/reinventingpeace/2013/10/22/state-sponsored-violence-and-conflict-under-mahamed-siyad-barre-the-emergence-of-path-dependent-patterns-of-violence/>.

Connell, Dan, 2005. *Conversations with Eritrean Political Prisoners*, Trenton, NJ: Red Sea Press.

Connell, Dan, 2009. 'The EPLF/PFDJ Experience: How it Shapes Eritrea's Regional Strategy', in Richard Reid (ed.), *Eritrea's External Relations: Understanding its Regional Role and Foreign Policy*, London: Chatham House, 24–44.

Coolidge, Jacqueline and Susan Rose-Ackerman, 1997. *High-level Rent-seeking and Corruption in African Regimes*, Washington, DC: World Bank, Private Sector Development Department and Foreign Investment Advisory Service, Policy Research Working Paper 1780, June.

Copnall, James, 2014. *A Poisonous Thorn in Our Hearts: Sudan and South Sudan's Bitter and Incomplete Divorce*, London: Hurst.

Cotula, Lorenzo, 2013. *The Great African Land Grab: Agricultural Investments and the Global Food System*, London: Zed Books.

Couldry, Nick, 2012. *Media, Society, World: Social Theory and Digital Media Practice*, Cambridge: Polity.

Daly, Martin, 1991. *Imperial Sudan: The Anglo-Egyptian Condominium, 1934–56*, Cambridge: Cambridge University Press.

Daly, Martin, 2010. *Darfur's Sorrow: A History of Destruction and Genocide*, Cambridge: Cambridge University Press.

Debos, Marielle, 2008. 'Fluid Loyalties in a Regional Crisis: Chadian "Ex-Liberators" in the Central African Republic', *African Affairs*, 107/427: 225–41.

Debos, Marielle, 2011. 'Living by the Gun in Chad: Armed Violence as a Practical Occupation', *Journal of Modern African Studies*, 49/3: 409–28.

Debos, Marielle, 2015. *Combatants and the State in Chad: Governing the Inter-war*, London: Zed Books.

Deng, Francis Mading, 1989. *Cry of the Owl*, New York: Lilian Barber Press.

Deng, Francis Mading, 1995. *War of Visions: Conflict of Identities in the Sudan*, Washington, DC: Brookings.

Deng, Francis Mading, 2005. 'African Renaissance: Towards a New Sudan', *Forced Migration Review*, 24: 6–8.

Deng, Lual A., 2013. *The Power of Creative Reasoning: The Ideas and Vision of John Garang*, Bloomington, IN: iUniverse.

Denison, Edward, Guang Yu Ren and Naizghi Gebremedhin, 2007, *Asmara: Africa's Secret Modernist City*, London: Merrell.

de Waal, Alex, 1993. 'A Fitful Apocalypse', *Times Literary Supplement*, 26 March, p. 10.

de Waal, Alex, 1996. 'State and Power in a Stateless Somalia', African Rights Discussion Paper, available at SSRC Webforum, 2007, *Crisis in the Horn of Africa*, online essays, at: <http://hornofafrica.ssrc.org/dewaal/>.

de Waal, Alex, 1997. *Famine Crimes: Politics and the Disaster Relief Industry in Africa*, Oxford: James Currey.

de Waal, Alex, 2002. *Demilitarizing the Mind: African Agendas for Peace and Security*, Trenton, NJ: Africa World Press.

de Waal, Alex, 2003. 'Human Rights and the Political Imagination: How the West and Africa Have Diverged', *Journal of Human Rights*, 2/4: 475–94.

de Waal, Alex, 2004a. 'The Politics of Destabilization in the Horn, 1989–2001', in Alex de Waal (ed.), *Islamism and Its Enemies in the Horn of Africa*, London: Hurst, pp. 182–230.

de Waal, Alex, 2004b. 'Counter-Insurgency on the Cheap', *London Review of Books*, 26/15 (5 August): 25–7.

de Waal, Alex, 2006. '"I will not sign," Alex de Waal at the Darfur Peace Talks', *London Review of Books*, 28/23 (30 November): 17–20.

de Waal, Alex, 2007a. 'Darfur's Deadline: The Final Days of the Abuja Peace Process', in Alex de Waal (ed.), *War in Darfur and the Search for Peace*, Cambridge, MA: Harvard University Press, pp. 267–83.

de Waal, Alex, 2007b. 'State and Power in a Stateless Somalia', SSRC Webforum, *Crisis in the Horn of Africa*, Online essays, at: <http://hornofafrica.ssrc.org/dewaal/>.

de Waal, Alex, 2007c. 'Humanitarianism Reconfigured: Philanthropic Globalization and the New Solidarity', in Michel Feher (ed.), *Nongovernmental Politics*, New York: Zone Books, pp. 183–99.

de Waal, Alex, 2007d. 'Reflections on the Difficulties of Defining Darfur's Crisis as Genocide', *Harvard Journal of Human Rights*, 20: 25–33.

de Waal, Alex, 2010. 'Sudan's Choices: Scenarios beyond the CPA', in Heinrich Boell Foundation, *Sudan: No Easy Way Ahead*, Berlin: Heinrich Boell Foundation, pp. 9–30.

de Waal, Alex, 2013a. 'Sudan's Elusive Democratization: Civil Mobilization, Provincial Rebellion and Chameleon Dictatorships', *Journal of Contemporary African Studies*, 31/2: 213–34.

de Waal, Alex, 2013b. 'African Roles in the Libyan Conflict of 2011', *International Affairs*, 89/2: 365–79.

de Waal, Alex, Chad Hazlett, Christian Davenport and Joshua Kennedy, 2014. 'The Epidemiology of Lethal Violence in Darfur: Using Micro-data to Explore Complex Patterns of Ongoing Armed Conflict', *Social Science and Medicine*, 120: 368–77.

Dickinson, Elizabeth, 2014. 'The Case Against Qatar,' *Foreign Policy*, 30 September, at: <http://www.foreignpolicy.com/articles/2014/09/30/the_case_against_qatar_funding_extremists_salafi_syria_uae_jihad_muslim_brotherhood_taliban>.

Donham, Donald, 1999. *Marxist Modern: An Ethnographic History of the Ethiopian Revolution*, Oxford: James Currey.

Dörrie, Peter, 2012. 'Burkina Faso: Blaise Compaoré and the Politics of Personal Enrichment', *African Arguments*, 15 August, at: <http://africanarguments.org/2012/08/15/burkina-faso-blaise-compaore-and-the-politics-of-personal-enrichment-by-peter-dorrie/>.

Drysdale, John, 1994. *Whatever Happened to Somalia? A Tale of Tragic Blunders*, London: Haan.

Duffield, Mark, 2001. *Global Governance and the New Wars: The Merging of Development and Security*, London: Zed Books.

El-Affendi, Abdelwahab, 2013. 'Sudan: The Insecurity of Power and the Revenge of the State', in John Esposito and Emad el-Din Shahin (eds), *The Oxford Handbook of Islam and Politics*, Oxford: Oxford University Press, pp. 440–52.

Elbagir, Nima, 2008. 'Meet the Janjaweed', *ABC News*, at: <http://www.abc.net.au/foreign/content/oldcontent/s2464863.htm>.

Ellis, Stephen and Gerrie ter Haar, 2004. *Worlds of Power: Religious Thought and Political Practice in Africa*, London: Hurst.

El-Tom, Abdullahi Osman, 2011. *Darfur, JEM, and the Khalil Ibrahim Story*, Trenton, NJ: Red Sea Press.

El-Tom, Abdullahi Osman, 2013. *'Study War No More': Military Tactics of a Sudanese Rebel Movement*, Trenton, NJ: Red Sea Press.

Englebert, Pierre, 2009. *Africa: Unity, Sovereignty and Sorrow*, Boulder, CO: Lynne Rienner.

Englund, Harri, 2006. *Prisoners of Freedom: Human Rights and the African Poor*, Berkeley, CA: University of California Press.

Eubank, Nicholas, 2012. 'Taxation, Political Accountability and Foreign Aid: Lessons from Somaliland', *Journal of Development Studies*, 48/4: 465–80.

Ezzat, Heba R. and Mary Kaldor, 2006. ' "Not Even a Tree": Delegitimizing Violence and the Prospects for Pre-emptive Civility', in Helmut Anheier, Mary Kaldor and Marlies Glasius (eds), *Global Civil Society 2006/07*, London: Sage, pp. 18–41.

Fadul, Abdul-Jabbar and Victor Tanner, 2007. 'Darfur after Abuja: A View from the Ground', in Alex de Waal (ed.), *War in Darfur and the Search for Peace*, Cambridge, MA: Harvard University Press, pp. 284–313.

FDRE (Federal Democratic Republic of Ethiopia), 2002. *Foreign Affairs and National Security Policy and Strategy*, Addis Ababa: Ministry of Information, November.

Feinstein, Andrew, 2011. *The Shadow World: Inside the Global Arms Trade*, New York: Farrar, Straus and Giroux.

Ferguson, James, 1990. *The Anti-Politics Machine: Development, Depoliticization and Bureaucratic Power in Lesotho*, Minneapolis, MN: University of Minnesota Press.

Ferguson, James, 2006. *Global Shadows: Africa in the Neoliberal World Order*, Durham, NC: Duke University Press.

Flint, Julie, 1994. 'Somaliland: Struggling to Survive', *Africa Report*, 39/1: 36–40.

Flint, Julie, 2008. *Beyond 'Janjaweed': Understanding the Militias of Darfur*, Small Arms Survey, Sudan Working Paper 17.

Flint, Julie, 2010. *The Other War: Inter-Arab Conflict in Darfur*, Small Arms Survey, Sudan Working Paper 22.

Flint, Julie and Alex de Waal, 2008. *Darfur: A New History of a Long War*, London: Zed Books.

French, Ben and Nicholas Travis, 2012. *South Sudan: The Juba Compact*, London: ODI Budget Strengthening Initiative, July.

Gallab, Abdullahi, 2008. *The First Islamist Republic: Development and Disintegration of Islamism in the Sudan*, Aldershot: Ashgate.

Garang, John, 1987. *John Garang Speaks*, edited and introduced by Mansour Khalid, London: Kegan Paul.

Garang, John, 1992. *The Call for Democracy in Sudan*, edited and introduced by Mansour Khalid, 2nd edn, London: Kegan Paul.

Garang, Joseph U., 2010 (1961). 'The Dilemma of the Southern Intellectual: Is it Justified?', in Rogaia Abu Sharaf (ed.), 'What's Left of the Left: The View from Sudan', *South Atlantic Quarterly*, 109/1: 175–96.

Gassim, Gamal, 2010. 'Reflecting on Sudan's Higher Education Revolution under Al-Bashir's Regime', *Contemporary and International Higher Education*, 2: 50–4.

General Accounting Office, 1989. 'Somalia: Observations Regarding the Northern Conflict and Resulting Conditions', US General Accounting Office, GAO-NSIAD-89-159, May, at: <http://www.gao.gov/assets/220/211267.pdf>.

Geuss, Raymond, 2008. *Philosophy and Real Politics*, Princeton, NJ: Princeton University Press.

Gilkes, Patrick, 1993. *Two Wasted Years: The Republic of Somaliland 1991–1993*, London: Save the Children Fund.

Guigale, Marcelo, 2012. *Briefing, Marcelo Guigale, Director of Economic Policy and Policy Reduction Programmes for Africa*, Washington, DC: World Bank, 1 March.

Guyer, Jane, 2004. *Marginal Gains: Monetary Transactions in Atlantic Africa*, Chicago, IL: University of Chicago Press.

Hansen, Ketil Fred, 2013. 'A Democratic Dictator's Success: How Chad's President Déby Defeated the Military Opposition in Three Years (2008–2011)', *Journal of Contemporary African Studies*, 31/4: 583–99.

Harir, Sharif, 1994. ' "Arab Belt" versus "African Belt," Ethno-Political Conflict in Dar Fur and the Regional Cultural Factors', in Sharif Harir and Terje Tvedt (eds), *Short-Cut to Decay: The Case of the Sudan*, Uppsala: Nordiska Afrikainstitutet, pp. 144–85.

Hassan, Mohamed Aden and Caitlin Chalmers, 2008. 'UK Somali Remittances Survey', London: DFID and sendmoneyhome.org, May, at: <http://www.diaspora-centre.org/DOCS/UK_Somali_Remittan.pdf>.

Hirji, Karim F., 2010. 'Tribulations of an Independence Magazine', in Karim F. Hirji (ed.), *Cheche: Reminiscences of a Radical Magazine*, Dar es Salaam: Mkuki na Nyota, pp. 35–52.

Hobbes, Thomas, 1996. *Leviathan, Part 1* (Richard Tuck, ed.), Cambridge: Cambridge Student edition (first published 1651).

Hoehne, Markus, 2009. 'Counter-Terrorism in Somalia: How External Interference Helped Create Militant Islamism', SSRC webforum, online essays, at: <http://webarchive.ssrc.org/Somalia_Hoehne_v10.pdf>.

Hutchinson, Sharon, 1998. 'Death, Memory and the Politics of Legitimation: Nuer Experiences of the Continuing Second Sudanese Civil War', in Richard Werbner (ed.), *Memory and the Postcolony, African Anthropology and the Critique of Power*, London: Zed Books, pp. 58–70.

International Crisis Group, 2008. 'Somalia: To Move Beyond the Failed State', *ICG Africa Report*, 147 (December), Brussels: ICG.

International Crisis Group, 2010. 'Eritrea: The Siege State', *ICG Africa Report*, 163 (September), Brussels: ICG.

International Crisis Group, 2013. 'Eritrea: Scenarios for Future Transition', *ICG Africa Report*, 200 (March), Brussels: ICG.

International Crisis Group, 2014.'Eritrea: Ending the Exodus?', *ICG Africa Briefing*, 100 (August), Brussels: ICG.

Iyob, Ruth, 1995. *The Eritrean Struggle for Independence: Domination, Resistance, Nationalism, 1941–1993*. Cambridge: Cambridge University Press.

Jackson, Robert and Carl Rosberg, 1982. *Personal Rule in Black Africa: Prince, Autocrat, Prophet, Tyrant*, Berkeley, CA: University of California Press.

Jamal, Vali, 1988. 'Somalia: Understanding an Unconventional Economy', *Development and Change*, 19: 203–65.

James, Wendy, 2007. *War and Survival in Sudan's Frontierlands: Voices from the Blue Nile*, Oxford: Clarendon Press.

Johnson, Douglas, 2012. *The Root Causes of Sudan's Civil Wars: Peace or Truce?* Oxford: James Currey.

Johnson, Pat, Ken Menkhaus, Hassan Sheikh and Ali Joqombe, 2009. *A History of Mediation in Somalia Since 1988*, Geneva: Interpeace and Center for Research and Dialogue.

Johnston, Michael, 2005. *Syndromes of Corruption*, Cambridge: Cambridge University Press.

Johnston, Michael, 2014. *Corruption, Contention and Reform: The Power of Deep Democratization*, Cambridge: Cambridge University Press.

Jumpert, Maria Gabrielson and David Lanz, 2013. 'Globalized Rebellion: The Darfur Insurgents and the World,' *Journal of Modern African Studies*, 51/2: 193–217.

Kaldor, Mary, 2003. *Global Civil Society: An Answer to War*, Cambridge: Polity.

Kaldor, Mary, Terry Lynn Karl and Yahia Said, 2007. 'Introduction', in Mary Kaldor, Terry Lynn Karl and Yahia Said (eds), *Oil Wars*, London: Pluto Press, pp. 1–40.

Kameir, el-Wathig and Ibrahim Kursany, 1985. *Corruption as the 'Fifth' Factor of Production in Sudan*, Uppsala: Nordiska Afrikainstitutet, Research Report no. 71.

Kapteijns, Lidwien, 2013. *Clan Cleansing in Somalia: The Ruinous Legacy of 1991*, Philadelphia: University of Pennsylvania Press.

Karadawi, Ahmed, 1999. *Refugee Policy in Sudan, 1967–1984*, New York: Berghahn.

Karim, Atual, Mark Duffield et al., 1996. *OLS: Operation Lifeline Sudan: A Review*, Birmingham: University of Birmingham.

Keck, Margaret and Kathryn Sikkink, 1998. *Activists Beyond Borders: Advocacy Networks in International Politics*, Ithaca, NY: Cornell University Press.

Keen, David, 1994. *The Benefits of Famine: A Political Economy of Famine and Relief in Southwestern Sudan*, Princeton, NJ: Princeton University Press.

Keen, David, 2005. *Conflict and Collusion in Sierra Leone*, Oxford: James Currey.

Kelsall, Tim, 2013. *Business, Politics and the State in Africa: Challenging the Orthodoxies on Growth and Transformation*, London: Zed Books.

Kepel, Gilles, 1993. *Muslim Extremism in Egypt: The Prophet and Pharaoh*, Berkeley: University of California Press.

Khan, Mushtaq, 2012. 'Governance and Growth: History, Ideology and Methods of Proof', in Akbar Noman, Kwesi Botchwey, Howard Stein and Joseph Stiglitz (eds), *Good Growth and Governance in Africa: Rethinking Development Strategies*, Oxford: Oxford University Press, pp. 51–79.

Kibreab, Gaim, 2009. 'Forced Labour in Eritrea', *Journal of Modern African Studies*, 47/1: 41–72.

Komey, Guma Kunda, 2012. *Land, Governance, Conflict and the Nuba of Sudan*, Oxford: James Currey.

Konrad, Kai and Stergios Skaperdas, 2006. 'The Market for Protection and the Origin of the State', *Econ Theory* DOI 10.1007/s00199-101-0570-x.

Krause, Monika, 2014. *The Good Project: Humanitarian Relief NGOs and the Fragmentation of Reason*, Chicago, IL: University of Chicago Press.

Kulaksiz, Sibel, and Andrea Purdekova, 2006. 'Somali Remittance Sector: A Macroeconomic Perspective', in Samuel Munzele Maimbo (ed.), *Remittances and Economic Development in Somalia: An Overview*, World Bank, Social Development Papers, Conflict Prevention and Reconstruction, Paper No. 38, November, pp. 5–8.

Laitin, David D., 1999. 'Somalia: Civil War and International Intervention', in Barbara F. Walter and Jack Snyder (eds), *Civil Wars, Insecurity, and Intervention*, New York: Columbia University Press, pp. 146–80.

Lang, Sabine, 2013. *NGOs, Civil Society and the Public Sphere*, Cambridge: Cambridge University Press.

Larson, Greg, Peter Biar Ajak and Lant Pritchett, 2013. *South Sudan's Capability Trap: Building a State with Disruptive Innovation*, Harvard University Kennedy School of Government, Center for International Development Working Paper no 268, October.

Leeson, Peter, 2007. 'Better Off Stateless: Somalia before and after Government Collapse', *Journal of Comparative Economics*, 35/4: 689–710.

Lefebvre, Jeffrey, 1992. *Arms for the Horn: U.S. Security Policy in Ethiopia and Somalia, 1953–1991*, Pittsburgh: University of Pittsburgh Press.

Lefort, René, 2007. 'Powers – *mengist* – and Peasants in Rural Ethiopia: The May 2005 Elections', *Journal of Modern African Studies*, 45/2: 253–73.

Leonardi, Cherry, 2007. 'Liberation or Capture: Youth between Hakuma and Home during Civil War in Southern Sudan and its Aftermath', *African Affairs*, 106/424: 391–412.

Leonardi, Cherry, 2013. *Dealing with Government in South Sudan: Histories of Chiefship, Community and State*, Oxford: James Currey.

Levine, Donald, 1965. *Wax and Gold: Tradition and Innovation in Ethiopian Culture*, Chicago, IL: University of Chicago Press.

Lewis, Ioan M., 1961. *A Pastoral Democracy: A Study of Pastoralism and Politics among the Northern Somali of the Horn of Africa*, London: International African Institute.

Lewis, Ioan M., 1998. 'Doing Violence to Ethnography: A Response to Catherine Besteman's "Representing Violence and 'Othering' Somalia".' *Cultural Anthropology*, 13: 100–8.

Lewis, Mike, 2009. *Skirting the Law: Sudan's post-CPA Arms Flows*, Small Arms Survey, HSBA Working Paper 18.

MacIntyre, Alastair, 1981. *After Virtue*, Notre Dame, IN: University of Notre Dame Press.

Madut-Arop, Arop, 2006. *Sudan's Painful Road to Peace: A Full Story of the Founding and Development of the SPLM/SPLA*, Charleston, SC: Booksurge.

Mahgoub, Mohamed Ahmed, 1974. *Democracy on Trial: Reflections on Arab and African Politics*, London: Deutsch.

Mahmoud, Fatima Babiker, 1984. *The Sudanese Bourgeoisie: Vanguard of Development?* Khartoum: Khartoum University Press.

Mahrt, Michael, 2009. 'War, Spatiotemporal Perception, and the Nation: Fighters and Farmers in the Highlands', in David O'Kane and Tricia Redeker Hepner (eds), *Biopolitics, Militarism and Development: Eritrea in the Twenty-First Century*, Boulder, CO: Berghahn, pp. 17–33.

Mamdani, Mahmood, 1996. *Citizen and Subject: Contemporary Africa and the Legacy of Late Colonialism*, Princeton, NJ: Princeton University Press.

Mapolu, Henry, 2010. 'On Producing a Student Magazine', in Karim F. Hirji (ed.), *Cheche: Reminiscences of a Radical Magazine*, Dar es Salaam: Mkuki na Nyota, pp. 65–76.

Marchal, Roland, 2004. 'Islamic Political Dynamics in the Somali Civil War', in Alex de Waal (ed.), *Islamism and Its Enemies in the Horn of Africa*, London: Hurst, pp. 114–45.

Marchal, Roland, 2011. 'The Rise of a Jihadi Movement in a Country at War: Harakat al-Shabaab al Mujaheddin in Somalia', Unpublished report.

Marchal, Roland, 2012. 'Somalia on Hold', Unpublished report.

Marchal, Roland, 2013. 'Le Tchad entre deux guerres? Remarques sur un présumé complot', *Politique africaine*, 130: 213–23.

Maren, Michael, 1997. *The Road to Hell: The Ravaging Effects of Foreign Aid and International Charity*, New York: The Free Press.

Markakis, John, 1990. *National and Class Conflict in the Horn of Africa*, London: Zed Books.

Markakis, John, 2011. *Ethiopia: The Last Two Frontiers*, Oxford: James Currey.

Marx, Karl and Friedrich Engels, 2010 (1848). *The Manifesto of the Communist Party*, London: International Publishers.

Maxwell, Daniel and Nisar Majid, 2015. *Famine in Somalia: Competing Imperatives, Collective Failures, 2011–2012*, London: Hurst.

Mbembe, Achille, 2001. *On the Postcolony*, Cambridge: Cambridge University Press.

Menkhaus, Ken, 2003. 'State Collapse in Somalia: Second Thoughts', *Review of African Political Economy*, 30: 405–22.

Monga, Celestin, 1997. *The Anthropology of Anger: Civil Society and Democracy in Africa*, Boulder, CO: Lynne Rienner.

Moyn, Samuel, 2010. *The Last Utopia: Human Rights in History*, Cambridge, MA: Belknap Press.

Mwenda, Andrew, 2010. 'Uganda's Politics of Foreign Aid and Violent Conflict: The Political Uses of the LRA Rebellion', in Tim Allen and Koen Vlassenroot (eds), *The Lord's Resistance Army: Myth and Reality*, London: Zed Books, 45–58.

Natsios, Andrew, 2012. *Sudan, South Sudan and Darfur: What Everyone Needs To Know*, Oxford: Oxford University Press.

North, Douglass, John Joseph Wallis and Barry R. Weingast, 2009. *Violence and Social Orders: A Conceptual Framework for Interpreting Recorded Human History*, Cambridge: Cambridge University Press.

Nouwen, Sarah and Wouter Werner, 2011. 'Doing Justice to the Political: The International Criminal Court in Uganda and Sudan', *European Journal of International Law*, 21: 941–65.

Nyaba, Peter Adwok, 1997. *The Politics of Liberation in South Sudan: An Insider's View*, Kampala: Fountain Press.

Olson, Mancur, 1993. 'Dictatorship, Democracy and Development', *American Political Science Review*, 97/3: 567–76.

Omaar, Rakiya, 1994. 'Somaliland: One Thorn Bush at a Time', *Current History*, 93 (May): 232–6.

Pateman, Roy, 1990. *Eritrea: Even the Stones are Burning*, Trenton, NJ: Red Sea Press.

Patey, Luke, 2014. *The New Kings of Crude: China, India and the Global Struggle for Oil in Sudan and South Sudan*, London: Hurst.

Perham, Margery, 1948. *The Government of Ethiopia*. London: Faber and Faber.

Perry, Chris and Adam C. Smith, 2013. 'Trends in Uniformed Contributions to UN Peacekeeping: A New Dataset, 1991–2012', *Providing for Peacekeeping*, 3 (June), New York: International Peace Institute.

Phillips, Sarah, 2011. *Yemen and the Politics of Permanent Crisis*, London: International Institute for Strategic Studies.

Pinaud, Clémence, 2014. 'South Sudan: Civil War, Predation, and the Making of a Military Aristocracy', *African Affairs*, 113/451: 192–211.

Plaut, Martin, 2014. 'Eritrea: How the London Embassy Forces Eritreans to Pay the Illegal 2% Tax – Full Report', martinplaut blog, 16 February, at: <http://martinplaut.wordpress.com/2014/02/16/eritrea-how-the-london -embassy-forces-eritreans-to-pay-the-illegal-2-tax-full-report/>.

Polanyi, Karl, 1944. *The Great Transformation: The Political and Economic Origins of Our Time*, Boston, MA: Beacon Press.

Pool, David, 2001. *From Guerrillas to Government: The Eritrean People's Liberation Front*, Athens, OH: Ohio University Press.

Poole, Amanda, 2013. 'Ransoms, Remittances, and Refugees: The Gatekeeper State in Eritrea', *Africa Today*, 60/2: 66–82.

Porter, Michael, 2008. 'The Five Competitive Forces that Shape Strategy', *Harvard Business Review* (January): 86–104.

Powell, Benjamin, Ryan Ford and Alex Nowrasteh, 2006. 'Somalia After State Collapse: Chaos or Improvement?', Oakland, CA, *Independent Institute Working Paper No. 64*, 30 November, at: <http://www.independent.org/pdf/working_papers/64_somalia.pdf>.

Prendergast, John, 2014. Testimony of John Prendergast, Co-Founder of Enough Project, Senate Foreign Relations Committee, 'The Situation in South Sudan', 9 January, at: <http://www.foreign.senate.gov/hearings/010914am>.

Putzel, James and Jonathan DiJohn, 2012. *Meeting the Challenges of Crisis States*, London: London School of Economics, Crisis States Research Centre.

Quinlivan, James T., 1999. 'Coup-Proofing: Its Practice and Consequences in the Middle East', *International Security*, 24/2: 131–65.

Rands, Richard, 2010. *In Need of Review: SPLA Transformation in 2006–10 and Beyond*, Small Arms Survey, HSBA Working Paper No. 23.

Rawls, John, 1971. *A Theory of Justice*, Cambridge, MA: Belknap Press.

Reno, William, 1999. *Warlord Politics and African States*, Boulder, CO: Lynne Rienner.

Reno, William, 2011. *Warfare in Independent Africa: New Approaches to African History*, Cambridge: Cambridge University Press.

Riggan, Jennifer, 2009. 'Avoiding Wastage by Making Soldiers: Technologies of the State and the Imagination of the Educated Nation', in David O'Kane and Tricia Redeker Hepner (eds), *Biopolitics, Militarism and Development: Eritrea in the Twenty-First Century*, Boulder, CO: Berghahn, pp. 72–91.

Roeber, Joe, 2005. 'Hard Wired for Corruption: The Arms Trade and Corruption', *Prospect* 113 (28 August), at: <http://www.prospectmagazine.co.uk/features/hardwiredforcorruption>.

Roessler, Philip, 2014. *In the Shadow of the Coup d'Etat: The Strategic Logic of War and Peace in Africa*. College of William & Mary, book manuscript.

Roggio, Bill, 2012. 'Bin Laden told Shabaab to Hide al Qaeda Ties', *The Long War Journal*, 3 May, at: <http://www.longwarjournal.org/archives/2012/05/bin_laden_instructs.php>.

Roitman, Janet, 2005. *Fiscal Disobedience: An Anthropology of Economic Regulation in Central Africa*, Princeton, NJ: Princeton University Press.

Rolandsen, Oystein H., 2005. *Guerrilla Government: Political Changes in the Southern Sudan during the 1990s*, Uppsala: Nordiska Afrikainstitutet.

Schatz, Edward, 2009. 'Introduction: Ethnographic Immersion and the Study of Politics', in Edward Schatz (ed.), *Political Ethnography: What Immersion Contributes to the Study of Power*, Chicago, IL: University of Chicago Press, pp. 1–22.

Schatzberg, Michael, 2001. *Political Legitimacy in Middle Africa: Father, Family, Food*, Bloomington, IN: Indiana University Press.

Schumpeter, Joseph, 1954. 'The Crisis of the Tax State' (trans. W. Stolper and R. Musgrave), *American Economic Papers*, 4: 5–38.

Scott, James, 1976. *The Moral Economy of the Peasant: Rebellion and Subsistence in Southeast Asia*, New Haven, CT: Yale University Press.

Scott, James, 1998. *Seeing Like a State: How Certain Schemes to Improve the Human Condition Have Failed*, New Haven, CT: Yale University Press.

Scott, James, 2009. *The Art of Not Being Governed: An Anarchist History of Upland Southeast Asia*, New Haven, CT: Yale University Press.

Simons, Anna, 1995. *Networks of Dissolution: Somalia Undone*, Oxford: Westview Press.

Small Arms Survey, 2006–7. 'Anatomy of Civilian Disarmament in Jonglei State', *Sudan Issue Brief*, 3 (November 2006–February 2007). Geneva.

Small Arms Survey, 2009. 'Supply and Demand: Arms Flows and Holdings in Sudan', *Sudan Issue Brief*, 15 (December). Geneva.

Small Arms Survey, 2014. 'The Conflict in Northern and Western Bahr al Ghazal States: Describing Events through 10 October 2014', *Human Security Baseline Assessment for Sudan and South Sudan*, (October), Geneva, at: <http://www.smallarmssurveysudan.org/facts-figures/south-sudan/conflict-of-2013-14/the-conflict-in-bahr-el-ghazal.html>.

Snowden, John, 2012. *Work in Progress: Security Force Development in South Sudan through February 2012*, Geneva: Small Arms Survey, HSBA Working Paper 27.

Soré, Ramata, 2011. 'Charles Taylor Trial Ended, but Burkina Faso and Libya Incriminated', Thomas Sankara website, at: <http://thomassankara.net/spip.php?article1055&lang=fr>.

Spears, Ian, 2003. 'Reflections on Somaliland and Africa's Territorial Order', *Review of African Political Economy*, 30/95: 89–98.

Stiansen, Endre, 2004. 'Interest Politics: Islamic Finance in the Sudan, 1977–2001', in Clement Henry and Rodney Wilson (eds), *The Politics of Islamic Finance*, Edinburgh: Edinburgh University Press, pp. 155–67.

Stiglitz, Joseph E., 2002. *Globalization and Its Discontents*, New York: W.W. Norton.

Styan, David, 2004. 'Twisting Ethio-Eritrean Economic Ties: Misperceptions of War and the Misplaced Priorities of Peace', in Dominque Jacquin-Berdal and Martin Plaut (eds), *Unfinished Business: Ethiopia and Eritrea at War*, Trenton, NJ: Red Sea Press, pp. 177–200.

Tareke, Gebru, 1991. *Ethiopia: Power and Protest: Peasant Revolts in the Twentieth Century*. Cambridge: Cambridge University Press.

Tareke, Gebru, 2009. *The Ethiopian Revolution: War in the Horn of Africa*, New Haven, CT: Yale University Press.

Tarrow, Sydney, 1994. *Power in Movement: Social Movements and Contentious Politics*, Cambridge: Cambridge University Press.

Thigo, Philip, 2013. 'People, Technology and Spaces: Towards a New Generation of Social Movements', *Journal of Contemporary African Studies*, 31/2: 255–64.

Thomas, Edward, 2015. *South Sudan: A Slow Liberation*, London: Zed Books.

Tilly, Charles, 1985. 'War-making and State-making as Organized Crime', in Peter Evans, Dietrich Rueschemeyer and Theda Skocpol (eds), *Bringing the State Back In*, Cambridge: Cambridge University Press, pp. 169–87.

Tilly, Charles, 1990. *Coercion, Capital and European States, AD 990–1992*, Oxford: Blackwell.

Tronvoll, Kjetil, 2010. 'The Ethiopian 2010 Federal and Regional Elections: Re-establishing the One-party State', *African Affairs*, 110/438: 121–36.

Tronvoll, Kjetil and Daniel R. Mekonnen, 2014. *An African Garrison State: Human Rights and Political Development in Eritrea*, Oxford: James Currey.

Tubiana, Jérôme, 2007. 'Darfur: A War for Land?' in Alex de Waal (ed.), *War in Darfur and the Search for Peace*, Cambridge, MA: Harvard University Press, pp. 68–91.

Tubiana, Jérôme, 2011. *Renouncing the Rebels: Local and Regional Dimensions of Chad–Sudan Rapprochement*, Small Arms Survey, Geneva: HSBA Working Paper 25.

Tucker, Jonathan B., 1982. 'The Politics of Refugees in Somalia', *Horn of Africa*, 5/3: 20–31.

Turner, Victor, 1974. *Dramas, Fields and Metaphors: Symbolic Action in Human Society*, Ithaca, NY: Cornell University Press.

Tvedt, Terje, 1994. 'The Collapse of the State in Southern Sudan after the Addis Ababa Agreement: A Study of Internal Causes and the Role of NGOs', in Sharif Harir and Terje Tvedt (eds), *Short-Cut to Decay: The Case of the Sudan*, Uppsala: Nordiska Afrikainstitutet, pp. 69–104.

United Nations Monitoring Group, 2011. 'Letter Dated 18 July 2011 from the Chair of the Security Council Committee Pursuant to Resolutions 751 (1992) and 1907 (2009) Concerning Somalia and Eritrea Addressed to the President of the Security Council', UN Security Council, S/2011/433.

United Nations Monitoring Group, 2012a. 'Letter Dated 11 July 2012 from the Chair of the Security Council Committee Pursuant to Resolutions 751 (1992) and 1907 (2009) Concerning Somalia and Eritrea Addressed to the President of the Security Council', UN Security Council, S/2012/544.

United Nations Monitoring Group, 2012b. 'Letter Dated 11 July 2012 from the Chair of the Security Council Committee Pursuant to Resolutions 751 (1992) and 1907 (2009) Concerning Somalia and Eritrea Addressed to the President of the Security Council', UN Security Council, S/2012/545.

United Nations General Assembly, 2014. 'Approved Resources for Peacekeeping Operations for the Period from 1 July 2013 to 30 June 2014', UN, Fifth Committee, 68th session, Agenda item 147, A/C.5/68/21, 23 January.

US Embassy Asmara, 2006. Cable, 'Controlling the Market, Controlling the People: Hidri Trust Takes All', 27 June, Wikileaks 06 Asmara 553, at: <http://wikileaks/cable/2006/06/06ASMARA553.html>.

US Embassy Asmara, 2007a. Cable, 'Lifting the Veil on Corruption in Eritrea', 12 December, Wikileaks, 07 Asmara 936, at: <http://wikileaks/cable/2007/12/07ASMARA936.html>.

US Embassy Asmara, 2007b. Cable, 'Eritrea's Threadbare Economy', 18 December, Wikileaks, 07 Asmara 954, at: <http://wikileaks/cable/2007/12/07ASMARA954.html>.

US Embassy Khartoum, 2008. Cable, 'Parastatals – The Regime's Gray Companies', 8 March, Wikileaks 08 Khartoum 374, at: <http://wikileaks.org/cable/2008/03/08KHARTOUM374.html>.

US Senate, 1980. *An Assessment of the Refugee Situation in Somalia*, Washington, DC: Senate Committee on Foreign Relations.

Uvin, Peter, 2009. *Life After Violence: A People's Story of Burundi*, London: Zed Books.

Van de Walle, Nicolas, 2001. *African Economies and the Politics of Permanent Crisis, 1979–1999*, Cambridge: Cambridge University Press.

van Reisen, Mirjam, Meron Estifanos and Conny Rijken, 2012. *Human Trafficking in the Sinai: Refugees between Life and Death*, Oisterwijk: Wolf Publishers.

Vaughan, Sarah and Mesfin Gebremeskel, 2011. *Rethinking Business and Politics in Ethiopia: The Role of EFFORT, the Endowment Fund for the Rehabilitation of Tigray*, London: African Power and Politics Programme, Research Report No. 2.

Vaughan, Sarah and Kjetil Tronvoll, 2003. 'The Culture of Power in Contemporary Ethiopian Life', *SIDA Studies*, 10, Stockholm.

Warah, Rasna, 2012. 'New Report Reveals Somalia's Missing Millions', *Foreign Policy in Focus*, 31 July, at: <http://www.fpif.org/articles/new_report_reveals_somalias_missing_millions>.

Watts, Clint, Jacob Shapiro and Vahid Brown, 2007. *Al-Qaida's (Mis)adventures in the Horn of Africa*, West Point, NY: Harmony Project.

Williams, Isaac, 2014. 'Insights from the Management Theory of the Political Marketplace', blog entry, Reinventing Peace, 12 August, at: <http://sites.tufts.edu/reinventingpeace/2014/08/12/insights-from-the-management-theory-of-the-political-marketplace/>.

Wilson, Hamish, 1994. 'The Booraama Conference and Elections', Unpublished draft report, London: African Rights.

Woldemikael, Tekle, 2009. 'Pitfalls of Nationalism in Eritrea', in David O'Kane and Tricia Redeker Hepner (eds), *Biopolitics, Militarism and Development: Eritrea in the Twenty-First Century*, Boulder, CO: Berghahn, pp. 1–16.

Woldemikael, Tekle, 2013. 'Introduction: Post-Liberation Eritrea', *Africa Today*, 60/2: v–xix.

Wöndu, Steven and Ann Lesch, 2000. *Battle for Peace in Sudan: An Analysis of the Abuja Conferences 1992–1993*, Lanham, MD: University Press of America.

Woodroofe, Louise, 2013. *Buried in the Sands of the Ogaden: The United States, the Horn of Africa, and the Demise of Détente.* Kent, OH: Kent State University.

World Bank, 1983. *Somalia: Policy Measures for Rehabilitation and Growth*, Washington, DC: World Bank, Country Programs Department Eastern Africa Regional Office, Report No. 4081a-SO, May.

World Bank, 1991. *Somalia: Crisis in Public Expenditure Management: Volume I: Summary of Main Findings and Recommendations*, Washington, DC: World Bank, Country Operations Division, Eastern Africa Department, Report No. 8727-SO, March.

World Bank, 2003. *Sudan: Stabilization and Reconstruction, Country Economic Memorandum, Volume I: Main Text*, Washington, DC: World Bank, Poverty Reduction and Economic Management 2, Africa Region, Report No. 24620-SU, June.

World Bank, 2007. *Sudan: Public Expenditure Review, Synthesis Report*, Washington, DC: World Bank, Poverty Reduction and Economic Management Unit, Report No. 41840-SD, December.

World Bank, 2011. *World Development Report 2011: Conflict Security and Development*, Washington, DC: World Bank.

World Bank, 2012. *World Bank Summary of Financial Diagnostic Assessment of 'Audit Investigative Financial Report 2009–10'*, Mogadishu: World Bank.

World Bank, 2013. 'Public Expenditures in South Sudan: Are They Delivering?', *South Sudan Economic Brief*, 2 (February), Washington, DC: World Bank.

Young, John, 1996. 'The Tigray and Eritrean People's Liberation Fronts: A History of Tensions and Pragmatism', *Journal of Modern African Studies*, 34/1: 105–20.

Young, John, 2012. *The Fate of Sudan: The Origins and Consequences of a Flawed Peace Process*, London: Zed Books.

Zenawi, Meles, 2012. 'States and Markets: Neoliberal Limitations and the Case for a Developmental State', in Akbar Noman, Kwesi Botchwey, Howard Stein and Joseph E. Stiglitz (eds), *Good Growth and Governance in Africa: Rethinking Development Strategies*, Oxford: Oxford University Press, pp. 140–74.

Zenawi, Meles, n.d. 'African Development: Dead Ends and New Beginnings', Uncompleted thesis Erasmus University, Rotterdam, excerpts online at: <http://www.meleszenawi.org.uk/meles_legacy.html>.

Index

Note: Acronyms used in the index are explained on pages viii–ix; page numbers in italic refer to figures.